Praise for *The Sacredness of Questioning Everything*

David Dark is my favorite critic  ica
and the Christian faith. He bring ry
book he reads, every song he he a
discerning reverence — attentive to es
on them. He is also a reliable lie ce
in the book.

> EUGENE PETERSON, professor emeritus of spiritual theology,
> translator of *The Message*

David Dark is one of our wisest authors, and I plan to read everything he writes. *The Sacredness of Questioning Everything* will comfort
questioners, doubters, and skeptics with assurance that their questions
can be faithful, and it will challenge the complacent with an ethical
summons to wonder. It invites everything to give life — and faith — a
second thought, and did I mention that it's beautifully written?

> BRIAN MCLAREN, author of *Everything Must Change*

Brilliant and charming and insightful as always, Dark comforts both
my soul and my mind with this synthesis, part memoir and part essay,
of the culture around us and the culture within us.

> PHYLLIS TICKLE, author of *The Great Emergence*

We will never find the answers until we begin to ask the right questions. Most of us are skeptical of self-righteous folks (whether pastors
or politicians) who try to force their answers into you as if truth was
an enema. And if there is anything we can learn from both liberals
and conservatives, it's that you can have all the right answers and
still be mean people. This is not a book of answers. Here is a book of
questions — question everything ... including this book.

> SHANE CLAIBORNE, author, activist, and recovering sinner

This is what I need: a far-reaching Christianity that's not just for the Shiny Happy People but for me, questioning and doubting and trying to live into the mystery. I couldn't ask for a better fellow pilgrim than brainiac David Dark, who feels as comfortable mining *The Office* and *The Colbert Report* as he does Dostoevsky and Flannery O'Connor. This book is for everyone who quietly suspects that God is a whole lot bigger than the church would have us believe.

JANA RIESS, author of *What Would Buffy Do?*

In *The Sacredness of Questioning Everything*, David Dark serves up a unique blend of pop culture and high culture, generously seasoned with religious texts. The result is an immensely readable, profoundly subversive, and deeply prophetic book.

ANDREW BACEVICH, author of *The Limits of Power*

In *The Sacredness of Questioning Everything*, David Dark travels the lonesome highways of the American soul and finds signs of grace where many of us see only despair. Carry this book with you as a guide through these uncertain times.

CHARLES MARSH, author of *Wayward Christian Soldiers*

David Dark is a brilliant and respected cultural critic, and here, in this new work, he has done something that very few evangelical writers have done: he truly invites us — no, he calls us — to the holy task of thinking all manner of things through, of saying yes and no, of questioning and seeking and discerning what is most true. We need this kind of feisty, literate, and (dare I say it?) prophetic call, and we will be better — as people and as a Christian community and as a culture — if we take up this unsettling and liberating challenge.

BYRON BORGER, owner of Hearts & Minds bookstore, Dallastown, Pennsylvania

Dark wanders through the landscape of theological inquiry with brilliance, taking us into uncharted valleys where questioning, confusion, doubt, and promise intermingle. This book is a call to action, a resounding yell of encouragement, to all types of Christians.

CHRISTOPHER R. SMIT, assistant professor, Calvin College

The Sacredness of
Questioning
Everything

DAVID DARK

ZONDERVAN®

ZONDERVAN.com/
AUTHOR**TRACKER**
follow your favorite authors

ZONDERVAN

The Sacredness of Questioning Everything
Copyright © 2009 by James David Dark

This title is also available in a Zondervan audio edition.
Visit www.zondervan.fm.

Requests for information should be addressed to:

Zondervan, *Grand Rapids, Michigan 49530*

Library of Congress Cataloging-in-Publication Data

Dark, David, 1969-.
        The sacredness of questioning everything / David Dark.
            p.   cm.
        Includes bibliographical references.
        ISBN 978-0-310-28618-9
        1. Apologetics. 2. Questioning. 3. Popular culture — Religious aspects —
    Christianity. 4. Christianity and culture. I. Title.
    BT1103.D37   2008
    230 — dc22   2008036212

Published in association with the literary agency of Daniel Literary Group, LLC, 1701 Kingsbury Drive, Suite 100, Nashville, TN 37215.

Interior design by Beth Shagene

Printed in the United States of America

09 10 11 12 13 14 15 • 23 22 21 20 19 18 17 16 15 14 13 12 11 10 9 8 7 6 5 4 3 2 1

For Harmon

Contents

A question.
Since before your sun burned hot in space
and before your race was born,
I have awaited a question.

The Guardian of Forever to Captain Kirk,
***Star Trek*, "City on the Edge of Forever,"**
airdate April 6, 1967; stardate 3134.0

Never What You Have in Mind

Questioning God

What do I love when I love my God?
Augustine of Hippo

Remember to love your neighbor as you love yourself.
And if you hate yourself, then please —
just leave your neighbor alone.
Jon Stewart

Dig, if you're willing, this picture: a tiny town with a tight-knit community. The people share joys and concerns, woes and gossip. They keep a close and often affectionate watch on one another's business. They talk and talk and talk.

What an outsider would notice within minutes of listening in on conversations are constant and slightly self-conscious references to "Uncle Ben." A beautiful sunset prompts a townsperson to say, "Isn't Uncle Ben awesome?" Good news brings out how thankful and overjoyed they feel toward Uncle Ben. Even in tragedy, a local might say, in a slightly nervous fashion, "You know, it just goes to show how much we all need Uncle Ben. I know — we all know — that Uncle Ben is good."

Uncle Ben is always on their minds.

Even when the magnificence of Uncle Ben isn't spoken of aloud, he's somehow present in facial expressions and actions. It's the look of stopping a train of thought before it goes too far, of letting an uncompleted sentence trail off into awkward silence, of swiftly changing the subject. It's as if a conversation can go only so far. People hardly ever look one another in the eye for long.

At the beginning of each week there's a meeting in the largest house in town. Upon arriving, people get caught up in good fellowship and animated discussion of the week's events, with conversations straining in the direction of Uncle Ben. When a bell sounds, talk ceases. Everyone moves to the staircase and descends into the basement. Each person sits facing an enormous, rumbling furnace. Seated close to the furnace door, as if he were a part of the furnace itself, is a giant man in black overalls. His back is turned to them.

They wait in silence. In time the man turns around. His face is angry, contorted. He fixes a threatening stare of barely contained rage on each person, then roars, "Am I good?"

To which they respond in unison, "Yes, Uncle Ben, you are good."

"Am I worthy of praise?"

"You alone are worthy of our praise."

"Do you love me more than anything? More than anyone?"

"We love you and you alone, Uncle Ben."

"You better love me, or I'm going to put you ... in here" — he opens the furnace door to reveal a gaping darkness — "forever."

Out of the darkness can be heard sounds of anguish and lament. Then he closes the furnace door and turns his back to them. They sit in silence.

Finally, feeling reasonably assured that Uncle Ben has finished saying what he has to say, they leave. They live their lives as best they can. They try to think and speak truthfully and do well by one another. They resume their talk of the wonders of Uncle Ben's love in anticipation of the next week's meeting.

But they're limited, in myriad ways, by fear. Fear causes them to censor their own thoughts and words. Fear prevents them from telling anyone of their inner anguish and fright. Fear keeps them from recognizing in one another's eyes their common desperation. This fear is interwoven, subtly and sometimes not so subtly, in all of their relationships.

End of story.

I find this story both jarring and entirely familiar. It captures some of my worst fears concerning the character of God. And I suspect a good number of people live their lives haunted by a nightmare similar to this one. Perhaps you entertain fears like these. Perhaps Uncle Ben forms your image of the divine even now.

Something akin to the Uncle Ben image might be what a lot of people refer to when they speak of religion as the worst thing that ever happened to them, a nightmare that damages everything it touches. We might protest that there's much more to religion than such tales of terror. But I find it hard to deny that the image of Uncle Ben lurks within an awful lot of what is called popular religious belief.

Uncle Ben might be the best-selling version of an all-powerful deity, a great and powerful Wizard of Oz-type who refuses to be questioned and threatens anyone who dares to doubt or protest. Fear constrains many to call this God good and loving, ignoring what they feel inwardly. The less reverent candidly observe that this God is the perfect model for a brutal dictator, the cosmic crime boss who runs everything and expects us to be grateful. Trying to satisfy such a God while also getting through a workday, trying to balance a checkbook, and being moderately attentive to the needs of others can take a certain emotional toll.

Loving God

For a long time, I was in the habit of praying a prayer ("I love you, Lord") that was something of a gamble, like Pascal's wager.[1] I wasn't sure I loved this God at all. In fact, I believed this Uncle Ben-like God was unlovable, determined to consign most of humanity to eternal torment for believing the wrong things. But, given the terrifying outcome of not loving him, I sensibly said I loved and believed in him anyway. If, somehow, I succeeded in loving this God, lucky me. And if I didn't love him, I'd be more or less damned anyway.

Having faith in this brand of God is akin to Orwell's "doublethink"—a disturbing mind trick by which we don't let ourselves know what's really going on in our minds for fear of what might follow. We learn to deny what we think and feel. The resulting mind-set is one of all fear all the time, a fear that can render us incapable of putting two and two together. Never quite free to *say* what we *see.*

When we think of belief intertwined with such fear, we might begin to wonder if self-professed believers caught in the grip of unseemly ideologies, religious or otherwise, are as fully convinced of what they claim to believe as they appear to be. Many are trying to prove their ultimate commitment by eliminating doubt—and fear—ridding themselves of the last vestiges of independent thought through force of will. Responding to the push that demands as much can become a kind of survival instinct. We do it without thinking about it. We witness the loss of independent thinking in a wide variety of settings—in offices, training camps, schools, political parties, clubs, families, and other religious assemblies. We're instructed to believe and to silence our questions and our imaginations. Like Orwell's Big Brother, Uncle Ben thrives when questioning is out of the question.

Open-ended questions such as "What on earth are we doing here?" and "Are we going crazy?" might occasionally give us enough air to keep breathing, but we're very often suffocating. We have just enough religion to be afraid as we go through our days, as we wake up and fall asleep. We feel pressure to believe—or pretend to believe—that God is love, while suspecting with a sinking feeling that God likes almost no one.

William Blake captured this hateful spirit most effectively by naming him Nobodaddy (nobody's daddy, non-father, Father of Jealousy). As a being of hatefulness and perpetual accusation, Uncle Ben might be called a Satanic perversion of the idea of God. However we choose to name him, his voice (or its voice) is at work within our world.

For the record, I don't believe in the nonloving, fear-producing image that is Uncle Ben, but I hasten to add that I'm not without my own doubts. The intensity of the struggle ebbs and flows. When people ask, "Are you sure God isn't like Uncle Ben?" I tend to reply, "Most of the time."

Deliverance Begins with Questions

I readily confess that, in my darkest hours, the fear of an Uncle Ben, Nobodaddy-driven universe still has a hold on me, even as I hope and pray that my children and their children will find such an unworthy image of God to be almost comical. In my own religious upbringing, nobody ever told me that the Creator of the universe was a hellish handler of human beings. But as a child, I had a way of filling in the blanks with my imagination. Images sprang out of what I was told must be in the Bible somewhere. And some very dark ideas arose when talk of baptism and the age of accountability and assurance of salvation came up. I suppose such prospects motivated me, at least partially, to *share* my faith with other people. But would I really be doing others a favor if I managed to convince them of my own little nightmare? What should one do with a Nobodaddy on the brain? Is deliverance possible?

I believe deliverance begins with questions. It begins with people who *love* questions, people who *live with* questions and *by* questions, people who feel a deep joy when good questions are asked. When we meet these people — some living, some through history and art — things begin to change. Something is let loose. When we're exposed to the liveliness of holding everything up to the light of good questions — what I call "sacred questioning" — we discover that redemption is creeping into the way we think, believe, and see the world. This *re*-deeming (re-valuing) of what we've made of our lives, a redemption that perhaps begins with the insertion of a question mark beside whatever feels final and absolute and *beyond* questioning, gives our souls a bit of elbow room, a space in which to breathe and imagine again, as if for the first time.

I had specific convictions concerning God and sin and eternity, but I also understood that my concepts, however well I might articulate them, were flawed, broken, and always in need of rehabilitation. When I heard Leonard Cohen proclaim in his song "Anthem" that there are cracks in absolutely everything, I sensed he was describing my life. The cracks, Cohen croons, as if we should all know it by now, are how the light shines in, and it is only by remaining aware of our imperfections that we remain open to redemption and reform. When we have questions, illumination is possible. Otherwise we're closed and no light can enter.

My inner Nobodaddy remained. Something clicked when a woman in northern Ireland told me her own Uncle Ben story. She said she'd heard it from the Jesuit priest Gerard Hughes.[2] Until I heard her story, I didn't have a good way of talking about this binding, bad concept of God. I might even say that I didn't know this death-dealing negative image was there. I didn't know what had hold of me. The story, as stories will, prompted a lot of questions concerning the presumed goodness of God, the idea that God *is* love, and what it might mean to affirm, as I do, that God conquers rather than sponsors death.

The light began to shine through the cracks. Stories, I find, help the light to shine.

Move On

In no small way, I think I owe my ability to hear and interpret stories to my Granddaddy Dark, a farmer, a minister, and a math professor with precise ideas concerning the way the parts of the Bible all add up into the irrefutable, always logical word of God. He saw no use of musical instruments in the New Testament accounts of the early church, so worship services he conducted did not use them. It was rumored that he once broke with a congregation when a kitchen was to be added to the church—there being no mention of attached cooking facilities in his King James Version.

But near the end of his life, my grandfather spake unto my father a saving word that was handed down to me. Seated in the car with my father, he observed that all the straight lines he'd drawn in the sand concerning what God wanted and what the Bible said were drawn because, as far as he could tell, this is what the Lord had spoken. "But," he told my father, "if it ever turns out that I'm wrong about these things, any of it, move on."

I don't suppose Granddaddy Dark will ever be characterized as a postmodern Christian, and he wasn't what could be called a moral relativist. But he did understand he was a pilgrim whose progress would prove to be finite, limited, and all too human in the grand scheme of things. He had his religion—those practices and ideas to which he committed himself—but he also understood, religiously, that he didn't *have* God. He knew that his attempt to understand God was relative to where he stood in space and time and that God's purposes might be borne witness to even as they wouldn't be contained, exactly, by any religion. In this sense, he didn't want my father to feel duty bound to remain in a stagnant religion. My father's duty was to honor his father by questioning him and by keeping his view of God open to question too. And, should it ever prove necessary, he would honor him most by moving on.

As something of an open-minded fundamentalist, my grandfather held tightly to what he thought he knew in faith. What else can one do? But he also understood that *as far as he knew* and *as far as he could tell* weren't far at all. He even remained open to the possibility that he was most wrong when he was most intensely sure of his rightness. Call it a religious sensibility.

This admission strikes us as counterintuitive in a culture that so often views *staying the course* as a virtue in itself. This is the madness that comedian Stephen Colbert lampoons with the term *truthiness*, that sense of what's true that trades the demands of critical discernment for what Colbert calls "the gut brain"—go ahead with your gut no matter what and call it strength of purpose, improvising an insane justification for your own folly as you go. Against this all too common culture of insane self-assertion, the expressions "as far as I can tell" and "as far as I know" and "to my knowledge" signal a vigilant awareness concerning our own limitations. I'd like to see this self-criticism more frequently displayed by pundits, politicians, and professional religious figures who confuse their gut feelings for integrity and a changed mind for weakness. What the pundits call wishy-washiness, the Bible calls repentance. I understand there's no salvation without it. While pride and self-satisfaction might play well on TV, the Lord detests the proud face.[3] It's the look of impenetrable ignorance. It doesn't ask questions. It has no reverse gear and won't admit to ever flip-flopping. When there is no soul-searching, is the soul still there?

Various traditions affirm self-questioning as wisdom, the posture of being ever prepared to receive the revelation that you are deeply mistaken. My grandfather might have cited the apostle Paul's observation that we all see reality "through a glass, darkly."[4] The need to think otherwise — that we always know what we're talking about, that we're objective, that we know where we stand and where we're coming from — might be one of the burdens my grandfather believed he was being delivered from by the grace of God. Perhaps he hoped to help my father remain open to the sweet, saving realization that we don't actually understand much of anything. There is a joy in knowing that you're only a human being among other human beings, all of us dreadfully cracked and in need of mending. My fundamentalist grandfather, for one sacred, saving moment, confessed to his sense that, despite his sincerest efforts, he was doubtless a naive idolater in one way or another. My father took him at his word.

Sacred Questioning

As an inheritor of this sensibility, my father never met a joke he didn't like. He liked jokes because they have the power to break through our tidy realities and our small, defensive kingdoms. He suspected that the Bible and other religious texts, when read properly and seriously, would function like jokes, uproariously ripping down whatever we thought we knew about the way things are. He figured these religious texts were always building up something new, undoing our doctrines, taming our religious pride — in short, humbling our imaginations *and* liberating them. He found the comedy of it all to be divine. It was as if he believed lightness of spirit to be a biblical imperative, a religious duty.

I don't think of the Uncle Ben story as a joke, although when I tell it out loud, I sometimes do find myself laughing. It's not funny in a laugh-until-it-hurts way, but funny like a song by the Decemberists or a Terry Gilliam film, funny because it's true and all too familiar. Telling the Uncle Ben story aloud gives us the space to question it, to examine it, and, finally, to protest it.

There was a time in my life when I viewed the Uncle Ben story, despite its nightmarish quality, as an accurate depiction of the way things work. Protesting it would have seemed cosmically useless, given that this God doesn't suffer questions, doubts, or complaints. But I eventually came to suspect that any God who is nervous, defensive, or angry in the face of questions is a false god. I began to realize that I often ascribed to God the traits of people who are ill at ease, anxious, and occasionally hateful and who even presume from time to time to speak on God's behalf. I began to wonder if the Bible backs up the contemptuousness they carry around.

Over time, the Bible ceased to be a catalog of all the things one has to believe (or pretend to believe) in order to not go to hell. Instead, the Bible became a broad, multifaceted collection of people crying out to God—a collection of close encounters with the God who is present, somehow, in those very cries. Far from being an anthology of greeting-card material, those accounts of joy, anger, lamentation, and hope are all bound up in the most formidable array of social criticism ever assembled in one volume.

And Christianity, far from being a tradition in which doubts and questions are suppressed in favor of uncritical, blind faith, began to assume the form of a robust culture in which anything can be asked and everything can be said. The call to worship is a call to complete candor and radical questioning—questioning the way things are, the way we are, and the way things ought to be. As G. K. Chesterton observed, the New Testament portrays a God who, by being wholly present in the dying cry of Jesus of Nazareth, even doubted and questioned himself.[5] The summons to sacred questioning—like the call to honesty, like the call to prayer—is a call to be true and to let the chips fall where they may. This call to worship is deeper than the call to sign off on a checklist of particular tenets or beliefs. It is also more difficult.

Some version of the Uncle Ben story works its way like an ominous thread throughout history and is woven throughout various religious traditions. There is no proof against it. Natural and man-made disasters seem to confirm the logic of Uncle Ben. We can feel it. We can testify to it.

Life does, indeed, feel this way. It appears that only wickedness prospers, that might makes right, and that things don't seem to be changing for the better. The poet, the prophet, the psalmist, and the singer are among the first to say so.

This is an image of God that can be discerned in environmental devastation, cutthroat consumerism, and economic Darwinism, whose reflection is especially evident in the paving over of paradise with parking lots, whose will, it is assumed, underwrites the plundering of natural resources that advertises itself as progress and efficiency, whose affections don't extend to those consigned to an early death by virtue of where they were born, those the God of "progress" is willing to leave behind.

But this image of God *will not suffice*. We must resist, in word and deed, this God who is no God at all. Determined to look evil squarely in the eye, the tradition of sacred questioning is driven to insist: this can't be right. There's a conspiracy of hope afoot, a beleaguered assembly of voices determined to oppose the apparent power of evil in the world. There are cracks and fissures in the prison walls, and light is shining in. There's a way out, and the big, black boot of power (Orwell's image) won't be pressed on the human face forever. Another world—a world of hope and love—can exist among us. Maybe God isn't against such a world. Maybe God is *for* it, *behind* it, and *within* it in ways we have yet to understand. Maybe God is never *not* redeeming and has long been at work among people in our past and our present who cultivate more redemptive ways of being in the world. And maybe this redemption is even now under way, on the earth, as it already is in the heavens.

You *Have* to Believe It, and You *Hate* It

One of my favorite instances of an exchange between a dire, dutiful, fear-driven view of God and a lively, determined curiosity occurs in the back of a pickup truck in the film version of Katherine Paterson's *Bridge to Terabithia.*

Throughout the film, ten-year-old Jess Aarons has his sense of competitiveness, propriety, and what's fair questioned by a creative, free-spirited ten-year-old girl named Leslie Burke. In the woods adjoining their homes, they journey out on a daily basis to adventure in an imaginary realm they created. Their play, centered around an old dilapidated tree house they've reassembled, regularly calls into existence the magical kingdom of Terabithia.

One Friday, when they've been rained out, Jess laments that Saturday's chores will take precedence over Terabithia and that he's got church the next day. When Leslie asks if she can come, Jess feels certain she will hate church (females are expected to wear dresses), but Leslie insists, suspecting she'll find it all incredibly cool.

"I'm really glad I came," she observes on the ride home with Jess and his little sister, May Belle, in the back of a truck. "That whole Jesus thing is really interesting, isn't it? . . . It's really kind of a beautiful story."

Reared to believe that Christianity is never to be talked about in such casual tones, May Belle protests with an exasperated lisp, "It ain't beautiful. It's *scary*! Nailing holes right through somebody's hand."

Then Jess chimes in, "May Belle's right. It's because we're all vile sinners that God made Jesus die."

"You really think that's true?" Leslie asks.

"It's in the Bible, Leslie," Jess interjects with a tone of resigned finality, as if such grim consent to the bleak ways of the divine is where all rightly informed people eventually arrive.

"You *have* to believe it, but you *hate* it," Leslie notes with a puzzled smile. "I don't have to believe it, and I think it's beautiful."

"You gotta believe the Bible, Leslie," May Belle asserts, interrupting Leslie's meditation.

"Why?" Leslie asks.

"'Cause if you don't believe in the Bible, God'll damn you to hell when you die."

Taken aback by the image of God as an angry judge who would consign those who fail to believe rightly to eternal agony and by the difficulties of reconciling this image of a God known most fully in Jesus, Leslie asks for her source. May Belle can't quote chapter and verse, but she can turn to Jess, who reluctantly agrees that somewhere in the Bible it can be plainly discerned that failure to comply with its contents will result in a fate worse than death.

"Well," Leslie said, "I don't think so. I seriously do not think God goes around damning people to hell. He's too busy running all *this*."

And Leslie raises her arms (it seems to me in praise) to signal an awareness of the wind, the sky, the trees, and the entire bright and beautiful landscape through which they're driving.

Leslie doesn't step into this age-old conversation with an

argument; she enlivens it with a witness. She calls on her peers to behold along with her the majesty of the wonderfully weird world they're in. She asks them to consider the possibility that their view of the Creator might be limited, mean, and perhaps a little tacky. She dares to imagine that God's redemptive purposes extend to life *before* death as well as after. In her limited experience of their religious tradition, she senses that the call to worshipfulness continues outside of their weekly "worship service." She even reckons that, one way or another, "that whole Jesus thing" is a call to revere others, ourselves, and our surroundings more intensely, a call to esteem life sacredly.

Maybe questions are how it happens. Maybe God *likes* questions.

Politics of Reverence

Suggesting that questioning is crucial to a life of devotion to God runs counter to many accounts of the meaning of religion, but the notion is borne out in the deep, life-bearing streams of many religious traditions. The religious impulse begins with a sense of awe, a sense of not knowing the fullness of what we're looking at. It is only when we're blessed by a feeling of finitude that we can begin to perceive the holy, that sense of a whole before which our limited understanding is dwarfed.

A work of art such as *Bridge to Terabithia* can sometimes bring us to this place. A view of the Grand Canyon can too. Images taken from the Hubble telescope can shut us up for a moment. Take a talkative three-year-old to the zoo, and you will note that out of silence and a sense of awe come questions. Religion is born out of questions, not answers. Only a twisted, unimaginative mind-set resists awe in favor of self-satisfied certainty.

We often call such a mind-set "fundamentalist," but we might simply call it "bad religion." And for the sake of humility—a characteristic crucial to sacred questioning—we might do well to confess that we're capable at any moment of such bad religion ourselves. We're capable of reducing other people to a cartoon character or caricature. We tend to be unwilling to treat what we perceive to be the opposition in a proper manner. Instead of dealing with others with a sense of graciousness and fair-mindedness, we devalue them in the very ways we fear they devalue us.

More humility might characterize our talk of God if we believe that the whole truth can never be entirely ours and that our attempts to nail God down are always well-intentioned human constructs at best and idols at worst. We might become more self-aware and pay closer attention to how our ideas about God affect the way we treat other people. We might commit ourselves to asking and receiving questions. Living this way, *anyone*—even someone sporting an offensive bumper sticker—might be a bearer of the wisdom we need and a speaker of a word from the Lord. Perhaps we should occasionally place our hands together like Buddhists and bow to them. Or, as a Celtic prayer has it, we might sense the spirit of Christ in the heart of the one we speak to *and* the one we listen to.

When we don't speak agreeably to someone with whom we disagree and don't know how to ask questions because we think we already possess most answers, we're practicing bad religion. We aren't curious or kind (save to our fellow believers), and we can't be made to question, even for a moment, our fear-hardened beliefs. As best-selling atheist Christopher Hitchens put it, we're breathing in the religion that poisons everything.

This refusal to question, to listen, and to think past a certain point has tragic consequences, easily discerned in the morning headlines. Self-described people of God are wreaking havoc in our world. They revere their own faith, but their irreverence for the faith of others is the loudest voice in the room. Perhaps that irreverence for others is an unconscious attempt to make peace with the Uncle Ben God. The God of our false beliefs seems pitiless, so maybe we're supposed to be as well. Maybe that's how we get on his good side. Maybe that's how we (gulp) make peace with him. But at what price? Is dwelling in nervous, habitual hostility toward most people, the people with whom we disagree, a form of peace, salaam, or shalom in any verifiable or discernible way? Are we mistaking our religion for our God?

I believe the living God calls us to refuse to "make peace" with such idols. Instead, we're called to wrestle with a God more complex and more deeply affectionate toward all of life than whatever God we have in mind. Due reverence toward other people, in this sense, is a work that is never complete, a work that is ever before us. Anything less is bad worship, bad theology, and a plain old bad idea. As that very famous prayer involving debts and trespasses reminds us, the peace we make (or don't make) with others — those who vote differently or believe differently or who happen to have been born in a different country — is the same peace we have (or don't have) with our Maker. Peace with God and peace with others are never separate issues. When we say we love God while hating others, we lie and the truth is not in us.[6]

I'd like to suggest that the deepest call of most religious traditions is the call to reverence, specifically the revering of other human beings, no matter their creed or DNA or documentation. A call to revere God by revering the people who bear God's image is a call to revere all people.

This is very different from the way many religious groups grasp for power to protect their own interests. How can we challenge such deeply ingrained practices? No rabbi, Zen master, prophet, or saint ever said it would be easy. I'd like to think my grandfather somehow sensed this. I know my father did. We're called to revere. We're called to be afraid of ourselves, our own evil, our own tendency to pervert, to mischaracterize, and to bear false witness. And as we read, look, listen, and create, we're called to ask questions. We're called to remain open to moments of illumination — *religious* moments, if you will. We're each called to ask questions — in the name of life and hope — as if our souls depend on it.

Sacred questioning (and the reverence that generates such questions) makes witness to God possible. Without reverence, there is no witness.

· · ● ◉ ● · ·

Questions for Further Conversation

1. What's up with Uncle Ben? Does this story speak to your understanding of God? If it doesn't, how does your experience differ? What hesitations might accompany a radical break with the Uncle Ben image of the divine? What might be gained in such a break?

2. In the "Move On" section, Granddaddy Dark seems to make a distinction between what he understands to be the will of God and the God who always surpasses his understanding. How does this distinction function in his advice to his son? And what does the advice say about the nature of the God in whom Granddaddy Dark ultimately placed his trust?

3. How is sacred questioning an essential aspect of faith?

4. What's at stake in the conversation between the young theologians in *Bridge to Terabithia*? Does Leslie have a higher view of God than her companions? How would you distinguish between her sense of reverence and theirs?

5. How might people with an Uncle Ben–like view of God respond to the idea that questions—lots of questions—are a good thing? Is there a danger in becoming too attached to our questions? What are the pitfalls, and are they worth it? What do we lose when we don't ask questions?

6. How might our understanding of God impact our response to economic practices? Do we imagine that God is somehow divorced from economic concerns? Why might we find it necessary to imagine God's relationship to our world in this way? Does God's kingdom challenge our less than humane economic practices? If so, how?

The Unbearable Lightness of Being Brainwashed

Questioning Religion

Whoever is afraid of dialogue is hiding something.
Sheikh Reda Shata, Muslim imam

We shouldn't be mad at Chef for leaving us.
We should be mad at that fruity little club
for scrambling his brains.
**Children of *South Park*, eulogizing
the loss of their friend Chef**

As a wedding present, a Roman Catholic friend gave me a crucifix sculpture with a milky-white Jesus about as tall as an old-school G.I. Joe doll. I liked it a lot, but my wife, Sarah, and I were never sure where it belonged. Placing it prominently over the fireplace risked setting a tone with guests that, as much as we like talking about Jesus, felt a tad overbearing. Just laying it on a shelf somewhere seemed irreverent. So it landed on a filing cabinet next to my writing desk in the guest room, as if presiding over my literary aspirations.

In time, we crammed a couch in the guest room, and our then three-year-old daughter, Dorothy, took to standing, bouncing, and lounging on it while staring out the window. One day Sarah found her lying there with her hands behind her head, staring up at the pale Jesus nailed to the cross. "Hey, Mom. What happened to that little guy?"

Sarah and I are always grateful for questions like these from our children, but we're also freaked out by the prospect of responding badly and doing damage. Before we even know what to say, an overwhelming waterfall of Very Bad Answers floods the mind. (Sarah didn't tell Dorothy that it was interesting that she should ask because, as it turns out, her own sin, selfishness, and disobedience nailed him there.) Life-giving answers don't always spring to mind in these teachable moments—we're too busy thinking of what *not* to say.

Sarah can't recall how she responded, but I think my answer would have been, "It's a long story," followed by a silent prayer that Dorothy would put her sacred questioning on hold long enough for me to think of my answer.

Fast-forward to Dorothy's eighth year, and she's still at it. She wants to know which part of *The Simpsons* movie made me laugh the hardest, and I tell her it was the part where Grampa Simpson is seized during a church service by a restless spirit, and Marge begs Homer to do something—anything—to calm his convulsing, frothing-at-the-mouth father. Homer starts feverishly flipping through the nearest pew Bible and, in a typically Simpsonesque shot at popular religion, exclaims, "This book doesn't have any answers!"

Dorothy laughs dutifully and then pauses with a concerned look. "Well, of course, the Bible *does* have answers."

Believe it or not, this teachable moment took a very good turn or two *and* didn't end with Dorothy getting fed up with my tendency to belabor an issue. Through some miracle, it occurred to me to say that the Bible isn't like a phone book (this struck her as plainly true). And I told her that it doesn't give us answers the way we might want it to—that people sometimes try to make the Bible seem like a big book full of *easy* answers, but it isn't. It's a bunch of voices from the past that ask *us* a lot of questions about why we do things the way we do—so it's a collection of questions too, including questions we *still* haven't answered. Dorothy kept listening, and I was just warming up, but I was relieved when Dorothy stopped asking about the Bible and asked about lunch.

At this moment, you might be praying a prayer of mercy for a poor, harried eight-year-old whose father will likely intellectualize her into a place of intense loneliness, and you might be right to do so. But you should understand that this same eight-year-old, a few weeks earlier, asked a Presbyterian minister why God made Jesus.

If I could fast-forward to Dorothy's first semester of college—when, for many, questions come rushing with the force of a fire hose—I'd want to tell her that God is stranger and the biblical witness is richer than anyone can reckon. I'd want her to know that when people talk about guaranteed solutions, cure-alls, and instantly answered prayers, a meaningfully biblical faith isn't being practiced. And, in the interest of preventing brainwash, I'd want to hand down the same word that my forefathers handed down to me: When necessary, move on.

Losing My Religion

It's tempting to characterize my grandfather's advice to my father as a safety clause, an escape route from religious ideology, as if the only hope for the religious is the possibility that they might just get over it. But I don't think I'd be doing justice to my grandfather's story if I tried to suggest that his advice was somehow separate from his religion. Like many people, my grandfather tried to be faithful to a particular story. He told it and retold it. He tried to make it add up rationally. He wanted to bend his will toward a life of obedience to it. And—this is where it gets complicated—he tried to persuade people that much of what they *thought* was acceptable to God wasn't. He tried to call them, and himself, to repent. He felt compelled by the story as he understood it.

Most redemptively, he felt compelled to remember, as he told the story, that his own testimony wasn't the *whole* story. He sought God but knew he would never *have* God in the way one holds a copyright or a piece of property. God would never be the *object* of his search, because God, whatever God is, refuses to be objectified. My grandfather knew he was not a knower but only another pilgrim—a practitioner—of religious awe. Perhaps, in some fashion, this describes everyone.

Needless to say, one doesn't set out to cultivate a sense of awe. Awe happens. And out of that awe, religion happens—for better and for worse. My grandfather took his sense of religiosity seriously enough to handle it lightly, to hold his religion, at least on occasion, with an open hand.

"Losing my religion," in addition to being the title of an incredibly good song by the band R.E.M., is also a variation of a Southern expression. While the phrase is often employed in jest, it names a state of shock in which something so unsettling or unexpected has occurred that it calls for a paradigm shift and perhaps even a disavowal of certain truths once held as self-evident. It's the feeling of things falling apart, of the center no longer holding. The old binding ideas aren't working anymore. Like an encounter with a ghost or an extraterrestrial, it's as if everything we thought we knew about reality is wrong. There's more at work in the world than we've dreamed of in our petty little philosophies. It might even call for a formal break with one's religion.

As a high school English teacher, I like to tell my students that if their encounters with the Bible, Shakespeare, film, music, and poetry don't in any way undo their worlds or lead them to change their way of thinking (what's still occasionally called repentance), they're probably wasting their time. Kafka said a good book should be like an ice ax cracking away at the frozen sea inside us all. Jesus spoke of old wineskins that couldn't contain new wine and about losing your life to find it.[1] The apostle Paul talked about Christ-followers as having died to the old self.[2] In this sense, we should take advantage of every chance we have to lose our religion. As wonderful as our religion might feel, it's never so fresh that we should settle for it. A living religiosity will be sustained by questions, revelations, and a determination to be transformed by the renewing of our minds.[3]

Southern writer Flannery O'Connor once remarked that people talk about religious faith as if it's an electric blanket, cozy and available for quick and easy reassurance, an ever-present resource for avoiding the truth of the matter. In response to religion-as-sentimentality, she argued that a Christian faith is always more like a cross, a costly engagement with the world. The bearer of faith enters into the crisis of what's wrong with the world rather than glossing over it. In this sense, O'Connor's faith made her *more*, not less, realistic, more determined to see things as they are, not as we'd prefer them to be.

O'Connor insisted that it was her Christian faith that kept her skeptical. She says that the cultivation of skepticism is a sacred obligation because skepticism keeps us asking questions. Against whatever flavor of brainwash is popular, skepticism "will keep you free — not free to do anything you please, but free to be formed by something larger than your own intellect or the intellects of those around you."[4] This *redemptive* skepticism is a religious commitment to avoid being swept up by bad ideas, especially ones that wear a godly guise and demand absolute, unquestioning allegiance. Sometimes you have to lose your religion to find it.

Insert Soul Here

This idea is the stark opposite of what usually comes to mind when we speak of religion. Let's proceed carefully. By "religion," I'm speaking of an ethical summons, a calling out. Religious expression, for instance, is the expression that binds (*religio* means "binding influence"). In the positive sense, it is the expression that imaginatively challenges the status quo, breaking bonds with a different, wider angle concerning what is or should be out of bounds. It redemptively unsettles whatever unworthy authority currently holds sway. When Bob Dylan attests that, as a young man, he thought of Johnny Cash as a religious figure, he's describing a voice that grabbed hold of him, demanding a reappraisal of whatever he thought he knew about life and how to live it before Cash came into his life.

According to Dylan's own testimony, hearing "I Walk the Line" for the first time was like hearing a voice calling out, "What are you doing there, boy?" It was a voice from across history:

> Johnny didn't have a piercing yell, but ten thousand years of culture fell from him. He could have been a cave dweller. He sounds like he's at the edge of the fire, or in the deep snow, or in a ghostly forest, the coolness of conscious obvious strength, full tilt and vibrant with danger.... Johnny's voice was so big, it made the world grow small.... Words that were the rule of law and backed by the power of God.[5]

Is this the space of sacred witness? What do we think is going on here? Sending or receiving? Or both?

When we take in art religiously, we're listening for a wake-up call. Something grabs us—while listening to P. J. Harvey, watching a Martin Scorsese film, looking at a painting by Georgia O'Keefe, or reading Toni Morrison—and we are smack-dab in the thick of the religious. Whether by way of a lyric, a joke, an image, a sound, or a sentence, we're made to realize and to pay heed to a wider sense of the world by way of what someone is saying. We want to hear the voices that partake of and contribute to what I like to call the club of cosmic plainspeak,[6] an informal crowd that includes, for instance, Richard Pryor, Patti Smith, Mark Twain, and all the truth tellers you'll find crammed within these pages. There are so many people, dead and alive, to learn from, so many people out of whom the plainspeak, the legendary electricity, flows. Cosmic plainspeak is that disruptively truthful expression that engages our religiosity and gets through to our nervous systems, rearranging the way we see. Our hearts are made more open; something is awakening within. This isn't to say we're being brainwashed, but we are no longer mere spectators or consumers. We are being engaged. We feel moved, compelled, by something—even if it's only another human voice. What else is there? Religion happens.

Yale professor Harold Bloom observed that Karl Marx had it only partly right when he said that religion is the opiate of the people. More broadly speaking, it is the poetry of the people, both the good and the bad, for better and worse. According to Bloom, trying to attack or conquer such a massive target is almost as useless as blindly celebrating it. But religion can, and should be, objected to, questioned, and talked about. Contrary to many adherents who demand unquestioning respect for their faith, religion is perfectly and wonderfully objectionable. In fact, what else in life could be *more* worthy of objection? Interestingly, most religious traditions are constantly objecting to *themselves* over the decades and centuries, challenging old categories with new, religious proclamations. This is how religions work. Devastating criticism of religion is always *part of* religion. The religiously faithful aren't just permitted to critique and complain and reform; they're *bound* to do as much *by* religion. Without it, there is no faithfulness.

Of course, when religion won't tolerate questions, objections, or differences of opinion and all it can do is threaten excommunication, violence, and hellfire, it has an unfortunate habit of producing some of the most hateful people to ever walk the earth. Blaise Pascal once observed that one never practices evil so completely and with such cheer as one does when motivated by religious conviction. In this sense, religion isn't something good folks would ever wish on friends or enemies. It's something rightfully held in contempt by honest, well-meaning people all over the world. It's a washing over of otherwise decent brains. Who needs it?

But religion per se isn't something we could ever be strictly for or against. "Religion" by itself is a void-of-content term. The actual content of a religion can only be known by the everyday practice of the practitioners of particular faiths. Or as one religious tradition puts it, "By their fruit you will recognize them."[7]

This is a difficult prospect for many self-professed religious people because it means their personal, private faith is, in some sense, everybody's business, including those who don't share their religion. To put it more provocatively, the content of the faith that sits deep down in our hearts is verifiable and knowable only by the way we speak, the way we act, and the way we generally treat other people. It's talkaboutable. It's funny. It's open to investigation. Questionable. Deniable. Objectionable even. Like wars on terror, jobless rates, and the foibles of famous people, it's something we get to hold up to the light of everyday conversation. If we don't, we could hardly be more thoroughly brainwashed and intellectually dead, and, religiously speaking, we could be no more thoroughly damned.

To confess that I play Tetris religiously isn't to say anything pro or con about religion. But to do it more than once a day, visit the *Drudge Report* every hour, check my cell phone every three minutes, and listen to Rush Limbaugh more often than I listen to any other human voice and to then claim that these things have absolutely *nothing* to do with my religion is to be, to some degree, delusional. My religion *is* my practice. It's what I do.[8]

Because religion is how I am instructed (for better and worse), it is also the name of the con. The *con* game of the *con* artist is a matter of selling *confidence*. Religion happens when I give my heart and mind to a televised image, for instance, that will succeed in directing my behavior, my buying power, and the buttons I press in the voting booth. It really does work, after all. We know it does. We might be better equipped to know what's going on if we stop bracketing religion as an entity unrelated and somehow divorced from our everyday choices. We could recognize that a Mercedes commercial, for example, is a call to worship. Perhaps we should place a sticker on our televisions, computers, and cell phones that reads INSERT SOUL HERE. Religion is what's going on. Now we have to figure out a way to talk about it.

Become Aware of What's Going On in Your Mind

Religion can never be, strictly speaking, a self-contained issue because our religion is nothing more (and nothing less) than the way we order and understand our worlds. It's not just *what* we mean; it's *how* we mean. Our religion is our economy of meaning, and like every economy, it can always do with a little deepening. The Uncle Ben story describes, albeit in a *Twilight Zone* fashion, one way of ordering and understanding the way things are. It describes a religious experience. To a certain extent, it describes *my* religious experience. Religion is the name of the con game.

But hearing the story, receiving it, adding some details, retelling it, and considering it afresh is also religious experience, an experience whereby we begin to see the con we're in. Religion, then, is also the *naming* of the con. The religious voice *makes us more aware* of the con. It awakens the heart to what's happening. The con could be the Babylonian empire, a criminal justice system, a motion-picture industry, a pyramid scheme, a political party, or a military-industrial-entertainment complex, all equally unsound. Religion calls *us* out, and it compels us to place our confidence in something more sound. To be conned, after all, is human. To confess to having been conned is an act of awareness. To believe ourselves impervious to cons is to be in denial, to be dangerous, to perhaps have an especially telegenic personality, and, in our day, to be uniquely electable to public office.

Churches, governments, marketing schemes, and other unsound structures are always with us. Reforming them, deconstructing them, or renouncing their stratagems altogether will often be an ethical imperative. But to begin to get out from under a bad con isn't to escape into a place where everything is permitted, some religion-free zone void of awe or wonder or a sense of the holy. We break with sacred cows all the time, but when we do, it's generally because we've stumbled on something that strikes us as *more* sacred than what we once feverishly sought or bowed down to. This, too, is religion — ever inescapable, always worth talking about, questioning, and, perhaps, reaffirming. What do we hold as sacred? Is it worthy? Have we begun to ask the right questions?

Siddhartha Gautama, the Buddha, decided there was something more sacred than the material wealth and privilege that surrounded him in his formative years. Jesus of Nazareth taught that healing people on the Sabbath was more important than keeping the Sabbath rules. Muhammad asserted that the hypermaterialism of the ostensibly religious merchants of Mecca was displeasing to the one true God. Martin Luther King Jr. persuaded thousands that their worship of racial privilege was unjust, evil, and an abomination in the sight of God. Sacred cows are called into question. Community standards are confronted. Religion happens. You've got to lose your life to find it. You have to learn how to die.

The Only Game in Town

In the shouting matches involving pundits, career politicians, celebrities, and Senate committees, we often hear individuals announce in high-sounding phrases that they won't stand still while their morality, integrity, or religious beliefs are impugned. I understand that certain lines of questioning can take a turn for the hateful, but if we can't talk about the ideas and motivations behind observable behavior (read religion), what is there to talk about?

There are so many ways to shut down conversation and frustrate human connection, so many ways to miss each other. This break in communication serves only to maintain the cartoon realities, the caricatures, the stereotypes, and the untruths. How might we stumble on an alternative space? Where's the candor? Where do we find people who are *really* talking to each other?

"A poet's work" is "to name the unnameable, to point at frauds, to take sides, start arguments, shape the world, and stop it from going to sleep."[9] The voice that butts in, shakes nerves, rattles brains, unmasks pretensions, and takes down names isn't what we typically think of as a religious voice; yet it is this sort of voice that clears the space for sacred questioning. Call it religious or poetic or, if you must, religio-poetic. It's the voice that signals a shift and perhaps does the shifting. It's a public-service announcement. It's the voice that awakens sleepwalkers and daysleepers, calling out to anyone with ears to hear and eyes to see. In this sense, the poetic voice is that always more comprehensive way of putting things. And religion, following Harold Bloom, might be considered the stock inventory of word, image, and story, the always-moving river—never exactly a reservoir—that makes it possible to pull out the poetry to begin with. It's never static. You can never step into the same religion twice.

The sentence that begins the above paragraph is spoken by a character in that most objectionable of late twentieth-century texts *The Satanic Verses*. And the very name of its author, Salman Rushdie, is a reminder that religion is ever under way. Like language, rhetoric, and contracts, religion binds and lets loose all day long. Crying out loud through a multitude of media, religion—like poetry—is happening. It might be the only game in town.

C. S. Lewis once observed that while many people *use* art, only a very few *receive* it.[10] The texts that get called *scriptures* by various religious traditions are often *used* by individuals (mostly quoted out of context) to pepper speeches, buttress bad arguments, and, on occasion, to avoid awareness of responsibility for our actions. We read and quote selectively to better justify what we've already decided to do. Where is the self-awareness in any of this, the sense that our scriptures can, and should, change how we think and act? Will we allow a religious critique of our practice of religion? Are we up for a redeeming word? Show me a transcript of the words you've spoken, typed, or texted in the course of a day, an account of your doings, and a record of your transactions, and I'll show you your religion.

Religion, in this sense, is the whole deal, so it is clearly an exercise in futility to try to locate the places where religion intersects with, say, politics, as if there are a fixed number of interesting spots where religion actually interfaces with the everyday world. Instead, our world is all religion all the time. The exclusive categories of modernism—economics, politics, and so on—do not, in fact, work. They're just different terms for the same thing, the slippery stuff of human existence. Religion is what we have, what there is. Religion is the air we breathe. It's our most immediate and demanding subject matter.

Human Resources

"The most sacred thing I do is care and provide for my workers, my family. I give them money. I give them food. Not directly, but through the money. I heal them." Thus spoke Michael Scott, manager of the Scranton branch of Dunder Mifflin, as he prepared to pick "a great new health care plan" for his employees. On this episode of *The Office*, we watch Michael Scott, portrayed by Steve Carell, bend and mostly break under the strain of trying to believe such words against the evidence of everyone's eyes. His employees are less delusional concerning the gravity of the situation. They know what's going on. And they know how to smile politely or pretend not to notice when Michael observes aloud that he owes his boss status over them to his big heart, keen sense of humor, and overall awesomeness. A guiding trope or theme at work within the series is the suggestion that this delusion, which he wears like a suit five days a week, might be the most important component of his unwritten job description.

So when asked by his superior, Jan Levenson, if he's decided on a plan, Michael casually asserts that he has, of course, decided on "the Gold Plan," a plan neither Michael nor Jan has access to. Ever in the throes of an existential plight, Michael cannot bring himself to admit that it's *his* job to simply pick the cheapest plan and bring the bad news to his underlings. It's what bosses do. When he protests that she'd never do a thing like that, Jan observes, "I'm doing it. Right now. *To you.*"

This begins the process by which Michael tries to keep his

self-image intact by passing the responsibilities of bad news bearing to someone else. Jim Halpert declines and notes that, if he found himself promoted to the level of being implicated in such decisions, he would have to throw himself in front of a train. Dwight Schrute eagerly agrees to it and only regrets that he doesn't get to fire someone ("I slashed benefits to the bone. I saved this company money.... I don't believe in coddling people. In the wild, there is no health care."). Michael locks himself in his office, closes the blinds, and pretends to be overwhelmed with phone calls. As his employees begin to figure out what's afoot, he tries to quiet their disgruntledness with the promise of good news before the end of the workday, "trying to give the troops around here a little bit of a boost." "Operation: Surprise," he calls it. A self-styled genius of comic improv, Michael observes it's when he's backed into a corner that he really comes alive.

When Michael arrives with ice cream sandwiches, he is questioned: "This isn't the *big* surprise, is it? Because we've been having a pretty horrible day." And so, having abdicated his responsibilities, and having supposed that ice cream would make up for a slashed health plan, Michael locks himself in his office again and binges on the unwanted treats. At five o'clock, as everyone lingers to vent their frustration with the diminished coverage, he emerges from his office to loudly and publicly rebuke Dwight for cutting the benefits everyone knows he told him to cut. When he's asked about the big surprise, which he still insists is just around the corner, we're treated to his attempt at the sound of a long drumroll, clapping as if he's warming up, and then an embarrassed silence during which everyone begins to leave. As they walk past him, he rubs his eyes, and no words come.

Strangely, this concluding scene of sad epiphany is interrupted by Michael's narration in which he returns to his identity as a boss/cheerleader/performance artist. Somehow, the dejection brings to mind a hero of his whom, he seems to think, would know what to do. Michael would like to imagine himself to be in a similar league of improvisational charisma: "Robin Williams. Oh, man, would I love to go head-to-head with him. Oh! That would be exciting. 'Hi. I'm Mork from Ork.' Well, *I'm* Bork from Spork. Nanoo, nanoo. Jibelee, baloobaloo."

With this scene of corporate gloom and low expectations, which are never quite low enough, the sudden springing to mind of Robin Williams' ability to make light of just about anything is, in the thinking of a despondent branch manager, only out of place if our world is one of neat, tightly held, easily maintained categories—a world in which show business (maintaining appearances, habitual artificiality) is somehow confined to the entertainment industry and religious hopes can be quietly sequestered within churches, temples, and mosques, a world that bears no resemblance to the world we're in. With that observant, satirical edge that tells it so well by simply telling it like it is, *The Office* performs the function Salman Rushdie accords to poetry. It names the unnameable, articulating what was heretofore unarticulated, and it helps us to look harder and more humorously at the contradictions we sustain and the fraudulent behavior we accept as normal and even inevitable.

The highs and the Kafkaesque lows of Michael Scott and his employees aren't *a separate issue* from religion, because *The Office*, like all great storytelling, has an awareness-expanding function. It expands our sense of what's happening. It might even move us to view one another more compassionately. It *shows*. It interrogates the perversity of a phrase like "human resources" and places a question mark next to a seemingly self-evident saying like "health care." Like the plays of Arthur Miller or the novels of Dostoevsky, the TV program generates questions about society, the way people are commodified, the way we lose ourselves in false definitions of success, the way we see ourselves wrongly. Questions of meaning, of brainwashing, of justice — these are religious questions. Are we receiving them? Are we asking them?

We only receive art when we let it call our own lives into question. If the words of Jesus of Nazareth, for instance, strike us as comfortable and perfectly in tune with our own confident common sense, our likes and dislikes, our budgets, and our actions toward strangers and foreigners, then *receiving* the words of Jesus is probably *not* what we're doing. We may quote a verse, put it in a PowerPoint presentation, or even intone it loudly with an emotional, choked-up quiver, but if it doesn't scandalize or bother us, challenging our already-made-up minds, we aren't really receiving it. Not *religiously* anyway.

The Possibility of Mindfulness

In the interest of better reception and livelier perception in these times — as inundated and overloaded with information and images as we are — we need to rethink and recast our talk of religion. We need to recognize our failures of imagination. To imagine one another well requires a serious (call it religious) commitment to rightly hear the voices that come to us in conversation, in texts, in song, and even on television. Voices of anxiety, tragedy, and hope. Voices with wounds in them. Voices that might prove to be a means of grace. Voices that might save our lives. Voices we miss at our breakneck speed.

It should be obvious that our sense of what is sacred is tragically deficient if it remains closed to all but the most familiar people, places, and ideas. If we aren't reaching toward a fresh understanding of the world through the questions we ask, we remain pretty well zombified in the cold comfort of a dead religiosity. Fresh questions and new acts of imagination are our primary means to encounter love and liveliness, to discover integrity and authenticity. Without them, we're pretty well done for. We have to exercise and exorcise our imagination with questions.

But who has time to look into all these things? A few of my favorite people tell me that the dysfunction on display on *The Office*, for instance, strikes them as a little too close for comfort. They can't watch it, they say, because it only serves to bring them back to the insanity of their everyday reality, a workplace culture they hope to escape for at least a few hours each day and for two days at the end of the week. They fear becoming mere functionaries to management systems that serve to *almost* pay the bills. They boundary up their lives ("*That's* my 9 to 5, but *this* is who I really am"). I must say I hear you, and, for the record, me too.

I will only add this: Let us not forsake the possibility of mindfulness, a commitment to submit everything we're up to, at work and play, to the discipline of sacred questioning. I understand the temptation to leave well enough alone, and I don't want to naysay whatever health and happiness we *do* manage to cultivate at home, at leisure, or more avowedly in worship communities apart from and in spite of the quiet desperation (that *other* worship service) that is our working week—whatever it is we're doing when we think we're *not* worshiping. But if, in the name of maintaining what *feels* like an emotional equilibrium, we lose the habit of asking ourselves hard questions about our everyday practices and the worlds we fund and perpetuate with our lives, our religion becomes little more than a dim-witted maintenance of the status quo. We develop a resistance to anything and anyone who calls our lives into question. Our religious faith, what's left of it, becomes difficult to distinguish from the sentimental coziness of the warm electric blanket Flannery O'Connor warns us about, an anesthetizing presence in our lives.

At their best, all living religious traditions in some fashion offer a challenge to become aware of what's going on in our minds. They invite us to refuse to settle and to resist the reality-distorting media that perpetuate debilitating forms of self-satisfaction. In this sense, living religious traditions are like arsenals, renewable resources for rethinking our lives in light of the ethical demands of more sacredly conducted living—a way of living that confronts the disfiguring generalities of *mere* business, religion, politics, economics, and other deluding categories. But as we understand only too well, it is often the case that the redeeming power of religious witness is sabotaged, squandered, or ignored altogether by those who claim to speak for their religious tradition. For some, their religion is nothing more than a special interest group, a bastion of offendedness and anger, the powerhouse of the saved rather than a place from which life can be viewed and lived more redemptively. Overcoming this tendency—the drive to mistake intensely felt offendedness for *lived* morality—is the subject of the next chapter.

· · ● ● · ·

Questions for Further Conversation

1. What is it about religion, popularly understood, that makes it the ultimate conversation stopper? What do we risk when we talk about it? What might we gain? What makes it difficult for others to broach the topic of religion in our presence?

2. What might it mean to discuss religion redemptively? What ground rules come to mind?

3. If religious appeal is at work whenever the INSERT SOUL HERE pops up in image, word, or advertisement, what are some examples of unacknowledged religions at work in our world?

How might we cultivate a heightened awareness of the religious stakes involved in advertising, governments, and various broadcasts? What are the implications at work in the claim that religion might be "the only game in town"?

4. How do you distinguish between *receiving* a religious witness—in scripture, literature, or art—and merely *using* it? How does the popular understanding of religion and everything we often take to be *outside of* the religious sphere undermine the possibility of real reception? Can you think of examples of biblical texts or song lyrics or quotes being used rather than received?

5. In the "Human Resources" section, we consider the ways in which a comedy such as *The Office* can expand the space of the talkaboutable in the same way a novel or a lyric or an especially jarring image can. How might we carry the prophetic power and the ethical heft of a good television program into our everyday interactions? Can you think of other forms of media content (film, music, literature) that also speak to the sometimes-perverse use of a strange phrase such as "Human Resources"? Can you think of other disfiguring generalities that pepper the way we talk about people, the world, life, and how to live it?

Everybody to the Limit

Questioning Our Offendedness

Demons are known to work on men's imagination
until everything is other than it is.
Thomas Aquinas, *Summa Theologica*

Guys like us, we don't pay attention to the polls.
We know that polls are just a collection of statistics
that reflect what people are thinking in "reality."
And reality has a well-known liberal bias.
**Stephen Colbert, at the 2006 White House
correspondents' dinner**

When I was first spotted reading the thick Russian novels of
Fyodor Dostoevsky as a teenager, people began to look at me as
if to say, "Wow. Aren't *you* all smart, serious, and substantial?" It
never occurred to me to say, "What I hold here in my hands is the
surefire drama of people going crazy," or, "It's all about the snappy
dialogue." But it was and is. The big book was like the human
mind laid bare. The true-to-lifeness of the exchanges turned my
young head. Dostoevsky's endlessly defensive characters with their
self-justifying chatter were just like me and my friends. They got
worked up the way we got worked up. This apostle of shame and
self-consciousness captured the feverish anxieties and escalating
insecurities of so many people I knew, people who didn't care

what *anybody* thought and wanted *everybody* to know it. He got to the bottom of the madness that gets hold of us. He told it like it was. Everything, it seemed to me, was there. It was as if Dostoevsky had us all on microphones. The wicked grin that crept onto all of his characters' faces was my own. Not only did I find that I could understand Dostoevsky; *he* understood *me*. And it was all incredibly funny. Like all great novelists, he illuminated the whys and the hows of my emotional landscape. His nineteenth century was *so* twentieth century. The times I was living in felt downright Dostoevskyan. They still do.

The Office wasn't around when I was growing up, but Woody Allen was, and exposure to his films, it seemed to me, let in the air the way a comedy like *Arrested Development* does now. They satirize what we do and the way we do it, offering exposés of real-live ignorance. They do what Dostoevsky did—show us ourselves by dramatizing and rendering comical the otherwise incoherent facts of the way we feel, the secret shame that quickens the pulse. They shine a light on our screwiness, and by doing so, they are a ministry to us. Like the literature that comes to be called classic, they expand the space of the talkaboutable.

In *The Brothers Karamazov*, *Notes from Underground*, and *Demons*, Dostoevsky gives us characters who show up at parties and stay too long to spite the people they imagine don't want them there. They borrow money to buy clothes they hope will make winning impressions on the ones they will love or hate, depending on the confidence they do or don't feel from day to day. They knowingly manufacture feelings of offendedness out of sheer boredom and for the purposes of entertainment. They *decide* to fall in love. They constantly mistake what they merely *feel* for what they *know*. His internal monologues are like typed transcripts of our anxious thought processes. Friedrich Nietzsche said Dostoevsky's prose possessed the voice of blood. We can only imagine what Dostoevsky would have made of the social dynamics at work in text messages and blogs and Facebook.

Dostoevsky describes, names, and engages the spirits that make us crazy and mean. I suppose this is what I'm looking for in all my literary, musical, and audiovisual dabblings — my intelligence gathering, as it were. Which brings to mind a novelist who captures as well or better than just about anyone the weirdness of our own day and our troubled relationship with electronic media and all it hath wrought within and upon our hearts and minds. That novelist is William Gibson. He's the fellow who coined the term *cyberspace* more than twenty years ago. While he is most often referred to as a science fiction writer, I think it appropriate to place him within that genre only if it means we take him more, not less, seriously. Gibson has watched technological developments accelerate to the point that his material is no longer science fiction in the popular sense. Or rather, the times have taken a turn for the sci-fi.[1] The high-tech brainwash is on.

One particular exchange between a daughter and her mother in his novel *Spook Country* spotlights the concern of this chapter amazingly well. The daughter, Hollis Henry, is the former lead vocalist of a popular early-nineties punk band called The Curfew who has taken up a career in journalism. The following cell phone exchange occurs when she checks in on her parents. Her mother assures her that all is well, except for a certain strangeness in the moods of her father, a retiree in his late seventies, who has developed a fierce and uncharacteristic interest in politics. Sound familiar? This interest, her mother tells Hollis, seems to engage his passions more than anything else does, but it renders him angry and disagreeable most of the time.

> "He says it's because it's never been this bad," her mother said, "but I tell him it's only because he never paid it this

much attention before. And it's the Internet. People used to have to wait for the paper, or for the news on television. Now it's like a tap running. He sits down with that thing at any time of the day or night, and starts reading. I tell him it's not like there's anything he can do about any of it anyway."[2]

"Like a tap running" is worthy of Marshall McLuhan.[3] All anxiety all of the time. It keeps the mind going, but going *where* and to *what end*? It's not as if the media junkie is moved to volunteer to tutor underprivileged youth or serve food at a homeless shelter. Media junkies immerse themselves in the news—like soaking in a warm bath—and remain there all day and into the night.

Hollis tells her mother that it's better than nothing: "It gives him something to think about. You know it's good for people your age to have interests."

Her mother's response is vintage William Gibson: "You aren't the one who has to listen to him."[4]

I don't have any solution for our national addiction to news that only ineffectively agitates, the steady stream of stories that offend and titillate without helping us redirect our lives in any positive direction. I don't have answers, but I do have comedy, especially when we're saying the same things over and over again and our sanctimoniousness is going nowhere. We need to stop and take note of our own ridiculousness. We need to remember that a fanatic is someone who *can't* change his mind and *won't* change the subject. Some of these spirits that get hold of us might be driven out by questions and laughter and prayer—and maybe a few tears (not necessarily happening all at the same time). We need a talking cure, and the possibility of redemption lurks in any number of unlikely corners. Comedy might puncture a harmful delusion or two by means of a carefully constructed celebrity fool who's never met a fact he can't deny with his gut feelings of personal infallibility. Ladies and gentlemen, I give you Stephen Colbert.

Concerning Truthiness

When Stephen Colbert opens *The Colbert Report* with the threat, the promise, and his own personal guarantee of Truth-o-cution, "two maximum strength tablets of Truth," or a ride on the Truth-Coaster, it might be important to note, for the more easily offended, that he isn't making fun of the possibility of truth, strictly speaking. He is, however, having a good time lampooning the notion that any celebrity talking head, news network, or religious authority might own truth's copyright. And I hope it's becoming obvious why such lampooning is not only a good thing but absolutely necessary if we're to avoid an unexamined life, mass hypnosis, and uncritical surrender to our preferred forms of newspeak. Colbert channels and engages the spirit that insists there's an international, multicultural assault on truth, and only a loud man in a tie can save us. For his expert satire, submitted alongside the broadcasts of the psychotic, self-promoting truth-meisters of our day, I want to thank him whenever his truthisms enter my mind: "It's time to jump down, turn around, and pick a bale of Truth." "Knock knock. Who's there? The Truth. No joke." "If beauty be Truth and Truth beauty, then I look fabulous tonight."

When he celebrated the proud triumph of "the Truth *unfiltered* by rational argument" in front of the president at the White House correspondents' dinner, it was a largely unprecedented interface between the knowingly theatrical productions of comedy and the less avowedly fabricated production of political press conferences. I suspect the text of Colbert's speech will find its way into an anthology of political satire perhaps a few pages over from Jonathan Swift and Mark Twain. The play's the thing, one sensed all too well. *Whose* truth and *which* rationality will reign from one moment to the next will often be a matter of which gentle mortal has access to the microphone. A radically democratic moment, it seemed to me, and a redemptive bit of fair play if we affirm, as one source has it, that all the world's a stage.

I don't think we can joke about this sort of thing too much—all the vain, self-satisfied, insane ways we carry on about truth, as if we know exactly what we're talking about, as if we have access to a God's-eye view of what's really going on. We don't know our own minds from one minute to the next. We're mad to think we've got hold of truth like nobody else or that we *want it* more or that our relationship to the Almighty trumps everyone else's. With such atmospheric conditions surrounding our speech, we need jokes like we need clean air. We can't live or think sanely without them. We need something or other to rearrange the hierarchies of supposed seriousness, to remind each and all that we're just sorry saps—in some sense, "poor existing individuals," in Kierkegaard's phrase, like everybody else. We need jokes to keep it all talkaboutable.

A joke can clear a space for candor, and without candor there can be little in the way of conversation (or, for that matter, conversion). In this sense, we might make the right to make a joke an inalienable one for the purposes of truthful talk; we might make the right to find one another funny or problematic in what we say and do a right that must be accorded all comers in civil discourse. Or, to put it another way, no one gets to insist on the right to not feel silly. We will treasure one another's testimonies, even past the point of feeling offended. We'll risk it in the hope of truth. And we might even go so far as to confess that actual conversation, genuine listening, and authenticity aren't states toward which many of us tend. Instead, we ought to seek out the company and conversation of folks who'll dare to disagree with us, people who will tell us (perhaps with our encouragement) when they think we're wrong, confused, or hateful. The risk of feeling offended comes with the territory. It's worth it.

When we refuse to take the risk, we develop a built-in resistance to any information that refuses to fall in line with our preconceived notions. As a masterfully wrought caricature of this mind-set, Colbert demonstrates how such insanely foolish hardheadedness can dull our minds to the point that the information won't even register. To hilarious effect, Colbert considers his invincible ignorance to be his strongest character trait. This parody of the way many of us are shut up and closed off within our minds hits what might be the cultural bull's-eye of our time, our enthrallment under what T-Bone Burnett terms "the black mass media." Colbert holds up a mirror to how fickle and hastily improvised our interpretations of the world are and how emotionally persuasive our refusal to see what's in front of us can be.

It's a catch–22. We might already be way past the point where someone has the nerve, the optimism, or the mad hope to dare to disagree with us. Have we lost the habit, the skill of listening for anything more than a breath or a pause so we can jump back in with our own argument? Are we listening, or are we planning a response? Can anybody get through to us? Might the madness on display in the Stephen Colbert character somehow mirror our own?

I Find You Offensive

Admittedly, we all walk around feeling comforted and assured by specific certainties, but our sense of assuredness as true believers (whatever it is we claim we believe) need not preempt the possibility of feedback. "We condemn as unacceptable ..." is the opening phrase intoned by various groups in response to all manner of pictures, programs, or prose they view as offensive. Are we unwilling to endure the pain of a drawing? Does the pristine intensity of one's faith require that any question or jibe pointed toward its content be ruled as impertinent and out of order? If we won't entertain disagreement, how can a conversation ever occur? What is anybody's faith for? Isn't openness to the dangers of feeling offended a prerequisite to an actual relationship?

As we consider the escalating furor that accompanies word of Muhammad depicted in Danish cartoons; the portrayals of Jesus, Satan, and Scientology on *South Park*; and (if you can remember this far back) Andrew Serrano's crucifix submerged in urine, it might be of interest to note that the earliest known pictorial depiction of Jesus on the cross was a cartoon. Often referred to as "The Alexamenos Graffito," it's a crude drawing of a human figure raising a reverent hand toward a crucified individual with the head of a mule.[5] Discovered on the plaster wall of an ancient Roman school, this second-century parody of a certain Jewish Messianic movement includes, scrawled beneath the caricature, a taunt perhaps best translated as "Alexamenos worships his god."

I wish this particular cartoon could find wider distribution because it dismantles the image of the Christian, historically speaking, as a member of a special interest group, a sleeper cell for a political party, or a power constellation of offended people looking for something to boycott. In its place, we have a fellow named Alexamenos who's gotten caught (or accused of) believing that there's something dignified and praiseworthy in the career of a publicly executed Jewish peasant revolutionary.

Under the jurisdiction of the Roman Empire, where it was often believed that might alone made right, Alexamenos's purported conviction was (note my use of this phrase) *objectionable subject matter*, which is to say, subject matter able to be objected to. Peculiar convictions like those of Alexamenos are like that.

They're vulnerable, of human interest, and open for debate, ridicule, and adoption. This is how people get freed up, converted, disabused, and discipled. Things get talked about. The anonymous graffiti artist voiced his objection by implying that Alexamenos's adoration of Jesus was tantamount to worshiping a dying donkey. He might have hoped to cajole him toward a more sensible, less offensive worldview, something more decent and in line with the right thinking of people who knew what was what. Perhaps Alexamenos found this objection objectionable. Maybe the drawing hurt his feelings.

But it probably would have been out of keeping with the presumed ethos of the Jesus who Alexamenos dared to admire to angrily condemn the ridicule as unacceptable (with a hint of violent reprisal). If the Sermon on the Mount is any indication, Jesus taught his followers that suffering public denunciation is part of the deal. Proclaiming the kingdom of God does not include shouting down anyone who finds your proclamation unconvincing. After all, how would the Nazarene's revolution differ from all the others if it had chosen to silence, censor, and eliminate all opposition? What would make it any different from the groups of folks (in Jesus' case, "the Gentiles") who hate anyone who disagrees with them? The late comedian Bill Hicks was once cornered outside a bar by some self-described Christians who didn't like his Jesus jokes. When it became clear that they were threatening bodily harm, a thought occurred to him. He asked them if they were indeed Christians, and when they responded in the ambivalent affirmative, he borrowed a notion occasionally associated with their professed faith: "Well then, I have an idea. Forgive me!" Thrown into confusion by this novel suggestion and the details of what they were so sure they were offended about, they glanced at one another uncomfortably and left. And Hicks gained more winning material for his routine. I think he was on to something.

Selective Fundamentalism

The feeling of offendedness is invigorating. It might even be an effective way to bend a population toward a tyrant's will. But we must never settle for it. We must not confuse an accelerated pulse rate for the presence of the Holy Spirit in our hearts. We must interrogate our offendedness, hold it open for question. Complaining about Harry Potter or getting worked up over *The Golden Compass* (Philip Pullman's literary response to the damage done to people's imaginations in the name of religion) or pitting ticket sales of the Narnia films against *Brokeback Mountain* is a much less complicated call than that whole business about loving neighbors, to say nothing about loving enemies. If we're more opposed, for instance, to what we take to be "bad language" and nude scenes and films about gay people than we are to people being blown up, starved to death, deprived of life-saving medicine, or tortured, our offendedness is out of whack. We have yet to understand the nature of real perversion. We aren't as deeply acquainted with our religion as we might think.

Feeling offended is a reassuring sensation. It's easier than asking ourselves if the redeeming love of God is evident in the way we communicate with people. It's easier than considering our relationships with the huddled masses throughout the world who find themselves on the wrong end of our economic policies and other forms of warfare. Perhaps our cutthroat ways bear some relationship to our confused notions of God. Maybe we think God, as an intergalactic economist, is a survival-of-the-fittest type. And if we believe the Uncle Ben version of God is the only God out there, we might even think that being offended and angry and on the defensive is to be more firmly aligned with the Almighty.

I return to the Uncle Ben tale because I sense his spirit in our offendedness. Is this nightmarish God-view the root cause of our rage? Is it discernible in the meltdowns we see on YouTube among angry fathers at sporting events and television presenters whose teleprompters are making them feel less presentable, less capable of inspiring confidence? The bottom falls out when complexity rears its ugly head. Uncle Ben at least lets us know what we have to keep straight in order to get by. It's "the infinite gangster weight of God,"[6] in Michael Chabon's phrase, that gets things done. The threat of infinite violence is a strong persuader. Flying off the handle might feel a little Godlike when we notice how powerful and effective one can be by having a little available rage. One might even call it authority or gravitas. Someone's got to show these people what's what. Someone's got to have some standards.

While there is no lasting security in the dubious affections of the Uncle Ben God, who is a whirlwind of hatred and offendedness, he does have a way of simplifying things. Who's in and who's out is never a question. Getting right with God is a matter of believing the right things and keeping your questions to yourself. By this logic, we can't view ourselves as interpreters of truth or members of a pilgrim species learning their way through life. We are instead holders of absolute truth, possessors of the *saving knowledge* of God (as if it's *our* knowledge that saves) who hold to copies of the scriptures even though we aren't inclined to read them too closely. We feel most in line with the faith when we are most afraid. We view as a threat those voices that don't easily coincide with what we think we have to believe to be saved. They aren't safe voices. Music, films, and literature that don't fit our categories might cause us to lose whatever hold we still have on our religion. It's as if old Nobodaddy is just waiting for us to slip up—by way of a wayward imagination, an unsafe thought.

To keep it all simple and safe, we often become selective fundamentalists. We know where to go to have our prejudices explained as just and sensible, our convictions strengthened, our group or political party reaffirmed. We process whatever already fits the grid that is hardwired (or *re*-hardwired) in our heads. It's difficult for anything else to get through. We're easily offended. Maybe we're *looking* to feel offended, which can make us feel better about ourselves. Feeling offended summons a sense of being in the right, a certain strength, a kind of power, an espresso shot of righteous indignation. And if the image of God hardwired into our nervous system is easily offended and put off by certain people and their offensive behavior, there's a feeling of being that much closer to the winning side, that much more likely to be numbered among the elect, the saved, the documented.

We can live, if we choose to, with a kind of Styrofoam casing around our imaginations, an informational echo chamber. We can and do surround ourselves with people who think the same things we think, people who won't challenge us, and people who've learned to avoid certain topics while in our presence. It's a natural, understandable, deeply human need to have our thoughts and opinions mirrored to us in verbal exchanges. We all need positive reinforcement.

But if we feel deep affection only for people who tell us we're right and only give high fives to the like-minded, all we've done is joined a club. We risk becoming incapable of the give-and-take of genuine conversation. If all our friends and news sources require of us is a "Ditto" and "I think what you think," we might be in danger of becoming impenetrable to wisdom, immunized against the sensation of sympathy, resistant to the pleasure of being amused by our own ignorance, and closed to the joy of being wrong.

We seek out and even pay for our own hypnosis. Via television, radio, the Internet, and print, we receive our news product, fashioned and delivered by people who tidy up reality for us. If it isn't sufficiently tidied up, prepackaged and shrink-wrapped to fit our fearfulness, if our minds don't click into place quickly enough to satisfy our stunted attention spans, we change the channel or move to another site. We move swiftly from scenes that might call into question our exclusively saved, right-thinking status.

Contrary to the Uncle Ben image of our worst and most violent impulses, the God tradition calls Immanuel is both *with* us and *for* us. The God in whom love and justice meet, the God whose love radically exceeds whatever low definitions we settle for when we think we're loving God, is the God who is most present among us when we're having a go at that complicated practice of loving one another well. You've probably seen the God-talk on T-shirts and stickers that draw from dairy product promotional imagery by asking, "Got God?" It should probably be observed that, in the deepest sense, nobody's *got* God. God can't get gotten. And Jesus' gospel is never at our command, under our copyright, or contained within an -ism, an ideology, or any well-intentioned human construct.

The question is always whether Jesus' rare ethos has gotten hold of us in any discernible way. To answer that question we must stop defining ourselves by all the things we're against. We might also ask what, other than getting saved in the shallowest sense, we actually stand *for*.

What We Have in Common

If we've deluded ourselves into thinking that our angry mass emails or conversation-stopping talking points serve as a ministry or carry out the purposes of God, we need to slow down and take a breath. Are we merely perpetuating violence, anger, and alienation through the way we talk? In our proclamations and posturings, our offended feelings, what are we bringing to the table? When we go public with our convictions and opinions, are we up for countertestimony? Or have we developed a habit of rendering hasty verdicts? Do we find some people inadmissible? Have we made space in our heads for a wide variety of hearts and minds? Do we want fellowship or submission? Do we remain capable of conversation?

Perhaps our big ideas (religious, economic, political) take a murderous turn when we think they're more important than people's lives — the lives of those who aren't convinced of the rightness of whatever it is we get all trembly about. When we're ready to hurt someone, if only in our minds, for not getting in line with what we take to be our values, we need a gadfly (a Socrates, a Jesus, a Stephen Colbert) to make fun of our vanity, our arrogance, and our pretensions toward Godlikeness.

We need forgiveness too. (For we know not what we're doing exactly.) Otherwise, we're stuck within our little jihads and our other presumed wars on terror. These struggles are authentic only to the extent that they're a blessing to people who don't share our opinions. We need the freedom of people talking. Disagreeing agreeably. Everybody and everyone. To the limit. We get to try to see straight and think straight together. We get to ask all kinds of questions — especially open-ended ones.

An open-ended question is often the beginning of a relationship, and without relationship, there is no witness. Witness will involve something profoundly antithetical to the madness of offendedness. It will be the opposite of a stacked deck. Fordham University philosophy professor Merold Westphal puts the matter rather beautifully:

> If I am a good listener, I don't interrupt the other or plan my own next speech while pretending to be listening. I try to hear what is said, but I listen just as hard for what is not said and for what is said between the lines. I am not in a hurry,

for there is no pre-appointed destination for the conversation. There is no need to get there, for we are already here; and in this present I am able to be fully present to the one who speaks. The speaker is not an object to be categorized or manipulated, but a subject whose life situation is enough like my own that I can understand it in spite of the differences between us. If I am a good listener, what we have in common will be more important than what we have in conflict.[7]

"What we have in common will be more important" than defensively dissociating ourselves from those who might somehow call our rightness into question. And being capable of discerning what we have in common with the people who challenge our sense of decorum will involve silencing the tape, the inner monologue, that tells us why we're right and others are wrong, even as we pretend to listen by nodding knowingly. Our momentarily stilled tongues might genuinely signify the reception of another person's witness. And if they do, it could be that God's kingdom, where two or more are gathered in this way, is already present.

"In the end," Thomas Merton assures us, "it is the reality of personal relationships that saves everything."[8] And the reality comes unto us when we cast aside our categorizing impulses and our armored suits of offendedness (powerful feelings though they may be) and enter into the dangerous and redeeming space where people, all kinds of people, enter into the blessed work of actually listening to one another.

Human Interest

I once had a student, an outspoken redheaded young man, who salvaged many a classroom discussion by offering an impassioned word of disagreement with whatever I was going on about when most of the class just stared at me with the dull intensity of distracted people who would have given me money if I'd only end class early and let them get out their cell phones. After graduation, he admitted to me that he hadn't read a single assigned book in its entirety, but this bit of trivia never stood in the way of his willingness to challenge me aloud when I was otherwise unsuccessful in inspiring listless teenagers. He knew I'd never met a tangent I didn't like, and he would happily bring up topics (disgraced politicians and sports figures, *Saturday Night Live* skits, annoyingly popular musicians) in the hope that I'd take the bait, hold forth, and attempt to wrangle it all back, eventually, to Shakespeare. I can't recall ever not taking the bait. He knew I would because I never tired of saying that everything is connected to everything else.

During his senior year (he'd been my student as a sophomore), I sat in on a discussion between our theater director and a few students, including my redheaded friend, concerning an upcoming production of Arthur Miller's *The Crucible*. There were concerns about the ostensibly objectionable subject matter (witchcraft, demons, murderously hateful Bible-quoting religious fanatics) and possible complaints among parents. This conversation was intended to let in a little air in advance. What might Miller have hoped to accomplish by writing the play during the Communist scare of the McCarthy era? When might controversy be a good thing? The teenagers weren't responding, so the theater director took a different approach. "When is art dangerous?"

"Art can't be *dangerous!*" my student blurted out in an exasperated tone. The question had struck a nerve, and he elaborated with a boldness that, I suspect, surprised even himself. Unless you're poking someone's eye out with a picture frame, braining them with a statuette, or suffocating them with a scroll, we hold this truth to be self-evident: art *can't* be dangerous. It's somebody's *ex-*

pression, he insisted. Any harm anyone decides to feel in response to that expression—out of a sense of offense, outrage, impugned integrity, or whatever—is *their* responsibility and *their* problem. An expression is just an expression. You have to let it be. If we don't, everyone's muffled and nobody's free.

While I managed to remain silent, my heart swelled with something approaching the satisfaction of a proud parent. And I'm just arrogant enough to believe that the young man's rant might have had some connection to the times I'd repeated Lenny Bruce's adage "There are no dirty words, only dirty minds." Humankind's accounts of human experience—the human witness that is a story, an image, a lyric, a sentence, a prayer, a stammering, or even a curse—are never *merely* offensive or inappropriate, any more than any person, by God's lights, is irredeemable. It's all an occasion for hearing well, seeing better, and doing justice by one another's enigmatic output. It's all within that wonderfully broad genre of human interest. The blessedly, overwhelmingly idiosyncratic assemblage that makes up the *biblical* witness should make this observation all the more convincing.

I hasten to add that my own children understand the impropriety of bringing up particular nuggets of goings-on—crude, tragic, tragicomic, or overly tied to bodily functions—in certain company, but I'm determined to instruct them away from the mind-set (sometimes called religious) which implies that certain aspects of human life and certain human beings themselves are so beyond the pale of God's interest and affection that they can't be appropriately mentioned in prayer or included in the sphere of the talkaboutable. Without shame or hellfire, I hope to instruct them and be instructed myself in the direction of a growing awareness of what God finds offensive, namely, the perverse reduction of other human beings created in God's image. Most importantly, I hope we might all together be delivered from an ever-present fastidiousness, an easy offendedness that is *not* righteousness even though it will often feel like it. I understand that being delivered from this particular evil probably requires at least a lifetime. I suspect this deliverance too begins with and is perhaps even driven by the work of sacred questioning.

Kurt Vonnegut once observed that a joke is an excellent way of breaking into a conversation. I concur. I would also say that the space of the talkaboutable, the blessed zone of observational candor, is inaugurated and expanded by the art my young friend insisted should never be deemed dangerous. We might find someone's witness weird, but maybe the weirdness is our nearest avenue — a sign even — of transcendence, of that which will often leave us at a loss for words. The weirdness is crucial to the possibility of a civilization that redeems. Or as the wise old aunt in Shannon Hale's *The Goose Girl* observed, "If we don't tell strange stories, when something strange happens we won't believe it."[9] File under "Cosmic Plainspeak."

In my own thick and unwieldy file, somewhere alongside Vonnegut and such wonderfully weird witnesses as David Lynch, Gwendolyn Brooks, Rod Serling, Annie Dillard, Charles Bukowski, Werner Herzog, and Townes Van Zandt, I place the Nashville filmmaker Harmony Korine (*Gummo*, *Julien Donkey-Boy*, *Mister Lonely*), who recently described his filmmaking process like this:

> It's the mistakes and awkwardness of real life that I've always been attracted to. But I'm not waiting for it to happen. I like to instigate it. It's like a real world that's slightly tweaked — a subtle science fiction. It's like when you put chemicals in a jar and shake it up, and then you document the explosion.[10]

Korine's films include the lyrical wits of homeless people, brutally honest accounts of people emotionally abusing one another, a Michael Jackson impersonator performing for the residents of a nursing home, and nuns jumping out of planes. To those who find his work strange to the point of being off-putting or even offensive, I like to ask the question I bring to all the storytelling I receive: Is it truthful? And if it is, might the offendedness we feel be the beginning rather than the end of our interaction with the story? When an episode of the *Twilight Zone*, a painting by Salvador Dali, or an unsettling documentary brings our reasoning powers to an impasse, is it not a good thing? Might the awkward and the unconventional be a portal to a new way of seeing—and even living within—our weird and wonderful sweet old world?

I believe that, to some degree, an offending strangeness might be the surest means to seeing, hearing, and receiving a *redeeming* witness—a witness at work, for instance, in what Karl Barth refers to as the *strange new world* of the Bible. Does the Bible in any way dislocate our imaginations or prove to be an affront to what we consider seemly? In a certain sense, we might say that weirdness alone redeems, because it is that which strikes us as *un*seemly that forces us to *re*deem—or *re*evaluate—our vision of reality, our sense of what's appropriate. Are we willing to have our vision undone and redeemed? Are we up for the religious experience of feeling offended?

This is why I'm so moved and inspired by the testimony of English poet W. H. Auden. His characterization of his very unconventional but deeply invigorating belief in the paradoxical authority of Jesus of Nazareth is worth examining: "I believe because he fulfills none of my dreams, because he is in every respect the opposite of what he would be if I could have made him in my own image." No other voice within history or literature manages to "arouse *all* sides of my being to cry 'Crucify him!' "[11]

This is the opposite of knee-jerk sanctimoniousness. Auden feels compelled to try to seek the kingdom of God made known in Jesus precisely because he finds the life Jesus invites us to so revolting, so contrary to what he's inclined to want, so against his own, all-too-loud sense of what's appropriate. The mere thought of Jesus left him feeling unhinged or, rather, more in touch with a habitual unhingedness exposed and scandalized by an encounter with the Man of Sorrows/Prince of Peace/the One in whom, Auden believed, the fullness of the deity was pleased to dwell.

In an age where people regard their faith as a cause for boasting and think of their witness as having something to do with getting angry with people for saying "Happy Holidays" instead of "Merry Christmas," I'd like to commend Auden's self-deprecating way of taking Jesus seriously. Auden did so by taking his own fragile hold on the truth of things *less* seriously. In his constant return to Jesus' basic demand—the largely unheeded call to have a go at loving people—Auden, in my estimation, *out*-conservatives the most self-described conservative and self-described religious people among us. Auden: "One thing, and one thing only, is serious: loving one's neighbor as one's self."[12] An especially difficult task for those who are primarily offended by people other than themselves.

What it might mean to have a go at loving someone is, as ever, a larger, more demanding question than whether this someone (their language, their driving, their voting record, or their immigrant status) offends us. But it is also the question that makes a meaningful life, in practice as well as in big ideas, possible. The question should accompany us throughout our time-consuming relationships with computer keyboards, television remote controls, and angry voices on the radio. Keeping the question alive and kicking in our heads might keep us attuned and invested in human interest, in the deepest sense, and awake to the practice of being *humanely* interested.

· · ● ● ● · ·

Questions for Further Conversation

1. How does a TV show like *The Office*, films like *Knocked Up*, or a novelist like Dostoevsky shine the light on our otherwise unexamined dysfunction? Might these forms of media serve redemptive ends? Why or why not?

2. Via a fictionalized cell phone exchange, William Gibson describes the role of electronic media in the life of one man and the way it has to a large degree hijacked the possibility of a meaningful conversation with his wife. Describe similar situations in your own family or community. How does this happen? What might be done in the way of helping, healing, and recovering real relationship?

3. Where does Stephen Colbert, or the character Colbert plays, fit into this crisis of escalating offendedness? Where might we locate the role of the knowing fool in relation to Salman Rushdie's understanding of the poetic vocation—the work of naming the unnameable, pointing at frauds, taking sides, starting arguments, and stopping the world from going to sleep? In this sense, what does comedy have to do with religion? Might comedy spur sacred questioning? How does comedy widen the sphere of what can be talked about?

4. When we consider "The Alexamenos Graffito," what might it mean to remember that the earliest known pictorial representation of Jesus is a ridiculing cartoon? Might this be a strangely appropriate notion for a deeper understanding of the meaning of Jesus in the life of a self-described Christian? How might this bit of history challenge the pervading offendedness among people who claim to be tight with Jesus?

5. Consider Merold Westphal's description of the good listener. What thought-habits and ways of talking about the world will have to be overcome before good listening becomes possible?

6. If being offended by a work of art, the Bible, or a film is the first stage of receiving its witness, what might the next stage(s) look like? What lies beyond Auden's initial revulsion to the life of love Jesus calls his hearers to? In what way does the call, if we mean to discern it in an ever-renewing way, *remain* revolting and offensive? How does the intoxication of feeling offended over people, ideas, and issues compete with the biblical imperative to conduct ourselves with love and mercy?

Spot the Pervert

Questioning Our Passions

We have sealed ourselves away behind our money,
growing inward, generating a seamless universe of self.
William Gibson, *Neuromancer*

We all believed in the supremacy of being liked.
Questions were not encouraged. Instead we occupied
ourselves by dutifully repeating advertising catch-phrases like,
"Be Positive." … How could we have known the seemingly
innocent slogans we swallowed whole were part of a national
mood that gave birth to some very questionable ethics, namely,
replacing human attachments—usually fleeting and always
complicated—with the accumulation of money and objects.
Diane Keaton, *Mr. Salesman*

I think it was in Northern Ireland that I first learned how to talk
back to my television, or to put it a little more academic sounding,
where I settled into a firm commitment to the joys—and ethical
imperative—of critical engagement. On a mountainside over-
looking the small, seaside town of Newcastle, I lived and worked
with other volunteers at a YMCA center for outdoor pursuits.
We'd take young people canoeing and rock climbing and clam-
ber into a small space—"the staff room"—at the end of the day
to unwind and watch television together before making our way

down to a pub called The Anchor. It didn't matter what was being broadcast, because anything was good fodder for jokes, amused observations, and shouting back at the nonsense being foisted on our souls. The electronic soul molester — television — scored no easy victories over our affections.

Clever irreverence was the unspoken rule for all of our communal TV viewing. Nothing televised was sacred. During a commercial for a humanitarian project of some sort, which featured the sound of John Lennon's song "Imagine," my friends were uncharacteristically silent until Lennon intoned that, while he certainly knows and understands all too well that he's a dreamer, he'd also like to assert, with dignity and solidarity, that he's not the only one. At this, a young man from Dublin jeered, "That's what *he* thinks."

This was the early nineties, and I remember feeling homesick for this sort of talk-back upon returning to the States and seeing something similar transpire between a man and a couple of robot puppets watching bad movies on that glorious cable television series *Mystery Science Theater 3000*. Talking back to the screen or even dwelling at length in thoughtful conversation at what had just come through to us was an entertaining, liberating, and even revolutionary activity. There are ways of raging against what Leonard Cohen calls "that hopeless little screen."[1] There are ways of being a little *less* lost within it.

Yet this isn't how it usually works. Televised content works its strange will by way of mind massage on millions. I began to wonder how democracy — government of, by, and for the people — could survive against what James Joyce prophesied in the phrase "impovernment of the booble by the bauble for the bubble."[2] Do certain technologies increase the risk of developing a citizenry who reside in their own private, sealed-off, informational echo chambers? In a similar vein, Michael Franti's band, the Disposable Heroes of the Hiphoprisy, proclaimed television to be the drug of the nation ("United States of Unconsciousness," Franti opined in 1992). This struck me as exactly right. We let the commercialized reality of television into our hearts to the point that it's the only reality we know. As sci-fi as it sounds, commercial imagery becomes what many of us mean by *realistic*. It becomes what people have to transform into (telegenic?) to reach the masses, to sell products, to win votes. Our whole society becomes, in Philip Rieff's masterful phrase, "a dictatorship of the empty by the phony."[3]

I wanted to make sure that I never stopped talking back to the TV transmissions. If I did, if I ever got into the habit of receiving the content of electronic media without talking about it, without critically engaging it, I figured I'd be in serious trouble. Something crucial would be lost. I began to collect phrases and analogies to articulate forms of resistance — cosmic plainspeak on napkins and notepads.

One particular evening back at the Newcastle Y remains fixed in my memory. As I was descending the mountain in the company of a slightly older fellow volunteer, I asked him if he'd enjoyed the film we'd just seen broadcast. The film was Penny Marshall's *Big* (1988), starring Tom Hanks as a young boy who finds himself grown into an adult body overnight. I'd liked it, and he said he liked it well enough. But after a moment of silence, he added that a certain falseness, a contrived quality, had left him feeling a little depressed. I asked him to clarify. The film struck him, he explained with a bit of reluctance, as "a waste of perfectly good emotion."

What a way of putting it! He'd given a name to a certain, mildly insidious something I'd had no way of naming before, and I made a note to myself to employ this phrase at the first available opportunity. Emotions are ... what they are. They're inevitable and blessed and wonderful. But there's a way of playing to them, of preying on them, that is a bridge too far. There's a sentimental-izing of matters that is an affront to the possibility of dignity. It's an undermining, by way of unreal endearment, of our ability to hold one another dear, a way of drawing us away from a sense of what's real. Films like *Big*, *Patch Adams*, and *Hope Floats* are inter-esting enough, but if such sentimental fare is what mostly consti-tutes our media diet, our affections might slowly become — hear this! — merely theoretical, sentimentality preying on our nervous systems from one day to the next. We get to the point that we save our strongest emotions for people who don't exist. Or in the case of sports figures, celebrity politicians, and radio talk show hosts, we get most worked up and alive (if you can call it being alive) by way of people we don't know and who in all likelihood don't want to know us. The living, breathing people next door or in the next cubicle or in the same house who might benefit from our showing up to them emotionally get left behind. "A waste of perfectly good emotion," he said. And it worked on so many levels. My moral vocabulary had been expanded.

Lust in Action

As I acquire these lines and phrases, I drop them into my ex-changes with anyone who'll lend me their ear. When I started teaching high school English, students became an especially good means for fulfilling this need in my life, because they have to at least pretend to listen to me. They're a captive audience. We tell each other about what we've seen and heard, with occasional emphasis on the readings assigned the previous day. We share our findings with one another in preparation for the water coolers that await them in their near future. It goes well when I can cajole them into disagreeing with me. It's as if a disagreement is the only way a good conversation can break out.

The best words I have to offer on the subject of wasted emotions come, as they usually do, from Shakespeare. He's the indisputable authority on passions, and his wisdom seems to precede and surpass whatever we think we know about ourselves as a species —all expert opinion, all the professionalization of our supposed knowledge of -isms and -ologies.[4] On the squandering of passions that might have been harnessed in the direction of something worthwhile, Shakespeare has a bit of breaking news. It's Sonnet 129, and I quote it in full. Look at what he says about lust in action:

> The expense of spirit in a waste of shame
> Is lust in action: and till action, lust
> Is perjured, murderous, bloody, full of blame,
> Savage, extreme, rude, cruel, not to trust;
> Enjoyed no sooner but despised straight;
> Past reason hunted; and no sooner had,
> Past reason hated, as a swallowed bait,
> On purpose laid to make the taker mad.
> Mad in pursuit, and in possession so;
> Had, having, and in quest to have extreme;
> A bliss in proof, and proved, a very woe;
> Before, a joy proposed; behind, a dream.
> All this the world well knows; yet none knows well
> To shun the heaven that leads men to this hell.

I commend memorizing this sonnet and reciting it to oneself while walking through shopping malls.[5] It's so intensely applicable to our entire world. But if we have to isolate a single money quote out of all these dazzlingly informative phrases, out of this complete meditation on the way we devalue and get devalued in our desiring, the one that comes closest to my friend's description of a sentimental film is Shakespeare's take on lust: "the expense of spirit in a waste of shame." Our deluded wanting, we're reminded, is often all we feel, and worse, it blinds us to what's in front of us, objectifying and commodifying reality to the point of fantasy. As Mr. Spock of *Star Trek* reminds us, amid his own lifelong struggle with passions, "having is not so pleasing a thing as wanting. This is not logical, but it is often true."[6] And ashamed of our own fetishizing impulse, we hold in contempt those people and things we still have yet to regard healthily and properly — the world we've looked on with our deluded vision but have yet to really see.

Shakespeare's sonnet is an elaboration on Jesus' assertion that we have to lose our lives — let go of them — to find them.[7] The sonnet even seems to be a sort of midrash on the apostle Paul's confession in his letter to the congregation in Rome concerning the distance between the good he wants to do — the good he means to do — and what he actually does.[8] In our failure to value one another properly, it's as if we can't even manage to *mean* well. Our misdirected passions can falsify and make a false god out of just about anything and anyone.

I'd like to travel back in time to figure out if Karl Marx, who I know to have been a Shakespeare enthusiast, might have had Sonnet 129 in mind when he wrote of commodity fetishism. We lose one another in our misapprehensions, our transmogrifying[9] of people into things and things into objects of worship. A false consciousness is cultivated. A genuine reality-based consciousness of ourselves and one another slowly slips away. What does it profit us to gain a whole world of objects and forfeit our souls? Are we willing volunteers in our own liquidation?

In their words on lust in action, Shakespeare, Marx, and Spock effectively popularize the ethical insights of the Hebrew prophets who speak so powerfully and poetically against the ways we offer human lives as living sacrifices to big ideas in wars and legislation and marketing schemes. These graven images are unworthy of our passions. They're broken cisterns that can't hold water. Our ideologies are blind, deaf, dumb, and murderous, sabotaging the ways that make for peace. And our unacknowledged perversions in speech and action so stunt our attention spans that we can neither live long, in any meaningful and redeeming way, nor prosper.

Somebody in a Body

Pervert is a verb, and we do it all the time. To pervert is to degrade, to cut down to size—and we do it to people in our minds. We devalue them. We reduce them to the limitations of our appetites, of our sense of what might prove useful to us, of our sense of what strikes *us* as appropriate. As I noted in the preceding chapter, we often only file them away—these living and breathing human beings—into separate files of crazy-making *issues*-talk. When we think of a person primarily as a problem, a potential buyer, a VIP, a celebrity, or an undocumented worker, we're reducing them to the tiny sphere of our stunted attention span. This is how perversion works. Perversion is a failure of the imagination, a failure to pay adequate attention.

While perversion appears to be the modus operandi of governments and the transnational corporations they serve—and the language both speak in their broadcasts—the reductionism implicit in perversion doesn't ultimately work. It doesn't do justice to the fullness of what we are. We, the people, are always more than our use value. Like the God in whose image people are made, people are *ir*reducible. There's always more to a person—more stories, more life, more complexities—than we know. The human person, when viewed properly, is unfathomable, incalculable, and dear. Perversion always says otherwise. Perversion is a way of managing, getting down to business, getting a handle on people as if they were things. A person reduced to a thing has been, in the mind of the perverter, dispensed with, taken care of, filed away. Perversion is pigeonholing.

At the risk of sounding puritanical, I'd like to suggest that our perverting tendencies too often go unquestioned in the words we casually employ in our characterization of a person, for instance, as *hot*. We do well to praise beauty and voluptuousness (conventional or unconventional) in myriad ways, but what have we wrought with our talk of who's hot? Reducing a person in this way is perversion, reducing them in the worst way to an image for visual craving; it is a taking of the human form to market. A not-to-be-objectified beauty is reduced to the easy access of the voyeur whenever a person is primarily good for looking at. It's the opposite of the affectionate gaze for which we long. People become mere means to particular ends. As U2 lyricizes in "Fast Cars," we're all accustomed to seeing *bodies* on film and in person, but we aren't used to seeing *somebody* in a body.[10] It requires an act of attentiveness, a holding of an image as *sacred*—a skill many of us appear to have frittered away.

Perversion is standard operating procedure in a merely mercantile world. The casual practice of perversion (though we don't call it that) seems as if it is the way to be successful and effective and realistic. It's a way of getting ahead. A well-stocked arsenal of eloquent objection to perversity is ever available to us in the plainspeak of Shakespeare, the Bible, and any religious or literary tradition, but we're mostly deaf to the alarm bells of such witnesses while we're doing it, while we're, as the saying goes, getting down to business. As reported from Abu Ghraib prison or fictionalized during an interrogation on *24*, perversion strikes us as eminently realistic and—we might say with a grim sense of pride—necessary. On magazine covers, in conversations, and in planning meetings, the perversion is on.

I tried to share some of this with my high school students, and a fellow who's always quick with an encouraging, conspiratorial smile walked up after class (always a rewarding experience) and said, "So we're all perverts then."

"Yep," I said. "But we aren't *only* perverts. We certainly underestimate each other, misperceiving and misrepresenting other people from one moment to the next. But we also get it right sometimes. We aren't *just* perverts. In fact, if we say of someone that he or she is a pervert and nothing but a pervert, we're being perverts speaking perversely as perverts do." Here I had to take a breath. "Like calling someone a fool or an idiot. It's one of those things Jesus tells us to never ever do. Calling someone a pervert without acknowledging our own inner pervert might lead to the destruction—or at least the perversion—of our own soul. We become perverts in our determination to catch a pervert."

Familiar with my habit of belaboring a point beyond all reasonable bounds, he knew I'd rave on until he politely excused himself. This was the kind of ground we'd covered before via some tangent or other. The tangents are the sunshine, after all. And this one, I think, was born of Kafka's *The Metamorphosis*. When we give our attention to someone like Kafka, he provides what all cosmic plainspeak affords: an occasion to question our own thought patterns, our perversions, and our passions—an opportunity, in some cases, to find *ourselves* ridiculous. It can be an enriching, morally invigorating thing.

Get Fresh Flow vs. Plastic on My Mind

High school English class, as I pitch it, is a special place for narrative interruption and lyrical intervention, a place where the best words have a chance to break through. It's like a compulsory book club that, we pray, might somehow be viewed as a *get to* rather than a *have to*. I like to think of English class as potentially a deeply entertaining storytelling think tank *against* perversion, a place to try to become aware of what's going on in your own mind, a place to consider the nature of real love, where you learn to think of lust as a waste of perfectly good emotion, an expense of the spirit in a waste of shame. English class is a space of sacred questioning where everything is rendered a little more talkaboutable, where one's consciousness might be transformed and enlivened by word and song and rhyme and reason — the space of the talkaboutable, the space called literature.

We get to listen with sympathy and solidarity to other people's words, getting a better hold of our own desires, our own fears. How do we distinguish whether we're feeling love or lust? How do Ralph Ellison and J. D. Salinger and Jane Austen do it? Might literature throw lifelines to students drowning in a sea of noise and feelings? Might paying attention to other people's words make us feel within our hearts the depths we didn't know we had?

My students understand all too well that *The Matrix* has them, but that movie is *so twentieth century*. They need a new word, a new way of putting it. They know they're being engaged, pummeled by brands and images and talking points that seek to mold them to particular patterns of consumption. How does one stay sane? How might we reclaim our attention spans?

I teach the sacredness of questioning everything, the sacred obligation to pay close attention to the world and our actions in it. By reading, thinking, and listening, we develop an arsenal of words and images against perversion. One name for the resource that assists us in *not* living life this way is *the poetic*, the innovative language at work in what comes to be called religion. Cosmic plainspeak, that ever-growing collection of common decency available to us in more ways that we can count. To be well versed in cosmic plainspeak is to cultivate—through narratives, lyrics, pictures, and sounds—a habitual, lighthearted, redeemingly self-critical awareness of our own tendency to pervert.

Nobel Prize-winning author Elias Canetti once said that his job as a writer is to show his readers just how complex selfishness is.[11] This takes self-awareness, critical thought, and the inbreaking of good words and important news. "A work of art is someone's act of attention, evoking ours," literary scholar Hugh Kenner tells us.[12] There are so many inspiring works of attention, so many sounds and sentences out there. And they're ours for the reading, reciting, and downloading, if only we'll pay attention. They're in poems and country songs and ballads.

In our unchecked passions, which advertisers and political campaigns prey on, we're in desperate need of what I call Get Fresh Flow—a flow of word and image—which can also do with some Jigsaw Jazz, some flotsam to mix with the jetsam. In teaching, I strive to practice and cultivate among the dear souls kind enough to consider themselves my students a sense of discernment, an awareness of the timely word—the expression that helps us pay better attention to what's happening and to sense how our perversions obstruct the possibility of real vision.

To somehow conjure up the redeeming potential of other people's art (their acts of attentiveness), I often turn my students' attention away from printed lines of textbooks to that other, slightly more haphazard, shifting collection of everyday sounds and words which enters the room by way of the artificial intelligence at work in the random selection of my iPod shuffle (the iPod god, my wife calls it). It's an open demonstration of Get Fresh Flow, Jigsaw Jazz, and other feats of intense attentiveness. These terms come to us through the naming powers of Beck, the artist who probably appears on my iPod most often.[13]

The phrase that often comes to mind in association with the question of perversion and the possibility of confessing our perversions in the hope of being less perverse appears at the conclusion of "Where It's At" on Beck's 1996 album *Odelay*: "I got plastic on my mind." What a confession! What sense this bit of nonsense brings! We allow people and ideas and objects into our minds only to the extent that we can use them, failing entirely to pay attention to what they actually are. As the sixteenth-century essayist Montaigne observed, "Who so hath his mind on taking, hath it no more on what he taketh." There is no fact so stubborn, no human face so beautiful and dignified, that we aren't capable of liquidating it, melting it down to size. As Shakespeare understood, we have a nasty habit of superimposing what is not there on what is, of misperceiving, of misrepresenting the reality of other people to suit our desires. Our minds betray us little by little. And the temptation to engage *un*critically, to carefully avoid an awareness of our own perversions, is as near as the nearest news product. The little everyday neglect of imagining other people well can add up to a lifetime of flawed, perverted vision, an expenditure of soul in a waste of emotionalism. It's on sale everywhere, and we're buying.

Let Me Tell You a Story

If perversion is a failure of attentiveness—a devastating devaluing of the infinitely valuable human form—it might be feats of attentiveness that best call us out of our perversity. Paying better attention, in this sense, becomes the primary activity by which we might behave morally, with ethical integrity. With this in mind, we might get the drift of what Thom Yorke of Radiohead means when he describes his band's creative output as a form of bearing witness. This is work worth doing. It's looking hard, gathering thoughts, and trying, for the sake of God and goodness and the possibility of justice, to pay attention. Yorke describes his own songwriting process, often undertaken in an Oxford pub:

> I sit there, on the way in, because it's a really nice little table. And then I get out my scraps of paper and I line them up. I need to put them into my book because they're just scraps of paper, and I'm going to lose them unless I do it. So am I writing here? Probably. I don't know yet. I'm just collating information. This is a nice, relaxing thing to do, and it also keeps your mind tuned in to the whole thing. And you see things you didn't know.[14]

To make sense of plastic on the mind and to develop a resistance to the perverse patterns that will otherwise run our worlds for us, I believe an activity of this sort—by way of a blog, an especially redemptive conversation with a coworker, a water coloring, or a playlist—is absolutely crucial. It can be done. And when we do it, we begin to see things we didn't know. We have to try to make sense. We have to make time for artful analysis, which is the way we clear a space for the possibility of sanity. It is an outlet for honesty. There are feats of great attentiveness around every corner. There are observant people everywhere, people like us, trying to talk about what's happening to them, holding reality up to question, pointing out things we aren't supposed to see. I want to be counted among them.

I trade stories—my own and those of others—with people when I talk about music and film and literature and whatever works of art are currently getting through to me. It's education and entertainment. It's the way we connect to each other. And more often than not, it's the way we talk to each other about our behavior, the way we provide input to one another. "It's like that episode of *Lost*," we might say. Or, "It's like that Joanna Newsom line." We have our preferred analogies, and popular culture appears to be our *lingua franca*.[15] What we're reading or listening to or, rather, what we're *getting into lately* is in some sense the most profound question we can ask each other. It's all seamlessly related to the question of how we're doing, and what it is that has hold of us, and how our passions might be channeled in a redemptive direction (and be good for something) rather than being tossed to and fro by the powers of passionate distraction.

Many of these people write their own stories and songs and collect and collage and paint into better ways of picturing things, but the informal sharing of story, if there's to be friendship worthy of the word, is nonoptional. It's the way we have of ringing true to other people. It's the way we harness our passions and salvage our obsessions toward the just. It's the way we get critically engaged.

In this sense, there's no hope without story and without carefully practiced story-*receiving* abilities. We have to quiet our minds long enough to hear what someone else is saying. Listen for the possibility of connection. Something registers. Someone is revealed. And our strongest and most passionately held impressions often disintegrate under closer, humbler inspection. We find out we were wrong about any number of things—other people, other countries, particular works of artistry. This is how we wake up. This is how we repent. The story opens the world anew.

Neighborhood Tunnels

The way my friends and I get through to each other is related in one way or another to the music and film and literature we're taking in. You'll understand, then, what I mean when I say we share a perfectly silly, carefully cultivated-over-the-years pop music snobbery for which we make fun of ourselves even as we air it out. I say "silly," but we're true believers. And we're serious when we speak of Suzanne Vega, Lou Reed, Laurie Anderson, Jane Siberry, Elvis Costello, or a Terence Trent D'Arby album shaping the way we view the world, informing our decisions, and revolutionizing our imaginations. So it was a very big deal when three of my friends—Gar, Todd, and Geoff—agreed behind my back that a band called Arcade Fire had accomplished, with its first full-length album, *Funeral* (2004), something on par with *OK Computer, Blonde on Blonde,* and *Joshua Tree,* something culturally crucial. I hadn't heard it yet, but I'd heard it touted by folks unduly swayed by whatever Pitchfork christens—not that Pitchfork Media isn't often wonderful. I was prepared to take them all on by way of a one-versus-three intervention if they'd lost their minds and there was nothing but hype-driven, bandwagonesque folly behind their bold talk. This was a question of ethics. How could I count on them again if they were getting this wrong? As a ministry unto the as-yet-ungospeled me, Gar was kind enough to leave a copy of *Funeral* on my front porch.

Gar was so right. Arcade Fire had me at "Hello." It felt somehow medieval and fresh and urgent all at once, with strings and electric guitar, marching band, minstrel-gypsy-troubadour fare coming out of a tavern full of clear-eyed, optimistic, coed worker priests. It felt wise and young and in unself-conscious continuity with some long-forgotten, undeniably authoritative ancient broadcast, a dusty, old, strong-as-an-oak culture. The band is very much a communal activity (sometimes with as many as ten people on stage), but they appear to be led by a married couple—lead vocalists Texas-born Win Butler and Régine Chassagne of Montreal—coming at us like a good news, deadpan circus.

I felt that I'd been formed by this kind of thing. To back up a little, there was a moment in the late eighties when pop music took on an earnestness, a sort of seamless social justice concern that later came to feel, for no good reason, somehow embarrassing.

Some might say that only U2 and R.E.M. survived it, but I happen to think it has aged wonderfully. Human-interest pop, we might call it. I'm thinking of the following vagabond voices: Hothouse Flowers, Lone Justice, 10,000 Maniacs, the Cure, Ocean Blue, the Water Boys, Midnight Oil, Big Country, and (if I may be indulged) Tears for Fears. They were waxing therapeutic and worrying over global warming long before the need to do so was becoming self-evident. And in a very moving way, Arcade Fire's *Funeral* felt like a vindication of and a majestic return to all of this. They herald a redeeming realization: It's time to apologize to eighties music. It was right all along.

Imagine fifty-nine-year-old David Bowie (or YouTube it) joining the band on stage to sing *Funeral*'s slow-rocking Springsteen-leading-an-orchestra-and-children's-choir anthem, "Wake Up." As the song goes, some insidious something out there has filled our hearts with nothingness, and someone's instructed us to refrain from feeling anything too deeply, to avoid lamentation, and to get it all under control. This instruction, Bowie and company proclaim, was a lie. It's time to get busy being born again. It's time to rock. It's time to wake up. The time is now.

Throughout the album, there's a sense of generations having been handed a very bad blueprint concerning life, love, and meaning. We are up to our necks, all of us, in false covenants. And now we're trying fitfully to grieve the loss of wisdom, lament lost time, and gather together what goodness remains amid the risk of losing each other to vampires and a sleep epidemic. Think "Rock Album as Exorcism." The driving conceit of *Funeral* is the "Neighborhood," subjected to futility while awaiting—even in its ongoing, feels-like-dying dysfunction—the arrival of better days. There's a power outage ("Neighborhood #3 [Power Out]"). Unfeeling follows. But there's also the possibility of digging tunnels to one another's windows ("Neighborhood #1 [Tunnels]").

We might still get through to each other by talking into cans with strings poked through their bottoms, strings long enough to reach one another's windows. The means are there, even as the song points to the disconnect whereby one generation has grown so deaf to bygone voices of its own history that it can't come up with names for its infants. The line of associations—forgotten knowledge, hair grown long, thickened skin—culminates in the sudden recollection of having had people they called parents back there somewhere. Butler asks what befell them in a cry like a caterwaul.

The ethical heft of *Funeral* assaults the listener like a summons to memory and vigilance. While observing the Bowie footage over my shoulder (followed by the sight of David Byrne joining them for a Talking Heads cover), my wife casually observed, "They're helping them save rock and roll." I think she's on to something. The Get Fresh Flow is still getting through.

Antichrist Television Blues

And now we have Arcade Fire's *Neon Bible*. More of the same, in the best possible sense. More boulevards of broken dreams, more mass hallucination, and a full-scale poetic assault on what Butler refers to as "the *American Idol* world."[16] The music speaks of, to, and for a culture in the throes of a vast meaning problem, and within the comprehensiveness of the Arcade Fire vision, any attempt to draw lines of separation between religion, entertainment, advertising, and politics will always fail to signify. The categories aren't functional. It's all ideology 24/7. What are we going to do about it?

Inserted parenthetically within the second half of *Neon Bible* sits "Antichrist Television Blues," and to me it is an eye-opening feat of attentiveness, a powerful broadside that speaks to the madness of religio-entertainment like nothing else I can think of. The speaker within the song is a passionate, well-intentioned figure with what we can properly call a heart for ministry. Some observant fan close to the stage at an Arcade Fire performance found the song transcribed on a set list under the title of "Joe Simpson," a figure known on reality television (and in reality) as a former Baptist youth minister and the father/manager of Jessica and Ashlee Simpson, but the song isn't an instance of making fun of anybody. On the contrary, it's a deeply sympathetic, imaginative rendering of a very common prayerful impulse within the discourses of religion and entertainment, art and commerce. It's a hard-driving, toe-tapping, disarmingly catchy song. In fact, it's an impassioned plea for justice and revelation and a more righteous world that might yet come to realize the good purposes of a loving God. The protagonist within the song wants desperately to make a difference and prays fervently that God might see fit to let each of his daughters serve as lanterns of divine illumination. He wants God to *make them stars*. Why? So that the world might know that God alone is God, and that God alone is good. The protagonist wants to bear witness. He wants to make an impact. He wants to be *relevant*. As it happens, there's a lot of that going around these days.

The lyrics give voice to the impulse (native, we might say, to any of us who try our hand at show business) that imagines a redeeming, ministerial vocation at work in the quest for celebrity status and maximum airtime (which would then be an acceptable, effective means to a healthy evangelical end). But the figure who prays his prayer in "Antichrist Television Blues" senses something amiss in his heart the more he keeps his eyes on the prize. He wonders if he might be wasting his time, and he notes, insightfully, that the more airtime he acquires, the more supposedly successful his family becomes, the more he finds that "nothing tastes good."

At this point, he delivers one of the most devastatingly disturbing, double entendres of recent memory. He persuades himself that, by way of his daughters' sex appeal (he is pleased to note that they "look old for their age"), he might hold up a mirror to the masses, and, that way, they'll be able to see themselves inside his little girls. We need not linger here long to receive the insight, the all-too-relevant breaking news, that something tragic and perverse is afoot in our attempts to make a big splash, to make God somehow more attractive, successful, and appealing. Selling units, proliferating one's image, and acquiring a massive audience (an audience to *what* exactly? we have to ask) becomes the means and the end. Throughout the album, we have figures who work for churches while their families deteriorate, those who cry out "Hallelujah!" with debilitating fear lurking in their hearts, and people for whom MTV has proved to be a source of multifaceted false covenants. The medium became the message, an expense of spirit in a waste of shame. Everything takes a turn for the demonic.

Other than the moments when the father chastises his child (backstage) for being ungrateful and for failing to understand how long and hard he's worked to give her opportunities, most of the song fits into the category of prayer.

It ends with the father asking if, despite his sincere intentions, he might have haplessly assumed the role of Antichrist. He wants—needs—to know. His ability to ask the question is a credit to his powers of self-discernment, still alive somehow. With this question, a good number of demons at work in show business are powerfully unmasked in under six minutes. Butler has spoken in interviews of the whole audiovisual culture moving in a "violent-porn direction," as far as the law will allow, with no aspect of human life left uncommodified.[17] In an age of escalating anxiety, *Neon Bible* serves as a creative, visionary response.

How do we live and love well? How do we discern what is

human amid an ocean of noise and violence? How do we think and see truthfully and freely? These are among the questions generated by Arcade Fire (and all purveyors of cosmic plainspeak), and never without mirth and joy and passion. The Jesuit activist-poet Daniel Berrigan once observed that brainwash is "that species of untruth which lies so near to the truth as to be able to wear its clothing."[18] And in the theater of Arcade Fire, there's the sense that brainwash — the name of the global con game — is never far away, always broadcasting in a fine frenzy rolling through our heads, 24/7, always appealing with its calls to worship, always as close as the jugular vein.

Surviving it all requires communal resistance and a determined, daily revaluing of what's in front of us. It requires poetic and lyrical multimedia proclamation. Arcade Fire delivers all of this, knowingly and powerfully, never underestimating the myriad ways in which power will play on our desires and our fears, never forgetting that in our in-between times the price of freedom will be a constant questioning vigilance.

So what is the *Neon Bible*?[19] I wonder if it might be the seemingly all-encompassing, false radiation of our bad, death-dealing interpretations of religious texts ("religious" in the broadest sense imaginable), the bad news that sells itself as the good news of escaping the weakness and the failure of your fellow humans by believing the right things and grabbing your copy of hell insurance. The siren song tells us emphatically (without saying it directly) to make ourselves at home, to insert our souls into its imagery, only to swallow us whole. In an attempt to speak to this sort of thing, I like to write the following William Blake line on the board for my students: "The vision of Christ that thou dost see / Is my vision's greatest enemy."[20]

Once they've pieced it together in their heads, they're amazed by the nerve of somebody saying, "What you worship as the holy one is actually the anti-holy. You are exactly backwards. The God you fearfully try to love is actually no God at all, a false god. Call him Nobodaddy, for God's sake. You're worshiping a perversion." Do people really get it *that* wrong? Do we? I then name any number of figures in history—reformers and revolutionaries whose names they know—to point out that this is how religious, political, and poetic visions work. Win Butler remarked that "this idea that Christianity and consumerism are completely compatible ... is the great insanity of our times."[21] Do we see the contradiction? Can we discern the cosmic plainspeak, old and new, that bears witness against it?

Valley of Decision

One reason "Antichrist Television Blues" is crucial in our consideration of mass hypnotism is because it interrogates the madness of the age from within it. The protagonist manages—it might be considered an act of heroism—to question his own dearest passions. He considers the possibility that, in his high-powered shot at being pleasing to God (of making a difference), he has tragically and paradoxically become an enemy of God. Might our most intense moments of perceived worshipfulness be the opposite of what we feel they are? How do I discern, as my friend Tom Wills once put it, the difference between the voice in my head and the voice of God? How do you know if you're possessed?

This is where I'd like to see Auden's testimony (page 65) recounted more frequently because it locates the lordship of Jesus solidly in Jesus' ethical demands, demands largely ignored by some of the very people who rant the most about how much they love Jesus. Auden seeks to follow Jesus because, in some sense, he finds the life Jesus commends and exemplifies so terribly *un*lovable—a life characterized by the *downward* mobility of unsuccess that constitutes the very different, counterintuitive honor, power, glory, and worthiness of the messiah the self-described orthodox executed or, as the book of Revelation puts it, the lamb who was slaughtered. It would be revealing to ask politicians if the *way* of Jesus, never to be separated from the affirmation of Jesus as the truth and the life, shocks and offends them. Or would they dare to claim that Jesus is unobjectionable, that Jesus' demands can be incorporated into our foreign policy, our immigration programs, and our practice of capital punishment.

Perhaps real wisdom only comes to us in a counterintuitive fashion, very often running contrary to our prevailing passions. In my listening, reading, viewing, and thinking, I mean to develop a taste for what comes *un*naturally. Wisdom will often feel incongruous, incompatible with the fullness of our feelings that *feel* somehow right even when they function mostly to insulate us from the reality—the consequences—of our doings. Wisdom will not only not get through but will be held in lively contempt when our feelings are the primary measure of what we allow in. Wisdom will not be let in when we edit reality itself to suit our sense of self, when we've grown unaccustomed to receiving information that might call our lives into question.

By way of an appetite for the unsavory, in this sense, we can admit Auden's strange confession and no longer reduce our story/image/lyric reception to whatever our egos find soothing. The clear-eyed sensibility that informs Auden's more robust worshipfulness is in line with better thought patterns that readily admit their perversions, minds that can receive "Antichrist Television Blues," Sonnet 129, and critical assessments of the false worship of commodity fetishism. When we refuse these newscasts and the wisdom they proclaim, we remain deaf to their source material—the wisdom of Jesus and the prophets—which Rowan Williams, archbishop of Canterbury, describes as "the hidden logic, the hidden unity, of the world."[22] Will we have eyes to see and ears to hear when wisdom comes to us, when it gets revealed? Are we alive to the spirit that is holy in the valley of decision?

My favorite example of wisdom getting through in what might be appropriately called *religious reading* comes to us from the mind of Ursula K. Le Guin, the storyteller I tend to think of as our greatest living philosopher. Her landscapes are often intergalactic, with all manner of traditions, economies, and religiosity coming into contact with one another and any number of sacred cows (patriotism, gender, race, religion) getting unsettled over and over again. Like her readers, the characters in her worlds are made to encounter themselves through other worlds and the presence of other people, just like them, who inhabit them. It's as if her science fiction landscapes serve as thought experiments that speak to the cross-cultural spaces of our time. Shallow worldviews are undone by the undeniable fact of other worlds, other cultures on other planets. These close encounters with otherness engage all that's been taken to be inevitable, the "just the way things are" in the lives of Le Guin's protagonists. As we ourselves often experience a shift when we take in a story, a lyric, or a poem, the unexamined passions that underwrite the perceived inevitabilities, the have-tos, and the common sense of all that once seemed obvious undergo a lively interrogation. This is what the Bible refers to as repentance, turning the mind around, allowing a rearranging of one's mental furniture. We have a script for what seemed realistic and right, and the script gets flipped.

In *Four Ways to Forgiveness*, Yoss, a middle-aged woman in a dilapidated house in a war-torn village, is reading what we could call an interplanetary version of *National Geographic*. She lives alone with her pet, Tikuli. She's giving herself a moment of pause. She knows that what she's reading is fair and balanced. To suggest, as people often do, that the account she's reading is somehow biased is a luxury she feels she can no longer afford, given the military violence and environmental devastation that pervade her world. She's a reader who has lost her taste for tales that flatter her life or her culture. She is eager to be *dis*illusioned.

"On the planet O there has not been a war for five thousand years," she read, "and on Gethen there has never been a war." She stopped reading, to rest her eyes and because she was trying to train herself to read slowly, not gobble words down in chunks the way Tikuli gulped his food. "There has never been a war": in her mind the words stood clear and bright, surrounded by and sinking into an infinite, dark, soft incredulity. What would that world be, a world without war? It would be the real world. Peace was the true life, the life of working and learning and bringing up children to work and learn. War, which devoured work, learning, and children, was the denial of reality. But my people, she thought, know only how to deny. Born in the dark shadow of power misused, we set peace outside our world, a guiding and unattainable light. All we know to do is fight. Any peace one of us can make in our life is only a denial that the war is going on, a shadow of the shadow, a doubled unbelief. So as the cloud-shadows swept over the marshes and the page of the book open on her lap, she sighed and closed her eyes, thinking, "I am a liar." Then she opened her eyes and read more about the other worlds, the far realities.[23]

This is one of my favorite passages in all the literature I know. It's the sight of someone deciding to stop living inside a lie. I try to facilitate this sort of thing in my conversations inside and outside of classrooms. And when I'm really on my toes, I'm alive to the possibility of undergoing such apocalypses myself. It's the sound of repentance, the sense of salvation transpiring somewhere, someone realizing some freedom, someone paying heed to the power of someone else's voice. Someone is refusing to let their own confused passions outshout the whisper of revelation. Someone's getting saved.

Le Guin gives us the anatomy of an emerging mind. Yoss isn't just finding her own culture contemptible; she's opening herself up to risk—the risk that lets in the realities, the lives, that might make many of her past decisions feel devastatingly foolish. She is going to see and hear, come what may. She will let the chips fall. She will *see better*. And the word for what's coming to her *and* the manner in which she receives it is *grace*.

· ∙ ● ● ∙ ·

Questions for Further Conversation

1. What experiences in your life come to mind when you consider activities or practices that could be rightly described as "a waste of perfectly good emotion"? Can you name moments that were unwastefully emotional or find examples of healthy passions?

2. When does desire become an "expense of spirit in a waste of shame"? Or how is it that our desires take a turn for the perverse?

3. As we hold our passions up to the light of sacred questioning, how might cosmic plainspeak in story, verse, or image invigorate us in the direction of paying closer attention to our own hearts and minds? In the work of "collating information," to use Thom Yorke's phrase, in the direction of prophetic resistance, do examples worthy of collection come to mind? Has a mixtape or a mix CD ever transformed your life?

4. How would you describe the visions of success in ministry and show business that reach an impasse in "Antichrist Television Blues"? Is Win Butler correct in his assessment of "the great insanity of our times"? Why or why not?

5. As we consider the passage in *Four Ways to Forgiveness*, can you think of moments in your own reading when the words on a page left you undone, when someone else's voice came to you as a kind of revelation? What habits of mind could make such occurrences more frequent in your life?

5

The Power of the Put-On

Questioning Media

Technology is the knack of so arranging the world
that we don't have to experience it.
Max Frisch, *Homo Faber*

Well, who you gonna believe? Me or your own eyes?
Chico Marx, *Duck Soup*

If you're like me, you rarely meet a conspiracy theory you don't like. You want to be in the know. You want to possess illicit information. Perhaps the line "The Matrix has you" ran down your spine ten or so years ago. And maybe the plight of Jim Carrey in *The Truman Show* struck you as eerily familiar. Is mind control the name of the global con game? Do the profit margins of the military/industrial/entertainment complex depend on forms of brainwash? Is my ability to perceive what's in front of me compromised by forces that intend to colonize my imagination with other people's talking points?

Well, of course! Is someone somewhere casting an eye on my spending power and buying habits and trying to bewitch me? Yes. Pretty much all the time.

"The media!" we cry. OK, calm down. What media are we thinking of exactly? Media is plural for the mediums through which someone or something is getting through (or trying to get through) to us. Let's name a few: letters, billboards, cell phones, novels, songs, newspapers, magazines, television, and emails. Are people trying to control *the media*? You betcha. We might even say that moneyed interests are trying to control as much media as they can. They're trying to place their brand on as many media platforms as possible. It's how inventories are sold, elections are won, wars are justified. Is someone putting us on, giving us an assortment of paradigms we feel strangely compelled to *put on* ourselves? Yes. The put-on is on.

Are these forces that pay top dollar to advertise their way into your consciousness making what we might call a *religious* appeal? Yes! It's all religion all the time. What else is there? But their ability to hijack your equilibrium depends on you because, fundamentally, you control the media. You cobble together your own media network, your own private broadcast system. The television doesn't turn itself on. Neither does your cell phone. And the rivers of the Internet in which many of us seem to live and move and have our being can't flow your way without your consent.

But the Internet might be made friendly. It might be viewed, at least in part, as a living witness, a resource. You have to do some intelligence gathering. An actual awareness of the world around you can't depend on the all-too-compromised mainstream news networks. You sense that the real news (as opposed to news *product*) will hardly ever be what everybody else is talking about. You're wary of best sellers, and whenever you find yourself on the majority side of an opinion poll, you get worried. You don't want to fit neatly into a marketing formula. You don't want to be that forever-lampooned figure of hip-hop—the Suckah. Suckahz be illin!

Are You Reality-Based?

In a now-famous piece in *The New York Times*, Ron Suskind described a conversation with an unnamed aide within the executive branch of the federal government.[1] The aide listened to Suskind's questions and eventually observed that Suskind and his ilk were a part of "what we call the reality-based community." The reality-based are those who *still* "believe that solutions emerge from your judicious study of discernible reality." Suskind agreed to the label, perhaps presuming it to be a compliment, and the aide cut him off:

> That's not the way the world really works anymore. We're an empire now, and when we act, we create our own reality. And while you're studying that reality—judiciously, as you will—we'll act again, creating other new realities, which you can study too, and that's how things will sort out. We're history's actors, and you, all of you, will be left to just study what we do.

Surprised? Manufactured realities are the business of governments, transnational corporations, and other top buyers of advertising space. Advertising isn't what they do with a small percentage of their budget after they've provided excellent manufactured goods and services; advertising is their primary vocation. As Marshall McLuhan taught, the mediums *are* the messages. We're soaking in them, as it happens. Did we expect a memo?

Two hundred years or so before we heard reports of a magically reassuring place called the No Spin Zone, William Blake talked about "mind-forged manacles," metal clasps forged by the mind and for the mind.[2] He heard the clank of the manacles whenever human beings opened their mouths. It's the sound of people letting other people do their thinking for them. It's the dirty trick whereby we keep perception safely at arm's length, denying ourselves the ability to think carefully and letting a talking head, a career politician, or an ideological authority do the work for us. As Simon and Garfunkel tell us, it's the way we hear what we want to hear and disregard the rest.[3]

News networks understand this. They have to sell the news. And what is news? Whatever they can sell us *as news*. They anticipate what it is that most people will watch and, for better or worse, deliver the audiovisual goods. If we want to hear about Lindsay Lohan's woes more than we want to know about genocide in Darfur, Lindsay Lohan's daily life will be the news. To survive, the networks have to play to our "felt needs." In this sense, *we* are the newsmakers—and the networks are just the sales force. They'll give us whatever they think we want. It is all they can afford to give.

But what about the reality-based folks who want to know things that the networks aren't selling—the names and places that are hard to pronounce and the stories that challenge the way we live? To be reality-based means to distrust in some way our own preference for the news that sits easily in our heads. The reality-based will hunt down uncomfortable facts that call into question assumptions about the everyday world. When the reality-based discover news that unsettles and challenges, they might even call it gospel—*good news*. Good because it's truthful, and if truthful, redeeming.

Sometimes uncomfortable facts *feel* biased. Because we're all standing *somewhere*, living within a particular culture, born and raised among particular people, certain facts feel biased because they challenge our self-esteem. It's as if real life elsewhere was somehow designed to make us feel guilty. When facts make us feel bad about ourselves (starving children, civilian casualties, impossible trade laws imposed on the so-called two-thirds world), will we have the wit and humility to look hard at them anyway? We'll always be free to call the facts "biased," but are we only interested in civilian death tolls that won't threaten our assumptions about our good-hearted foreign policy? If certain eyewitness testimonies call our presumed goodness into question, will we allow them into the witness box? Or do we only allow positive press? We're always free to turn away and go back to our preferred news sources (ministering to our "felt needs"). But if we're reality-based, we'll renounce knee-jerk defensiveness and look harder. We will be good intelligence gatherers. Even when revelations make us feel stupid because of who we voted for, we'll want the revelations anyway. If they're true, they're good. Even if they don't make us *feel* good instantaneously.

Radioactive Days

Given the tremendous amount of energy and resources expended by business interests and political parties to invent public reality, it will take serious strength of will to resist the informational echo chambers of our culture. If we're to be reality-based, we'll have to refuse the limited identities we've been offered on the treadmills of hyperconsumerism. Reality-based people will be distinguished by an eagerness to discover their own failings. And we will resist the vast feedback mechanism that tells us on a daily basis that we're never wrong, we've never been wrong, and it will always be *others* who are wrong. Instead, we get to live in anticipation of a great awakening. We get to listen to each other.

Genuine listening is rare. All too often, we find others uninteresting or irrelevant when they fail to say what we want to hear. It doesn't have to be this way. Remaining receptive to unpackaged reality will involve vigilance and curiosity and determined hospitality. It will require an eye and an ear for new stories, stories that may well lead us to regard as scandalous our own habits of consumption or the policies of our government.

Popular discourse suggests that certain people are unworthy of our attention. It's as if millions of people never enter our imaginations—not even as casualties. They don't enter the gates of our chosen media. We need to question ourselves. What content do I privilege? How many different kinds of people do I encounter? What am I taking in? To whom do I go to figure out what's going on?

These days, listening a little harder, looking with a wider-angle lens, and simply being slower to push the "I'm offended!" button might be revolutionary actions. Not content to deal in sound bites, we can aspire to be more reality-based. But like humility, it isn't a quality you have when you're sure you have it. When we claim to be without spin, we lie and the truth is not in us. It's a difficult task to want to know what we don't want to know.

We live in an audiovisual con game. In light of the con, it's often a pleasure to turn to *The Colbert Report* or *The Daily Show*, especially when we consider Jon Stewart's framing of his presentation, "And now … the fake news." It unmasks the con that is news production—news as whatever will momentarily soothe our minds, news that presumes to name itself unfake. While the paradoxical authority of satire's unseriousness would be undermined by a claim to legitimacy ("Listen to me! I'm serious now!"), it's hard to resist the suggestion that the real news is being broadcast through satire, that the only popular attempt at genuine truth telling is coming at us through comedy. The fake news *is* the news. Bill Moyers once remarked that he wasn't sure whether Stewart and his team were practicing an old form of parody or satire. Stewart replied that what they're actually practicing is "a new form of desperation."[4]

Circus Time

The power of the put-on, whether it's understood to be comedic, religious, or political, is the subject of the above exchange between Moyers, former press secretary for the Johnson administration and now a preeminent *news*man with PBS, and Stewart, a comedian who resists the labels of media critic and political commentator. Stewart prefers the label of "song and dance man" (like Bob Dylan and Andy Kaufman before him) over pretensions to significance and gravitas. In some sense, both Moyers and Stewart are the sum of the choices they made. And the task of those who aspire to be reality-based is similar to the work of discernment involved in the careers of these two. Perhaps it's the same work.

We all have the power to create our own media networks via the Internet and the postal service and our ability to put pen to paper, words to song, paint to canvas. It's all *our media*. What will we put on the air? What will our output be? Who *doesn't* work in media?

These questions come to mind when I recall a televised conversation between David Letterman and PBS's Charlie Rose.[5] When asked to draw a comparison between what he does and what was accomplished by Johnny Carson in his years on the air, Letterman remarked that what his team delivers is essentially "circus time," with things being lit on fire, dropped in water, and thrown from buildings. Letterman isn't happy with this state of affairs. It isn't as if trying to make conversation with the last person to get voted off the island is Letterman's preferred vocation, but an exhibition of literal nonsense appears to be what's required. He stressed that he could never really know for sure, but playing in the big leagues in the unending competitiveness of prime time seems to allow for no pause in circus time. He wants, after all, to stay on the air.

With heartbreaking candor, he expressed a preference for the kind of television associated with Tom Snyder and Rose himself, the exhilaratingly legitimate moment of people talking to each other and other people tuning in from far away. But could he risk it and keep up with Jay Leno and *The Tonight Show*? Would he remain commercially viable? He has to play it safe. Back to throwing stuff off buildings—back to whatever it takes.

Before the cameras, David Letterman can't talk to the kind of people he wants to talk to. He can't quite facilitate the stories he'd like to do. His show can't show what he wants it to show. He can't do what he wants to do without losing access. Access to what? Power? Influence? Like everyone else, he has to guess at what the biggest chunk of viewers want and then deliver it. And what haunts him is the feeling that his guess might be wrong. Maybe the viewers want what he thinks he can't give them. The medium, in this sense, is devastatingly limited. The competition for viewers is a race to the bottom. I'm reminded of Fred Friendly's observation that the producers of television broadcasts are so powerfully and amply rewarded for doing the *wrong* things that they aren't inclined to ask what might be *right* and *good* and promote psychological health. Success makes a failure of the medium's content.

Sellers of news product in newsrooms around the country may not honestly feel that a celebrity behaving badly is more important than Buddhist monks in Myanmar (formerly Burma) laying down their lives in nonviolent demonstration. Like Letterman, they might long for something different. They might sense the hope, the redeeming possibility, implicit in people talking to each other, sharing stories, and allowing their minds to be changed. But exploring such possibilities isn't in their job description. Network executives gain a world of ratings but forfeit on behalf of their shareholders the possibility of soul, the possibility of communicating substance.

If the name Fred Friendly didn't strike a chord, I'll mention now that he appeared as a character in *Good Night and Good Luck* portrayed by the film's director, George Clooney. The film chronicles the culture of the CBS newsroom of the 1950s, with particular emphasis on Friendly's relationship with his closest professional associate, newsman Edward R. Murrow. They seek out and broadcast the stories they feel the American people need to hear. For them, that which is most newsworthy is that which people might be able to do something about. Actionable intelligence, we might call it. Their career-long commitment to doing the job this way is legendary.

Friendly famously observed that it was the job of the journalist to create a pain in the minds of the audience so intense that it can only be relieved by thinking. That sounds about right to me. And I'd like to extend the job description to include any bearer of story, any bearer of witness. The storyteller's job is to bring the news (the new take, the new word, the strange report) and to bring it in such a way that it might change people's minds. As we receive it, the newsworthy story drives us to see our world and ourselves differently. Real news stories change *our* stories, our understanding of our own lives.

In the powerful speech that opens *Good Night and Good Luck*, Edward R. Murrow addresses a 1958 convention of radio and television news directors with an eye toward naming the responsibilities that come with reporting. He is deeply pessimistic concerning the effectiveness of his words ("This just might do nobody any good"), but the vision he shares brings the vocation of witness back to the promise and the hazards of people talking to each other:

> I have no technical advice or counsel to offer those of you who labor in this vineyard that produces words and pictures. You will forgive me for not telling you that instruments with

which you work are miraculous, that your responsibility is unprecedented or that your aspirations are frequently frustrated. It is not necessary to remind you that the fact that your voice is amplified to the degree where it reaches from one end of the country to the other does not confer on you greater wisdom or understanding than you possessed when your voice reached only from one end of the bar to the other. All of these things you know.[6]

While he observes, for the record, that he is an employee of the Columbia Broadcasting System, Morrow contextualizes these remarks as his own personal broadcast on the subject of the state of television broadcasting. As a broadcaster, his remarks are "of a 'do-it-yourself' nature," and while these words are less broadly cast than the ones that make it into the hearts and minds of millions, he wants to remind his listeners (and perhaps himself) that such grassroots exchanges (whether in bars, bus stops, or diners) are no less authoritative, no less worthy of being counted as wise, no less newsworthy. There's a whisper of revolution whenever people really speak to one another and really listen. Sending and receiving. Is this thing on? This revolution might even occur (Murrow hopes) via television. But things are looking grim.

Murrow imagines courageous souls with small budgets who might dare to tell the plight of Native Americans, news that the American public has yet to want to hear, news that is not deemed newsworthy. But if television remains a means to "methods of insulating while selling," Murrow argues, catering to "our built-in allergy to unpleasant or disturbing information,"[7] it will be a dead and deadening medium. Broadcasters function as sellers of advertising. Their broadcast content (often indistinguishable from the advertisements themselves) will be devoid of any suggestion that the untelevised might require the viewers' attention. One will have to look beyond those "wires and lights in a box"[8] to research what's going on and where it's at.

What's Going On?

Real news, I believe, is whatever drives us to think again. Most of us are on the prowl for it most of the time. I even hope for it via the television. I still count on Letterman for that unexpected response to the surreal status quo as he sits there hitting those cards against his desk. Like Stewart and Colbert, he isn't just making things funny; he's facilitating moments of reality within "circus time." He's staging something. In 2000, I watched him ask then-governor George W. Bush to distinguish between retaliation and due process of law, to acknowledge the fact of a melting polar ice cap, and to offer a word on how one could preside over so many executions in Texas—one hundred fifty-two—with such eerie self-confidence. He was asking harder and better questions than had been put to Bush in the 2000 campaign. He was bringing the news in a manner worthy of Murrow. An illumination was under way for anyone with an ear to hear. Real news won't always advertise itself as such.

Marshall McLuhan once quipped that anyone who tries to make a distinction between education and entertainment doesn't know the first thing about either. In typical fashion, McLuhan breaks down the high and low culture distinctions that sometimes get in the way of grappling with what's in front of us. A story (whether in a book, a thirty-second ad spot, a sitcom, or a song) isn't merely entertaining. It's telling you something. It has content. It seeks to feelingly persuade. It will colonize your imagination as you're sitting there laughing to yourself.

The media we admit into our lives are alive and signaling. Do we engage, or are we merely engaged? When we talk about literature or rave about a film, when we write something down or commit a line to memory, are we looking to open the doors of perception? If we don't talk about what we're taking in, why is it worthy of our energy? Have we lost the notion that Shakespeare is trying to tell us what's going on? Do we find the writing of Zora Neale Hurston trustworthy? Is Emily Dickinson a good intelligence gatherer in her poetry? Literature is a public broadcasting system. What is being proposed, made plain, revealed?

Shakespeare Is Country Music

What are we hoping for when we download a song? What sense of expectation do we have when we pay money to watch somebody belt out a chorus in a darkened room? What are we looking for in a book club? There's something so commonplace about our taking in of media that we tend to forget about the remarkable degree of faith, hope, and love involved. What I think we're looking for is a good word. We dare to believe that reality might unfurl before us by way of other human voices. We might even believe a soothsayer or shaman is about to show up. We're experimenting with an Amen.

In *Chronicles: Volume One*, Bob Dylan tells of finding Thelonious Monk sitting alone at the Blue Note with a large, half-consumed sandwich on top of his piano. When the young singer mentions that he plays folk music up the street, Monk responds as if commenting on the weather: "We all play folk music."[9]

Folk. Now there's a good word. It manages to somehow lift a burden. Folk is just folks trying to tell other folks what's happening in their heads and in the world. Folk is trying to tell truthfully what happened by telling it with slant. Folk *poetry*, if we want to put it that way. Folk *art*, if art and poetry are the highest praise we can give to someone's attempt to get through to us, to tell us what's going on. Do we have an appetite for plainspeak?

Ezra Pound once wrote that literature is "news that stays news."[10] Literature is the sound of full disclosure, an apocalypse, an unveiling, an unmasking. It's what we're after when we're looking for what's true regardless of who it privileges or *de*-privileges. It cuts across history and whatever divides we set up between people, people who are all just folks. Drawing on Pound's language, writer Lawrence Ferlinghetti challenges the poet (or anyone who wants to make things new) to write "living newspapers."[11]

The news-bearing lyrical word is not an edict from on high but often a disruptively truthful word about the way things are. It expands the sphere of sanity little by little. It breaks into monopolies on truth, overcoming the reigning myopia. I like to tell my students that anything they find in their literature textbooks should be viewed as no more or no less highfalutin than a trucker writing words of love or loss on a napkin at a Waffle House. Shakespeare *is* country music. The words weren't written and saved and passed down to make us feel stupid or estranged. In literature, there are no strangers. Everyone's invited. Everyone's allowed. The words on the page, the words of song, are all ways of paying attention, means to remembering some very important things, the means we sometimes call *media*.

A revelatory word can come from any quarter—from believer, unbeliever, and misbeliever alike. No hierarchy. No official words. Only testimonies. Poems. People being people.

We're on the prowl for inspiration. We want something extra-authentic, something to shake our nerves and rattle our brains. We need something to keep us from throwing in the towel and losing our minds—something to get us out of bed. Gospel, the news we call *good*, is always a media issue.

Build Your Own Reality Studio

This idea that media are only what we make of them returns us to the question of collage, of collating information and image, perhaps most wonderfully evident in that personalized, affectionate form of recommended listening we used to call the *mixtape*. Once mixtapes came along (I was fourteen or fifteen), there was no going back. What could be a more powerful blessing than to have vouchsafed on me a carefully orchestrated collection of songs (handpicked, painstakingly ordered with well-placed segues) by someone for whom I felt respect, someone who thought I would do well to hear *these songs*? The mixtape was, and is, like a handwritten letter or a little work of art. A cause for absolute euphoria. The sound of someone caring.

And I started compiling my own. I'd feign nonchalance, as if I'd accidentally recorded a collection of favorites with a particular person in mind. But I couldn't sustain the charade for long. Making a mixtape is the opposite of indifferent. It's heartfelt, purposeful—often a subtle form of flirtation. And it's downright embarrassing if these collections aren't treasured or at least paid a little mind, because the mixtape is a way of making yourself known, an interpersonal form of show business, of making news, of replicating sounds and words you find important. It's like poetry because poetry is what you can't say in any other way. At its most essential level, a mixtape is a way of getting through.

Making mixtapes—or playlists, now—is an instance of how the work gets done, how formative influences do their formative work. The recommendations ("You should check this out." "Have you heard this?") are how we find out what's going on. The true and truthful can seem elusive, so we stay on the lookout for revelation. We need art and stories and songs that break down, in Murrow's phrase, our long habit of reality insulation. And when we find them, we pass them on.

Murrow sensed that reality insulation was fast becoming the mode of operation for electronic media, an operation that deadens our ability to critically engage with news and information. He predicted a time when political strategists and other salespeople would observe, as a sort of truism, that perception is more important than reality. Reality, as he knew then and we know all too well now, could be manufactured, reinvented, to suit the agendas of political parties and transnational corporations and governments. But we aren't without resources in the work of critical engagement.

The forces that seek to shape popular discourse are ultimately only allowed the airtime we give them. There are the big, expensive reality studios (in the phraseology of William S. Burroughs), largely controlled by certain moneyed interests. But they broadcast meaningfully only when sufficient numbers of people pay heed. Our own broadcasts and our responses to the broadcasts of others can be beautifully local and interpersonal, less beholden to the concept of ratings. Our broadcasts can be the mixtapes, the lyricizing of reality, that come to us through music, stories, and image. There's an ancient conversation going on in a variety of forms, and there are so many ways of naming it: the space of literature, the religious sphere, the cosmic plainspeak, the poetic. Poet Cid Corman observes that poetry, in this sense, is the conversation we can't have in any other way.[12] There are so many ways of building your own reality studio. So many ways of raising your hand, picking up the microphone, tuning in. We need not be mere consumers, mere addicts. We can be producers, sharers, hunters, and gatherers. You are your own media mogul. People have the power.

Openness—and the production of plainspeak—is possible

only when we seek out and encounter others in all their stunning actuality, when we invite people to show up in conversation in the place where we share our news or our sense of the news. If we leave it to the major news media to have these conversations for us, most of what's being cultivated in our hearts and minds is a kind of escalating narcissism, tailor-made to fit our patterns of prejudice and insecurity. When we could be sharing stories, becoming more modest in our viewpoints, trying to redemptively process reality in one another's presence, we instead sit before the screen as addicts, watching beautiful people toss their hair in shampoo commercials. Our reality gets manufactured for us by forces that pose a kind of psychological health hazard. These media networks are carefully designed and redesigned to hold our attention by any means necessary. It's their job, and they do it extremely well.

But there are other networks, other reality studios, other media. They are as near as the nearest person, book, or blogosphere (to the extent that the blog isn't held captive by someone else's predetermined talking points). Hope is as near as the nearest work of art, the closest conversation, the person sitting nearby who wishes someone would ask her a question.

The People's CNN

To broadcast an honest word in our age often feels as if it's destined to be forgotten before it's even been heard. But if we can cultivate a more historical sense of the way the exchange of news works (via literature, folk music, poetry, whereby we speak to one another across the ages), we might begin to see that the lust for ridiculously large audiences, high ratings, and a fast track to immediate celebrity is a form of madness.

Like the understanding of religiosity discussed in the preceding chapters—our religion and spirituality is the life we're living—

our desire for trustworthy media sources seems to take us any-where and everywhere. We're pilgrims on a quest to find the story that speaks to our own world, the history we're swimming in.

Truth-telling broadcasts often fall on deaf ears. The best (whether books, folk songs, or paintings) will only rarely be best-selling within their creator's lifetime. But the songs remain the same. The broadcasts continue. The mixtape-making impulse is with us. We keep tuning in and hoping to hear a good word.

In *The Confidence-Man*, Herman Melville describes humanity as a "multiform pilgrim species."[13] That's a wonderfully broad way of naming our inner detective who is always looking for a story that will help us add things up, a story that might resolve all the incoherence, a story in which we might locate ourselves. We are all on a pilgrimage, always striving after meaning, hoping for a breakthrough. We want an epiphany, an adventure in precision, something that might kick down the doors of our dim-witted hypocrisy.

In my attempt to secure an audience for the voices of news-breaking, folkways tradition in my high school classroom, I've tried to pitch British literature textbooks as the equivalent of a wonderfully thick playlist, the "Greatest Hits" according to a cer-tain *tradition*. I tell my students that a tradition, according to G. K. Chesterton, is nothing more than "a democracy of the dead."[14] Maybe all those people knew something. Maybe there's some-thing tried-and-true in this collection. Maybe there's some news that's still news.

And to borrow a little from Chuck D of Public Enemy, folk tradition in this sense is the people's CNN. In the predominantly oral societies of ancient times (Roman-occupied, first-century Palestine, for instance), it was believed that words were infused with mystical powers. But it was often the case in those days, as in ours, that speaking truthfully, prophetically, or in an inspired fashion wasn't something just anyone could do. Only priests, prophets on the payroll, and other news professionals were permitted to make sure the right speech got spoken. Someone else decided what the news was, someone largely divorced from local concerns. Sound familiar?

We understand that these power brokers are with us always, hijacking our attempts to broadcast news to one another and co-opting our ability to function as communities. But folk expression (then *and* now) will cut through the noise. Art restores our sanity. And in-between the cracks of popular discourse, via blogs, libraries, live performances, and well-stocked iPods, better broadcasts are unprecedentedly within arm's reach. Grassroots concerns are a click away. There are so many ways of letting reality back in.

The painter Paul Klee once observed that art, in this sense, doesn't reproduce what we see; it *makes* us see.[15] It gives us something true to life. And now more than ever, this form of public-service announcement is always open to questioning, editing, embellishment, and retelling—and the results are wonderfully liberating. Our sense of what is newsworthy is too crucial to living a good and just life to be left to detached interests that will do whatever it takes to win the ratings race, which, content-wise, is a race to the bottom.

No Nobodies

As we consider the revolutionary and redeeming possibilities of mixtapes, blogspots, balladeering, and other forms of breaking news, I recall my discovery of a container, affixed to a wall outside a New England post office building, filled with Xeroxed copies of a one-sheet newspaper called *The Broadside*. For "one thin dime" placed in a metal box beside the container, anyone could have one. I was profoundly inspired. "*That's* what I'm talking about!" I remarked to myself. A Thomas Jefferson quote at the top of the page decreed the town meeting, of all things, to be "the wisest invention ever devised by the wit of man."

"Yes indeed," I said aloud, adding the words that were forming in my mind. "And the town meeting was invented by the early church."[16]

As is often the case, I spoke before I thought. But the thought beginning to form was this: it is good news—wonderful news—when people gather in small groups to say what they think and with a determination to give ear to all comers, an audience for every raised hand. This is how everyday people (in Sly Stone's phrase) begin to receive authority and feel a sense of dignity.

To better think through the sociological significance of the good news at work within the New Testament—and what on earth it might have to do with town meetings, the blogosphere, and folk expression—we might echo the befuddled and frustrated testimony of Flannery O'Connor's philosophizing serial killer, the Misfit, in "A Good Man Is Hard to Find": "Jesus ... thrown everything off balance."[17] He winces at the mention of a savior who single-handedly brought up the net value of human beings for every culture that takes him seriously. The Misfit sees how rumors of the Nazarene's notions mess with what passes as normal, expert, and professional. The whole mess, in the Misfit's view, can disturb a man's confidence. He figures that if Jesus were the real deal, there's nothing to do but drop everything and follow him. And if he weren't? "No pleasure but meanness."[18]

To the Misfit, Jesus' gospel isn't just another peaceful, easy feeling or a decent sentiment gently submitted for our approval. The good news is a blazing, bloodred question mark against whatever we consider common sense. Like a chain reaction (or a slow train coming), the gospel is a different sort of social imagination moving through history, breaking the pavement of countless cultural status quos, eventually searing even the conscience of the Misfit's Southern forbears, a slave-holding culture that believed itself to have the definitive word on how to read that thick, black, leather-bound book.

The ancient broadcast of Jesus of Nazareth, the Misfit laments, unsettles everybody's judgment, everything that *seems* right. What do you do with enemies? Love them. What do you do with your stuff? Share it. What about the foreigners and the strangers among you? Receive them. Look after their health. The Misfit is such a memorable character because, psycho killer though he is, he nevertheless takes Jesus' good news (the gospel) seriously. *More* seriously, we understand, than the self-described Christians who still make unfortunate distinctions when it comes to their fellow human beings—hardworking Americans/illegals, children of God/collateral damage, bearer of inalienable rights/enemy combatant, us/them. The many want the Jesus Christ whose name is a secret password into eternal bliss. The few will allow Jesus' gospel to actually infect the way they think about, talk about, and regard other people. The few will grapple (like the Misfit) with Jesus' always provocative good news broadcast.

If we do grapple with it, our sense of the newsworthy and of who we need to be listening to will be subverted and overturned. We will begin to sense a sanctifying presence in new places. We'll dream new dreams about ourselves. The remarkable and the holy will show up unexpectedly. Our sense of the world will become one where no human life is unsacred or uninteresting, and there are no nobodies. Every stranger has a story.

It's this very presumptuousness—that something worthwhile, cosmically significant even, is happening among the least of these —that brings us to the global broadcast called the Day of Pentecost. At Pentecost, Peter explains the very strange occurrence of mass communication among Jews of different languages, accompanied by the rush, rattle, and hum of a violent wind, by declaring that the Spirit of the Lord is being poured out on all flesh. In Acts 2, Peter goes on to say that the life lived by the agitator they've all heard about, the recently executed Jewish peasant revolutionary, Jesus of Nazareth, would not be held by the power of death, that God freed him from death, and everyone present is invited to enter into his way of doing things. They're invited to turn around, to step out of the presently crooked world orders by which they're enthralled and risk all on resurrection.

By the time of Jesus' death, Jesus' freedom to speak the truth aloud under duress was literally all he had left. And here's Peter telling the gathering that Jesus' word is the word of the Lord. That, like Jesus, they're called to speak and live truthfully and to let the chips fall even unto death. He's telling them that Jesus' mode of truthfulness, *this* mode of telling what is true, is an eternal liveliness, beleaguered, yet unconquerable. All too vulnerable, yet somehow invulnerable.

It's all we've got—all we've ever had. Bearing witness, telling the story of what happened and what's happening, is the genre of all genres. The only news. The only poetry.

Poetry and Pentecost

In a discussion of poetry and religion, Denise Levertov offers a vision of the poetic as the way people manage to communicate as they try to stay afloat and support one another within "the ocean of crisis in which we swim."[19] I find this image helpful and sobering. How do we communicate humanly? How do we discern one another? How do we figure out how to act justly?

As we consider the general devaluing of human life, it's helpful to consider the political significance of Pentecost as a revolution in the power of human speech (the breaking news that keeps on breaking). The events described in the book of Acts lead to the establishment of Jews *and* non-Jews (Gentiles) as, in Melville's phrase, a "multiform pilgrim species." No one infected by the event would "know their place" ever again. Any hierarchy we can name, any myth that keeps some people above other people, will in time be uproariously overturned. Call it democracy.

And lest we forget, the hope of democracy depends on actually practicing it. Without a polity, without an assembly of people who speak to one another, listen, disagree agreeably, and occasionally change their minds, democracy is just a high-sounding word employed by high-tech hypnotists. We have to do the work of critical reflection and communal discernment. We can't get wise all by ourselves.

It is rumored that the Spirit of the Lord is being poured out on all flesh and that all flesh shall see the salvation of God. With the word (sung or spoken) now radically possessed by the second-class citizenry, poetry and song become a witness more reliable than the "official" status quo. A new way of talking and listening is born. There are all manner of news networks, and the revolutions might occasionally be televised. The cosmic plainspeak that is everywhere will often help us overcome and articulate what Pete Seeger calls "the ocean of misunderstanding between human beings."[20] In the ancient Near East, the early church's word of life under Roman rule would have been very different from what the empire was in the habit of telling itself about itself. The subversively truthful report we call good news brings mythic realities down low.

People Talking to Each Other

This good news broadcast is multipartisan. Properly understood, it makes equal opportunity pilgrims of males, females, Jews, Gentiles, slaves, and the legally free. Nobody owns the copyright on the good, truthful, reality-bearing word. No label can contain the reach of the people's good news. In this sense, the gospel is a wider-ranging broadcast than we imagine it to be. Perhaps inevitably, the term would eventually be used for advertising purposes, but that doesn't mean we have to define it so rigidly. The biblical witness is a little muddier than the "spirituality" market allows. When we think of biblical broadcast as "religion" that exists primarily to "uplift" emotionally, we're missing the point. And gospel, in the deepest sense, can't exactly stay out of politics, as the saying goes, because the news bears witness with no neat divisions. Gospel speaks truth to everyone, high and low alike.

Take Johnny Cash who, as a kind of *news*man, purposefully sought to channel, in his words, "voices that were ignored or even suppressed in the entertainment media, not to mention the political and educational establishments."[21] That's a vocation, for sure, and we shouldn't reduce such a witness to a particular marketing genre any more than we'd characterize William Blake's prophetic verse as either religious or political. It's *all* folk music. The dichotomies don't fly when we're dealing with a human heart in conflict with itself—and that's *every* human heart. Folk expression is a way of staring down madness with mirth and death with determined truth telling. In this sense, there is no terrain outside folk's jurisdiction, no subject that's inappropriate or irrelevant to its stories and sayings and lamentations.

We're sold "news" that has the same effect on the human heart as foot binding had on women's feet in ancient China. When that which passes for news is untruthful—largely void of real investigative power—and never urges us to look harder at other people's faces or our own, we become people no longer capable of the give-and-take of human conversation. Such images and sounds don't invite real listening, only consumption.

To maintain some grip on reality, we have to constantly remind ourselves that the news is never what happened. It's a story *about* what happened, and it is only rarely worthy of it's own advertising. News product, usually quick and dependably shallow, will usually be the opposite of "in-depth coverage." We know this is how it works. What are we left with?

How about folk? A more reliable witness to what's going on, demanding to be inherited, committed to memory, sung around a fire, rehearsed, and recited. Folk isn't so arrogant as to view itself as a No Spin Zone because folk music understands that to spin is human. And those who think they're without spin have a nasty, high-ratings habit of casting the first stone. Folk music is a little more modest in its goals, but folk will try to tell truth as well as it can, even among the slow to believe. Folk invites our consent. And if we're willing, its gospel will become a part of the way we see, chastening and invigorating our way of looking at the world. It's the possibility of finding ourselves based in reality humanely mediated. Folk is good news. Folk is people talking.

· · ● ● ● · ·

Questions for Further Conversation

1. How does unexamined talk about the evils of "the media" sabotage the possibility of thinking properly about the world and one's place in it? Who benefits from our inappropriate use of this term?

2. What is it about the functioning of power in our brave new world that makes the "judicious study of discernible reality" (according to one source) an ill-advised, anachronistic way of finding out what's going on? What makes being "reality based" such a tall and complicated order?

3. Given the 24/7 tragicomedy of "circus time," can you think of media figures who "succeed" while simultaneously holding on to their souls? Are there ways of being in the world of "mainstream" media without being wholeheartedly of it?

4. Are there people you know personally or know of who bear true witness with their stories, their songs, or their sharing of their findings? What attributes characterize such people? How do they respond when people find their witness, for whatever reason, off-putting?

5. How might folk traditions, literature, or the ancient broadcasts of cosmic plainspeak be viewed as news networks? What do we gain when we come to think of folk music, for instance, as the people's CNN?

6. Describe a recent experience or encounter in which you believe you received an actual news transmission, an instance of actionable intelligence, that could properly be called *breaking news*. Who or what was the source and what was the content?

6

The Word, the Line, the Way

Questioning Our Language

> Language is a Trojan horse by which
> the universe gets into the mind.
>
> **Hugh Kenner, *Dublin's Joyce***

> Why is lenguage?... Lenguage is that
> we may mis-undastend each udda.
>
> **Krazy Kat's philosophical word
> to Ignatz Mouse, *Krazy Kat:*
> *The Comic Art of George Herriman***

The question I'd like to bring to language, my own and every-one else's, is the question of reductionism. Reductionism reigns when the words we use to give an account of people and events serve only to reduce, degrade, and devalue human beings in the interest of managing them, mischaracterizing our relationships with others to make them mean whatever we need them to mean to maintain our fragile ego structures. This is the perversity we employ—perhaps it employs *us*—when we reduce a person to a "just" ("So-and-so is just ...") or a "nothing but" ("You're noth-ing but a ..."), as if we've gotten to the bottom of all they are and ever will be. Eye-rubbingly broad generalizations are leveled in our talk of other countries, personal histories, and the petty mor-tal who just cut us off in the flow of rush-hour traffic. These are the death sentences that generate a sort of verbal totalitarianism, closing up and cutting off real-live people. The words that fail to do justice to the *ir*reducible complexity of whatever it is we *think* we're talking about. It's what we call *bad language.* Cursing words. The speech is dirty, if you like, because it deals in pseudo-reality, dimming an awareness of where we live, what we're doing, and what we're taking.[1] It demeans and disfigures with a feeling of control as it takes a turn for the contemptuous, DIS-membering experience in the telling.

But there are other utterances that counter the power of dis-membering death with wonderful words of life, words that serve to RE-member, restoring membership and belonging when they're spoken or sung aloud. Words that have the power to still lying tongues. The *good language.* It's a challenge, certainly, to keep such speech in our hearts and on our tongues, but it's the challenge that might be our only chance at love and life. The only real pleasure. The only kingdom coming down. Maybe we have to pray for the wit and imagination to RE-member people again and again. The hardened heart, I imagine, is the one that won't (or can't) RE-member, that won't quite grant a deep, personal reality to other people, the heart that finds it necessary to not RE-member others in order to survive, the heart no longer in tune with the notion, affirmed by every living religious tradition, that there is no available life in the universe that isn't connected to the practice of RE-membering.

The good words remember and represent. They repair our visions by making all things new. They make the world-at-large reappear in a dazzling new light, as if we didn't quite know, till the words came, what we were all about. When they are spoken aloud, we describe them by saying things like, "That's music to my ears." The good language uplifts the way bad language degrades. It's the life-giving authority of poetry. The Canadian literary scholar Northrop Frye speaks of poetic authority as the "authority which emancipates instead of subordinating the person who accepts it."[2] Frye isn't talking about an authority confined to libraries and bookstores; he's talking about the authority that redemptively rearranges life as we know it. When I try to bring my thoughts to bear on what I mean by the word *poetry*, I recall a televised exchange between the recently departed elder statesman of popularly understood American conservatism, William F. Buckley, and the Beat poet with a decidedly different vision of the meaning of conservation, Allen Ginsberg. In a freewheeling interview on his program *Firing Line*, Buckley interrupts Ginsberg's lyrical rant to suggest that such verbal outpouring fails to meet certain standards:

BUCKLEY: Well, you know what in my judgment is unsatisfactory about this analysis, I really don't think — incidentally it is not so much analytical as it is poetical …

GINSBERG: Oh, poesy is the oldest form …

BUCKLEY: Yeah, yeah.

GINSBERG: Analysis is a later form.[3]

In this exchange, Buckley appears to be on the verge of undercutting the authority of Ginsberg's cultural commentary by observing that Ginsberg's word on the world (politics, economics, religion, media) is not, strictly speaking, an analysis so much as it is a work of poetry. Ginsberg doesn't dispute this characterization of his output, but he does want to state for the record that Buckley's analytic posturing is the latecomer to meaning making, to all talk of flux and fire, to higher primates attempting to give an account of themselves to themselves. Ginsberg wants it to be understood that the lyrical precedes the analytical (underwrites it, in a manner of speaking), and his interruption asserts that it might be appropriate to occasionally remember as much, lest we get carried away. Poetry came first.

"Poesy is the oldest form.... Analysis is a later form." It has long been the case that there is something that passes for official, authoritative analysis, and then there's poetry. Ginsberg casually inserts that he means to function as a carrier for this, the oldest form of attempted awareness of whatever passes within our attention span as current goings-on, older than whatever distinctions Buckley might want to make between poetry and reportage, verifiable and unverifiable, fancy and necessity, hearts and minds. Poetry is here putting thought in its place, enlivening the scene, calling constructions into question. Poetry isn't merely representative of that which might momentarily escape rational analysis; it *generates* analysis as a form, and when heeded, it will awaken analysis to its own pretensions.

The plans of mice and men are challenged to humble themselves before a more ancient wisdom. These are the kinds of exchanges recorded in the scriptures we call sacred. This is why Ginsberg understood himself to be on the side of a more ancient conservatism when, in 1967, he issued a "Pentagon Exorcism" (delivered on the scene by Ed Sanders and Tuli Kupferberg) to protest his government's actions in Vietnam. He is attempting to be in line with a poetic/prophetic tradition that, often in necessarily unconventional ways, will engage madness in its myriad forms. What's a poet? Someone who makes things new. What's a prophet? Someone who tells the difficult truth. Poets and prophets speak and sing in tongues justified and ancient, calling past and future to the rescue of the present. Would that all of God's people were poets and prophets.[4]

When I consider Buckley's failure (or reluctance) to receive the drift of Ginsberg's point, I'm reminded of the interface of the modern with the premodern. In somewhat caricatured form, I think of Buckley as representative of the spirit of Enlightenment and Ginsberg stepping up to give voice to the bardic impulse, to the world going on underground, to older forms of knowing. Buckley would seem to be on the side of the traditional, seemingly aligned with the conventionally religious with its assumption of stable essences, always available to reassure us of certain certainties, absolute truths, to which the well-to-do have done well to be anchored. Ginsberg comes in with the unanchored chaos of one well-versed Jewish American harnessing what some Buddhist traditions call crazy wisdom, saying whatever comes to mind.

What's at stake in this exchange is the issue of whose words get to count. Will Ginsberg's poetic/prophetic word be received as significant? Will it be welcomed? The postmodern sensibility responds affirmatively and will even lean toward Ginsberg's mobile army of metaphors, because, unlike the brand of conservative often associated with Buckley, Ginsberg doesn't claim to *make* anything happen or insist that his side of a conversation is more responsible or realistic. He will call it like he sees it and admit that speech is all he's got. His words won't claim to go beyond words. Freed from the burden of cognitive certainty, the postmodern mind is determined not to fall for transcendental pretensions or any idolatry of concepts. It is perhaps all the more determined to listen for and receive that which eludes our categories and our perversions, all the more determined to be attentive.

Your Words Have You

To call my students to such attentiveness, we go around the room, sharing a short sample of whatever lines come to mind. It can be a commercial jingle, a quote, a lyric. They aren't graded for quality, but they do have to share one. To their surprise, they begin to understand that they're walking around with thick volumes of sentences within their consciousness. So many words linger in our minds. I want them to know that it wasn't only the ancient bards who could hold Homer in their heads. Whether it's a Bible verse, a hateful sentence once spoken to us, or a bad Vanilla Ice line, the words are there, naming the feelings we feel, narrating what happened, anticipating what's happening. It might be worthwhile to have a long look at them. Maybe there are better sentences to be had. Perhaps a revisioning is in order.

I recall a scene in Spike Lee's *Malcolm X* in which a younger Malcolm, played by Denzel Washington, is serving time in Massachusetts State Prison. He begins to spend most of his time in the library, where he has long and lively conversations with a Muslim inmate named Baines. Baines speaks of "the prison of your mind" and admonishes younger inmates, "You get used to this life, and it puts you to sleep."

Malcolm wants to know, "What's your angle?" Why does Baines act like he does? Why doesn't he curse like everyone else around the prison?

"A man curses because he doesn't have the words to say what's on his mind." This way of putting it is jarring, and the words come to Malcolm as a revelation.

"Ever look up the word *black*?" "Did you ever study anything that wasn't a con?" Baines asks. He takes Malcolm over to a dictionary. As his eyes scan the pages, the viewer receives a sense of the liberating and captivating power of words. What does a word like *black* mean?

" 'Black: destitute of light, devoid of color, enveloped in darkness, hence utterly dismal or gloomy, as, "The future looked black." ' "

"Pretty good with them words," Malcolm observes.

" 'Soiled with dirt, foul, sullen, hostile, forbidding, as, "a black day." Foully or outrageously wicked, as, "black cruelty." Indicating disgrace, dishonor, or culpability.' "

"That's something, all right."

"Let's look up *white*. Here. Read."

Malcolm reads: " 'White: the color of pure snow. Reflecting all the rays of the spectrum. The opposite of black. Free from spot or blemish. Innocent. Pure.' Ain't this something? 'Without evil intent. Harmless. Honest, square-dealing, and honorable.' Wait a minute. This was written by white folks, though."

"Sure ain't no black man's book."

"So why read it?"

"So you can *read the truth behind the words....* Here. Let's start at the beginning. We'll look them up, write them down, and *find out what they mean*."[5]

When I think of the poetic, I don't envision people wearing berets, speaking earnestly into a microphone, and occasionally snapping their approval. I think of people getting down to business with words, wrestling them back from mean meanings and crafting a moral vocabulary that dignifies people, cracking the pavement of the status quo, making language ring true.

The poetic addresses the itch that can only be scratched by dreaming harder, by thinking anew, by allowing our vision of what's possible to undergo deep reconsideration. The invitation to literature (or to a dictionary) is an invitation to rethink, reappraise, and redeem. We're made to see that the strange new world of the poetry, the story we're receiving, is the world we're living in.

Words, as Malcolm X came to understand, have hold of us inevitably and ineluctably. But for this very reason, words are *our way out*, even when the words we've settled for thus far say, with the awesome authority *we've* given them, that *there is no way out*.

Hateful mischaracterizations, bad sayings, other people's talking points, and thoughtless slogans come to our minds, blocking our perception just when we're on the verge of seeing and knowing something new. Sometimes they bubble out of our minds, and we hear the madness come to life on our own tongues. The plainspeak (in story, word, and song) testifies to this strange fact.[6] The flow of misrecognitions that runs through our lives of quiet desperation awaits some Get Fresh Flow, some jazz to redeem our jigsaw puzzlement, the sacred questioning that asks if we've ever yet looked beyond the world of con games.

By questioning our use of words, we ready ourselves for receiving language that makes things (our outlook, our estimation of ourselves and others, our seemingly irredeemable situations) new. If we're going to live and think freely, we get to seek out redemptive language, keep it in our heads, treasure it, and talk about it as if our very souls depend on this good, new, saving way of putting things. Ancient wisdom suggests that our souls do. We live (or die) by words.

I Thought You Knew I Was Joking

Long before I came to view language as the largely unacknowledged legislation of our worlds, I'd been taught to view words as holy, to be employed and always handled in a hallowed fashion. Every idle word, my tradition reminded me, would return to me. I'd have to give an account of every little thing I said seriously or unseriously in God's time. And to this day, I am to some degree haunted (cursed or blessed?) with a trigger in my head that won't allow me to let an untruth linger in the air. If I were to start a class by telling my students that I'd ridden into work on a Ferris wheel, I'd find it difficult to begin my lecture without whispering, "Just kidding."

As you can guess, there's a bit of the Uncle Ben inheritance at work in such obsessive behavior, but I in no way regret the nitpickiness handed down to me when it comes to words. On Sunday mornings, our children speak very naturally of going to the "church building." This habit is formed by an important distinction we've felt compelled to drive home: the building isn't to be confused with the people we know, the people with whom we live and work and dine and talk. These are people who mean to have a go at following Jesus in all they say and do, the called, the *ekklēsia*. We want them to have people in mind when they say "church," just as we want to *mean* what we say and *say* what we mean. We want to say and mean well. How to do so won't always be obvious. We might have to yak back and forth a little before we begin to get it right, before we can tell true and do justice to what we mean to say.

This brings to mind a recent day on the beach when I ran out into the ocean like a maniac in an effort to embolden my children to venture farther out. When I was up to my waist, I shouted that the drop-off would probably come when I least expected it. Then I pretended to fall into the ocean's depths and emerged on my knees to see that nobody was paying any attention.

Some time passed, and none of the kids had done more than get their feet wet (a surprise because they're all confident and capable in swimming pools). My daughter, Dorothy, held her arms up to me. She wanted to be carried out into the water. As we walked out, I assured her I hadn't spotted any jellyfish and noted that the waves in these shallow depths need not worry her. She continued to cling to me, and I tended to her needs in a way that had me feeling all responsible, sensitive, and fatherly (Anybody out there have a camera?). Then she nervously asked, "Is this where the drop-off is?"

Clearly, I don't share this scene to highlight the magnificence of my parenting skills. My heart sank, and I found myself saying words I hope I never have to say to any of my children ever again: "I thought you knew I was joking." I was chastened, and that whole biblical business about idle words came back to me. Self-satisfied wordsmith that I am, I saw how my own idle words had entered into the ancient, unredeeming cycle of talk that is cheap, talk that cheapens and dismembers. I had some reparation to see to.

I'd be willing to bet that a good number of the hateful and destructive sentences that still ring in our heads were followed by some variation of a grossly ineffective, "I was just joking." Our words go on and on, with consequences we can't measure, with reverberations beyond our control. Making our words do the right things, making them into a means for caring for one another, often involves stopping before we start or confessing that we didn't know what we were saying, that our words outran our limited wisdom.

There are expressions we overhear, and we sometimes realize, all at once, that we've heard it before, over and over, without stopping to wonder what it means, even as we hear ourselves say it. One came to me during a concluding scene on an episode of *Smallville*,[7] which featured two teenagers, Lex Luthor and Clark Kent, having a difficult conversation that forecast things to come between these two men of power. "I'm not about to debate semantics with you, Clark!" exclaimed Lex in a fit of exasperation, as if taking the time to get words right is a waste of valuable time.

But semantics might be all there is to talk about. The question of what our words mean, what we didn't mean, or what we didn't mean to mean, as tiresome as it all feels, is really all we've got. It's often our only hope of reconciliation. It's our only hope of ever really appearing before one another, of having a go at loving one another. If we're unwilling to reexamine or revisit the meaning of our words, if it wounds our pride to receive a talking-to concerning our ill-suited talk, what's left?

Mutual Hypocrisy

Language, after all, isn't just a tool for communication. Our language is, to put it strangely, our "lifeworld." And the limits of our language are, in some sense, the limits of our lifeworld. When our language is added to with a better way of putting things, we are expanding our lifeworld. We call this better way *poetry*. The poetic isn't the fancy stuff or the words the pretentious depend on to sound deep. Poetry is how our lifeworlds are made new. Poetry frees our speech and loosens our lips and our strangled imaginations. Poetry is called poetry because people decided to testify concerning the power of certain arrangements of words. They testified by calling these words, these testimonies, poetry.

Leonard Cohen once made this point when someone tried to call him a poet. He felt there was something inappropriate in accepting the nomination. Poetry is a verdict, not a choice, he said. It's the name for words (and the arrangement of words) that was decreed visionary for the fact that these words somehow widen vision and open up the possibility of seeing and hearing better. Poetry's beautifully humble beginnings, in this sense, are inextricable to poetry's paradoxical power. The words would not have meant anything if people hadn't let the words have meaning, if hearers weren't lending their ears, if nobody was paying attention, if nobody had received and borne witness to the power that is poetry.

In words well suited to this thought, Jacques Derrida observes, "A poem always runs the risk of being meaningless, and would be nothing without this risk of being meaningless."[8] Poetry evokes a strength made perfect in weakness, the risk of being misread, badly used, or misinterpreted that, we might say, characterizes all speech but which is especially necessary in the delivery and the reception of poetry. W. H. Auden reminds us that poetry doesn't *make* anything happen (or supply its own interpretation); it just "survives in the valley of its saying"[9]—maybe just powerless enough to change everything.

If the reader's sense of decorum will permit it, I'd like to place Derrida's and Auden's words alongside the scene in *Malcolm X*, Ursula K. Le Guin's depiction of a woman on a faraway planet hearing of a different way of doing things, and my discussion of the redemptive power of mixtapes and other healing ministries, other means of folk expression (the people's CNN). These are lyrical interventions. This is art keeping it all open, keeping everything talkaboutable. This is the power of the poetic/prophetic, helping us to reach outside of whatever we're currently caught up in—a space within which we can scrutinize ourselves and find ourselves amazed, sad, amused, moved, and open to the possibility of new encounters with ourselves and others. If being versified (in one way or another) is inevitable, the poetic/prophetic word makes us *well* versed. It's our multicultural inheritance.

And while I'm at it, I'll add to this motley crew a personal favorite, the song-and-dance man known as Tom Waits. In my collection of quotes and definitions for poetry, religion, and folk expression, I came across an interview he gave to Amanda Petrusich. His words on the oral tradition within which he delves, dabbles, and dares to be a part are better than anything I can devise:

> I make stuff up. There's nothing that you can say that will mean the same thing once it's been repeated. We're all making leaner versions of stories. Before there was recording, everything was subject to the folk process. And we were all part of composing in the evolution and the migration of songs. We all reached out, and they all passed through our hands at some point. You dropped a verse or changed the gender or cleaned up a verse for your kids or added something more appropriate

for your community. Anything that says "Traditional," it's "Hey, I wrote that, I'm part of that." Just like when a joke reaches you—how did it reach you? If you could go back and retrace it, that would be fascinating.[10]

To better lay hold of his drift, Petrusich asks, "So the second you write something down, it's fiction."
Waits has something a little more folksy in mind:

There is no such thing as nonfiction. There is no such thing as truth. People who really know what happened aren't talking. And the people who don't have a clue, you can't shut them up. It's the same with your own stories, the ones that circulate around with your family and your friends. We're all part of the same hypocrisy.[11]

There was a time in my life when I would've been entirely scandalized by Waits's word on there not being any such thing as truth. "What? But *God* is absolute truth. It just goes to show that moral relativism ..." I don't think like that anymore. I believe Waits would agree that there is such a thing as being truthful and, as the apostle Paul puts it, knowing in part (as through a glass, darkly).[12] And I think Waits is operating out of this very same heightened, deeply traditional awareness of our mutual failures of perception, our mutual screwed-uppedness, the descriptive inadequacy of our speech. Of absolute truth, none of us are knowers. And we often aren't especially good with the truth we *do* know. ("We're all part of the same hypocrisy.") This might have something to do with the biblical injunction against oath taking and for letting our yes be yes and our no be no.[13] Anything extra—those hand-over-heart assurances that we're real, we mean it, we guarantee satisfaction—is the con game. Someone's selling something.

The ones who really know what's up are too wise to pride

themselves on their supposed objectivity and unbiased reporting, their clearheaded analysis, or even their sound doctrine. They know how to keep silent. They know how little they really know. They also know how to tell a good story. They sense, though they might not put it this way, that the truth has no other way of getting through except through story. It won't be reduced to information, four spiritual laws, or a personal, private opinion. Truth depends, as is it always has, on those who bear witness. There are so many ways of being faithful and true, so many ways of doing justice to what's happening. Truth is "relentlessly narratival,"[14] to borrow a phrase from Walter Brueggemann, and it always demands fresh lyricization, new ways of putting it, new wine and new wineskins, new ways of listening for the word of the Lord. Were we hoping for something more easily possessed? More assured? More static? More easily advertised?

To put it a little differently, Eugene Peterson speaks of how the imagination informed by the biblical witness will take it as a given that the whole of life is "ultimately inaccessible to our five senses."[15] Metaphor, in this sense, isn't merely a tool for conveying a message or a "spiritual principle"; metaphor is the language that "conveys the indivisibility of visible and invisible, of seen and unseen, of heaven and earth."[16] It's the most reality-based way of putting things. Or, as Peterson puts it, in words that evoke Fred Friendly,

> A metaphor is a word that carries us across the abyss separating the invisible from visible. The contradiction involved in what the word denotes and what it connotes sets up a tension in our minds, and we are stimulated to an act of imagination in which we become participants in what is being spoken.[17]

A metaphor is never merely a metaphor, and a fable is always more than a fable. They're an invitation to locate ourselves within that witness, to hear and receive it faithfully, to receive instruction as we listen for the word of the Lord. It won't be mastered or possessed, but we can become participants, agents of witness, within the metaphor or the fable. It's how we lose our religions to find them. It's our way of being, speaking, and hearing true.

Without thinking, we fabricate to fill in the gaps of memory. We do this in spite of ourselves. We might at least do it a little more knowingly and with a good humor that acknowledges the various ways we employ fiction to justify our decisions. To strive for mastery of the truth, to insist on something more *behind* the story, is to be inhospitable to truth. The Reverend Cherrycoke, of Thomas Pynchon's novel *Mason & Dixon*, says that taking our fables seriously is the height of moral seriousness. He offers the following, which is reminiscent of Waits's words:

> Who claims Truth, Truth abandons. History is hir'd, or coerc'd, only in Interests that must ever prove base. She is too innocent, to be left within the reach of anyone in Power, who need but touch her, and all her Credit is in the instant vanish'd, as if it had never been. She needs rather to be tended lovingly and honorably by fabulists and counterfeiters, Ballad-Mongers and Cranks of ev'ry Radius, Masters of Disguise to provide her the Costume, Toilette, and Bearing, and Speech nimble enough to keep her beyond the Desires, or even the Curiosity, of Government.[18]

Emancipation Conversations

To bring it back around to Marshall McLuhan ("Anyone who tries to make a distinction between education and entertainment doesn't know the first thing about either"), the poetic word need not be a high-sounding phrase. But as witness, it brings us back to the question of whether something is trustworthy, good, or worth our time. Does the story—the poem, the song, the op-ed, the film—testify truthfully? Is it worthy of our allegiance? Does it shock us alive or keep us going? Can we affirm it as poetic?

A willingness to affirm the words of others as possessing a certain poetic/prophetic heft might be a prerequisite to understanding. Can we grapple honestly with one another's words if we've decided, in advance, that the speech won't overcome our critical distance? Or that it will only speak to us religiously, not politically (or vice versa)? We can begin our statements with "speaking as an economist" or "speaking as an English teacher," but the point of view we adopt can't contain the breadth of the subject matter. Are we hungering for righteous visions, for something true and good? Do we have the wit to hear what rings true?

"Mystery is a traditional fact!" decrees an exasperated Bob Dylan channeled by Cate Blanchett in Todd Haynes's *I'm Not There*. It wasn't a direct quote, but it is the kind of thing Dylan blurt outs when he opens his mouth on the subject of what it is he's taking part in with his broadside, boundless balladeering. As Czeslaw Milosz put it, to stick with the poetic, to live by it, is nothing less than to try to "be on the side of that stammering and mumbling with which human beings try to express themselves in their lonely helplessness."[19] It's the way we tap into a cultural memory wiser and truer than the nonpoetry (the raw propaganda) of corporations and nation-states.

The poetic/prophetic reserves the right to butt into anything and everything. The words invite us to view our world differently or to narrate ourselves *to* ourselves within a larger, truer story. The prophetic tradition, in this sense, is less concerned with predictions and more concerned with an enlivening, redeeming criticism. It begins with an intense self-criticism that, as Cornel West maintains, makes it possible to speak with candor and compassion.

The poetic/prophetic tradition invites us to tell the truth, even when it runs counter to reigning dogma—to say what we feel, not what we ought to say, what we know to be true rather than what feels appropriate or easily acknowledged. The force of words is why we are forced to think again. Words are mightier than swords. They're how we maneuver and get outmaneuvered mentally. As philosopher John Caputo observes, "The prophet lets us know what we do not want to know; he troubles and solicits us, makes us tremble, de-centering the 'I,' the arche/self, which has a tendency to organize everything around itself and to ensure that everything that it gives out is returned with interest."[20] With our egos momentarily and redemptively decentered, this news opens us up to the possibility of receiving an ethical summons, discerning a binding word, and entering into life-giving and loving relationships.

I occasionally employ the word *apocalyptic* to describe the expressions that call the world into question, that make things new in their way of telling truth, of speaking with such candor that one can hardly help but be sobered, often in the direction of renewed hopefulness. But the word *poetic* will probably do as well, maybe better. Milosz again: "Today the only poetry worthy of the name is eschatological, that is, poetry which rejects the present inhuman world in the name of a great change. The reader of today is in search of hope, and he does not care for poetry that accepts the order of things as permanent."[21]

Before we learned to speak of metanarratives and paradigms, prophecies and parables spoke of new worlds to those with ears to hear and eyes to see. Stories have always done this. As N. T. Wright put it, "They invite listeners into a new world, and encourage them to see their ordinary world from now on through this lens, within this grid. The struggle to understand a parable is the struggle for a new world to be born."[22] This isn't mere spirituality (whatever we mean by this word); it's the beginning of a whole new way of thinking and doing.

Or if you'll permit the language of another British storyteller, Philip Pullman:

> I have the greatest difficulty in understanding what is meant by the words "spiritual" or "spirituality"; but I think I can say something about moral education, and I think it has something to do with the way we understand stories.... "Thou shalt not" might reach the head, but it takes "Once upon a time" to reach the heart.[23]

Pullman is describing what comes to us by way of *emancipation conversations*—the exchanges in which we begin to be disabused of the bad ideas about life and love and God that keep us harried and afraid and inhumane. Lesser kingdoms lose their luster, and a new way to be human (a new way to speak, listen, act, and love) is inaugurated in the telling of stories, in paying heed to new social utterances—innovative and innovating—in pulling out the poetry. A new way that is at hand, coming, and among you. Emancipation conversations await us.

The words we affirm as true invite us to turn our minds around, and if we take it to heart, we will somehow, in some discernible fashion, act differently. We will give it something more than abstract consent. Its "Once upon a time" will become a part of the way we see because we will find it credible. It will chasten and invigorate. It unsettles our assumptions, haunts our conscience, and reorients our attention by addressing us with a summons to love.

Questions for Further Conversation

1. In the exchange between Ginsberg and Buckley, what is it that Buckley appears to treat dismissively and how does Ginsberg seem to outconservative him? Why are we often tempted to speak of the merely poetic or the merely entertaining, and what do we think we gain (or protect) by doing so?

2. Is it important to make a strong distinction between the poetic and the prophetic? Why or why not?

3. When you think of life sentences and death sentences (via lyrics, sayings, or proverbs), what words spring to mind? Why do you suppose these particular words have lingered there?

4. Can you think of a moment in your own life, similar to Malcolm X's dictionary epiphany, when the power of certain words struck you all at once? Describe.

5. What's behind the biblical injunction against idle words? Is there a sense in which examining our own speech (the meant, the unmeant, and all-too-meant) might be our most demanding, most costly, and most important work? Why do we resist this examining?

6. How is the biblical witness, or what we sometimes call "the word of the Lord," "relentlessly narratival"? How does this premodern understanding of the Bible interface (or conflict) with the way many religious people speak of absolute truth and/or "biblical principles"? Is one more faithful than the other? Can we have both?

7. What might Tom Waits mean when he suggests that people don't speak in nonfiction? What does it mean for the possibility of being a *faithful* witness as opposed to a possessor of absolute truth? How might fiction be a true story?

8. How is the struggle to understand a parable essentially a struggle for a new world to be reborn? What might it mean to be a good hearer of biblical stories?

Survival of the Freshest

Questioning Interpretations

It is in a chain of interpretation that what is not to be done
achieves its grip on the possibilities of human behavior.

**Philip Rieff, *Charisma: The Gift of Grace and
How It Has Been Taken Away from Us***

It is He Who has revealed to you the Book, with verses which
are precise in meaning ... and others which are ambiguous. As
to those in whose hearts there is vacillation, they follow what is
ambiguous in it, seeking sedition and intending to interpret it.
However, no one except Allah knows its interpretation.

The Qur'an, Sura 3:7, emphasis mine

In what turned out to be one of the best exchanges I'd had in all
my years as an English teacher at a Presbyterian high school, I
asked my students to define the word *agnostic*.

"Someone who doesn't want to believe," a student
responded.

The "doesn't want to" part threw me off. "Why the judgment call?" I asked. I wasn't sure what to say. I told the class to
try again.

"Someone who *chooses* not to believe," another student said.

I was beginning to sense a pattern. It wasn't unexpected. "No,
really, no. And I'm giving you a big hint when I say '*No*.'"

"Someone who doesn't *know*!" came a shout of mock enthusiasm.

And we were on our way. "That's right. Agnostics don't know. They might believe all kinds of things. And it can get to feeling like a crying shame sometimes, this lack of absolute knowledge, but they just don't know. Not much to be done for it, this not knowing business. Guess who's agnostic."

"You are," dared an especially avid young Presbyterian.

"Right you are. And please understand that I believe as much as the next believer. I can hardly even tell you how much I believe and how strongly I believe it. I believe, I believe, I believe [this with an intensification of my already sufficiently Southern accent]. I confess I find it hard to believe a lot of things sometimes. I'm riddled with doubts and uncertainties. But I see your smiling, approving faces, and I believe once more. Now I'm a believer. I believe again, as if for the first time. Belief. It's what I do. Guess who else I *believe* to be agnostic."

I had to wait this one out and gape at them goofily. One finally chirped in, with one eye squinted, "We are?"

"Yeah. But I think you think you have to pretend to *know* in order to not go to hell. And I want to tell you, in Jesus' name, that this isn't the case." And out of the silence, if memory serves, I made my way into the Uncle Ben story.

I hope it's clear that I wasn't invoking the name of Jesus lightly. I mean to invoke it again when I say, in the name of Jesus, that Uncle Ben is a false god. For love of God, as the expression goes, or, perhaps better, for love of humanity, I want to exorcise "the fear God," the Nobodaddy on the brain who keeps us afraid of our senses, wary of imagination, frightened of looking too hard at ourselves, and too fearful to think things through. This god who *isn't* love, made in our worst image, would keep us doubled up inside, putting on a brave face of fake confidence. This dysfunctional deity often interacts within our own semiconscious dysfunction and can render "religious types" into some of the saddest and most fearful, hateful, and damaging people in the world.

I want to announce the good news that God, the God in whom I believe, never calls anyone to playact or pretend or silence their concerns about what's true. I want to break through mind-forged manacles that render us incapable of seeing truthfully for fear we might let in the wrong information. God is not made angry and insecure by an archaeological dig, a scientific discovery, an ancient manuscript, or a good film about homosexual cowboys. Nor would I imagine God to be made angry or insecure by people with honest doubts concerning his existence. God is not counting on us to keep ourselves stupid, closed off to the complexity of the world we're in.

I encourage the use of whatever strong language might be employed in tearing down these idols, these false conceptions of who God might be. Damn this demonic Uncle Ben business. Damn it all to hell. May we bear it no more. Be explicit in bearing witness against such hellishness. Or pray, if need be, as Meister Eckhart paradoxically prayed, *God, rid me of God.*[1]

"God, rid me of God." Does this strike us as scandalous? Eckhart's prayer is scandalous to us only to the extent that we still believe that our conceptions of God—and not the grace of God—are what will save and deliver. As if our intellectual consent to certain truths is what will redeem, as if our faith in our own faith is the price of admission to eternal bliss. This madness degrades both the biblical witness and the possibility of sane thinking. Leaning on our own understanding of God in this way is idolatry, an inappropriate and unfaithful dependence on our pictures, concepts, and broken ideas that can't hold life-giving water. Nothing we claim to know or have hold of or pretend to believe as children or as adults places us on the winning side of God's affections. Maybe we're only called on to be honest. Maybe a vision of a God whose love transcends the limitations of our visions enables such honesty.

But if we believe that what separates us from chaos now and from eternal torment later is the tenacity of our hold on certain dogma, the conceptual humility that comes with being self-consciously agnostic will feel too costly. Standing firm in our beliefs will often take precedence over seeing what's in front of us. Even pressing matters of injustice and untruth, local and global, will pale in comparison to our personal, privatized salvation. A forthright honesty about how little we know is a luxury many of us feel we can't afford if right belief is our salvation, if we're saved because of the intensity with which we know we're saved.

I live in the hope that the God in whom I believe is the redeemer of the cosmos, that this God is never not redeeming in one way or another. There is, of course, a sense in which I'm willing to sing, as the words go, "I know that my redeemer lives." I believe it enough to try to act accordingly, to remember my baptism, to pray the Lord's Prayer, to say a number of creeds ("I believe ..."), to seek first God's kingdom and the righteousness of God in what I say and do, and to try—it's all trying—to bear faithful witness. I *believe* that I believe, and I believe, by God's grace, that I need not trouble myself with trying to believe more intensely. In matters of belief and knowing, I try to refrain from oaths, pledges, and swearing, lest I bear false witness, lest I claim falsely that I know something when I don't. Do I walk around knowing that my redeemer lives all the time? No. Do I think Isaiah and Paul and John the Baptist did? No. Do I still believe I'm being saved? Yes.

This business of having to feel a particular way or to feel a sense of absolute confidence in God or to pretend to know that God is there all the time is one of the things I've actually been saved —and am being saved—from. I'm not called to pretend at belief ever. I'm only called to try, with God's help, to be faithful; to try to love, and to try to tell the truth. I often feel a strong sense of confidence that the one who began this redeeming work in me will bring it to completion.[2] As I understand it, this is how salvation gets worked out. I'm not required to cut off my questions or try to uncritically place my faith in particular doctrines. The call to worshipfulness is a call to employ my imagination and therefore the whole of my practice. This call is a summons to mindfulness in all I say and do, a mindfulness that requires an engagement, a questioning of everything. It's a call to bring my wits to bear on the whole of life—be it "politics," "spirituality," "business," or that especially tricky area of "religion."

This call is a more comprehensive take on salvation (and perhaps more demanding) than what many of us are accustomed to hearing. It isn't exactly a personal, private relationship with God or a spiritual component or the religious belief politicians have to kowtow to if most Americans are to vote them into power. It's a call to the very honesty we often feel ourselves and others stepping away from when "religion" and "politics" show up in conversation, when a straightforward question becomes a perceived threat instead of an avenue of possibility and hope, a means to relationship.

What might have begun with open-ended give-and-take degenerates into the conversation stoppers we employ when the subject turns to things we're afraid of or unwilling to be questioned about. The redeeming possibility of dialogue ends when the monologue begins, and I don't doubt that this impossibly awkward moment is happening right now in cafés, bars, Bible studies, classrooms, work sites, and boardrooms the world over. People shut down. Things take a turn for the cultish—even if it's a cult of one. We sense when this artificiality takes hold. A tone of unreality possesses our speech. I believe we're called to fight it in ourselves and in others with determination and love. The monologuing must end before dialogue can begin.

What Else Is There?

I like to use the language of a call in the same way that I like to speak of sensing a summons. A call doesn't have to be presented as a big deal—"Suddenly I *knew!*"—or resemble what is referred to as a Damascus experience. It need not involve tears or perspiration. It can be an instance of discerning—in word, song, image, or real people—a voice to which one feels compelled to pay heed. You might sense a call in the way a community of people love one another or a sign of liveliness worth reciprocating in the way they've managed to love you. It can be a moment of discerning a presence in a text or a sermon or an account of the civil rights movement, the Truth and Reconciliation Commission in South Africa, or the community that formed around the life of Jesus and the events of Pentecost in the book of Acts. It doesn't have to be a solid grasp or an absolute guarantee in the language of insurance salespeople. In fact, if it's faith we're talking about, it probably can't be.[3]

Sometimes, in our discussion of scripture, history, God's will, military operations, or something a famous person said or did, an opinion is offered and, in response to the stated opinion, someone says, "That's just your interpretation." Technically speaking, this isn't a response at all. Unlike a question or an observation concerning the content of what was proffered, it only devalues and expresses disapproval of someone else's words, shutting down the possibility of a good conversation involving people good-naturedly sharing their interpretations with one another. The next time someone says it, I hope I'll have the nerve to say, "True enough. But what else is there?"

Unless we claim a direct line to God (and we'd do well to worry when we hear other people, especially our leaders, imply that they do), interpretation is all we've got, be it prayerful, prideful, dim-witted, or discerning. Admitting as much humbly and often might help us to become people less prone to reverting to monologue, that nonconversation that expects people to sit quietly and not interrupt. We might even enjoy listening to other people in the friendly hope of learning something we didn't know, with an expectation to better our own interpretations of what's happening, what's going on, and what's meant. Like belief, interpretation is an every-living-moment activity. Like our impressions, our interpretations can always do with a little refining. But if we're unwilling to have our interpretations questioned, we immunize ourselves to the possibility of wisdom. We fit the description, outlined in the Hebrew proverbs, of a fool.

When I speak of interpretation, I mean to return to a sense of the sensible way that people believe their way through life and the care with which folks pepper their speech with expressions like "as far as I can tell" and "as far as I know," being careful not to mislead or speak an untruth. In this vein, it might also be appropriate to entertain Friedrich Nietzsche's aphorism that there are no facts, only interpretations, and this too is an interpretation.[4] Many people allude to the first part without including the last bit.[5] But the last bit is crucial. What the purveyors of what's real (be they priests, presidents, or news producers) decree as facts are essentially interpretations by fellow humans. They are attempts at making sense. And it's what I'm doing, Nietzsche would say, right now. I'm a mere interpreter too. Aren't you? Will you join me in this confession? This is where we live, all of us—in a place of not knowing but believing and hoping and suspecting and interpreting. Might we admit for one mad, liberating moment that this is where we are? Is it a confession we feel we can afford? Can we renounce our pretensions to Godlike knowingness and speak again as humans? Doing justice to what's true, doing justice to justice.

There's that call again—a call I discern in everything I think of as an instance of cosmic plainspeak. It's a call to number oneself among our multiple pilgrim species, to be a human being among human beings, and to try to be truthful and loving among them. It's the call I'd like to think is occasionally detected or at least overheard in my classroom—a call to a freshening flow, to seeing with new eyes, to imagining our world differently.

Imagined Infallibility

But this call to be merely human—to know that we don't know much, even as we deeply suspect and fervently believe all kinds of things—isn't good enough for many of us. I'll confess that, in my attempts to get taken seriously and feel sufficiently affirmed (I know, it's a black hole), it very often feels less than satisfying. We're prone to speak beyond what we know, to overdo it, as if what we have to say and decree is more than interpretation, more than just humans trying to make sense of things. We want to come off as successful and informed. Despite the biblical injunction against oaths and excess verbiage, we lay it on thick. We're part of the put-on.

We fall into this because the language we know and are immersed in is often the language of the con game. We try to draw people in. We exaggerate. We deny our anxiety, even to ourselves, and we attribute inappropriate weight to the images and stories and ideas we concoct to give sense and meaning to life. We even drag talk of "God's will" into it. To keep the chaos at bay—a chaos we sense will have its way with us if all we're doing is interpreting—we develop what Ernst Becker calls "imagined infallibility."[6] We attribute an absolute infallibility and inerrancy to our interpretations to immunize ourselves against the madness, as a way of vying for immortality and keeping above the fray. Others, we might say, deal in opinions and interpretations, but *we* have convictions and gut feelings and strong intuitions. We get the job done. We know when we're right, and *we're right*. No doubt. No fear.

But the pretense of certainty comes at a cost. If we think our certainty is what drives success and, in the end, the very (so-called) faith that saves us, our honest confusion will become a source of shame and a sign of weakness. Yet we keep our doubts hidden. This is precisely where the biblical witness urges what I'm tempted to call a mandatory agnosticism. This is where we're summoned to know that we don't know. This is where we're called to confess.

While we're often rewarded in life for playing at absolute confidence, the pretense and the mind games are corrosive to the possibility of community, friendship, and redeeming love. Imagine letting go of the psychic burden of certainty. Imagine backing down from our imagined infallibility and assuming the mantle of a mere human. Imagine the poetic/prophetic way of relating that would be possible. We might become capable of questioning ourselves out loud. We might let a little air in. In the most life-giving sense, we might get a little religion.

Appropriations

In my early reading of the Bible, I somehow inherited a tendency to be a real stickler when it comes to context. I not only sought to read the Bible all the way through, but I was also committed to reading it correctly. I complained when ministers opened their sermons with a biblical reference and then talked about everything—stories, analogies, fishing trips—but what the passage might mean. I knew something was wrong when a person said, "Let's see what God has to say about this," and opened the Bible as if to say that whatever was there was inevitably God speaking. I knew that entire chapters of the book of Job, for instance, were only Job's friends speaking, the very friends God would insist were completely full of it.

Just quoting the Bible, I knew, was never enough. What's the context? Is it faithful? How do we make sure our use of biblical language now is in line with what was being talked about then? Are we understanding the proclamations of Jesus and the prophets? Are we good interpreters of these infinitely provocative texts? Something of my anxiety on biblical interpretation surfaced in my conversations after September 11, 2001, concerning patriotism, pledges of allegiance, and the distinctions made between pretensions of nation-states (in this case, the perceived self-interest of the United States) and the prerogatives of the coming kingdom of God. The lines, it seemed to me, were being blurred by people who considered themselves evangelical. In an attempt to address this crisis of bad interpretation, I wrote a book.[7]

That book led to an exchange that afforded me a revelation on appropriation. My wife and I were involved in a conference at Messiah College in Pennsylvania, and Jeff Tweedy of Wilco was closing out the weekend with a solo performance. That afternoon, I saw him standing on the lawn talking to people and decided I might take the opportunity to introduce myself and foist a copy of my book on him.

As I handed it to him, I observed, in an apologetic fashion, that I'd lifted a chapter title, "Bloodier Than Blood," from the song "Shot in the Arm," off the *Summer Teeth* album. I hoped he didn't mind.

Not at all, he assured me with a smile, and went on to observe that he had "appropriated" the line from novelist William H. Gass.

Tweedy's good-natured reference to the practice of appropriation hit me, pleasantly I hasten to add, like a ton of bricks. It was as if he was letting me in on a very big, deeply significant nonsecret that's been shouted aloud from rooftops all along and for some time. Appropriation. It's what Shakespeare did with the other versions of *Hamlet* and *Romeo and Juliet* and various histories. It's what Bob Dylan did with *Love and Theft*. It's what prophets, as avid fans of other prophets, do. It's only rarely in the footnotes. It's how the work gets done. Originality? You've got to be kidding.

A favorite lyrical wit of mine, Peter Case, has observed that the work of writing is the career of a magpie thieving material for the building of nests, bringing it all back home. We cobble together ideas, images, and songs. The material is all around us. It's why many of us like to have pen and paper nearby. It's why so much gets written on napkins and hotel stationery. It's the "folk process" Tom Waits alluded to in the last chapter—the collection of lines, images, and information. I think of folks in bars and cafés in Nashville eavesdropping on one another, making notes of the noteworthy. We're looking to write a hit. We want to be a hit.

The question, when we read the Bible, is whether we are appropriating and interpreting well. It's the same question when we hear a song or listen to one another. This is why Bob Dylan harbors the hope that he sounds a little like Charley Patton. It's why Dorothy Day hoped, when her life's work was done, that she might be remembered as someone who read Dostoevsky well. It's a question of living and lived inheritance, an anxiety of continuity[8], lines of succession in which originality is both out of the question and beside the point. Are we living within the continuum? Is the way we interpret the lines in line with what they—the bards, the prophets, the people of the books—were talking about? Will we be the conduits of ancient and redeeming transmissions? Will we be good recorders, servants, and scribes? Makers of meaning?

Something—some bit of important and even good news—has been sent. Are we receiving? Will the circle be unbroken?

Cosmic Plainspeak

The Bible isn't a static text demanding my dutiful submission, as if all the Bible requires is that I sign a statement saying I know it to be inerrant regardless of whether I've had a look to see what's in there. It is, rather, a living text that engages me with its questions even as it demands that I engage its witness with mine. It is, in fact, a record of sacred questioning in which everything is open for discussion. It houses traditions. And these traditions, if we have the wits to discern it, are talking to each other within the tradition we've come to call biblical. In some sense, the back-and-forth of "Thus sayeth the Lord" and "This is the fulfillment of . . ." is the biblical tradition. "You have heard that it was said. . . . But I tell you . . . "

Where is wisdom to be found? What is the Spirit of the Lord saying? How long until righteousness reigns over the earth? Will the righteous be slain alongside the wicked? These questions are our questions. The Bible records the voices of our cosmic contemporaries and affords us an opportunity to partake in cosmic plainspeak. Whether we walk on concrete or sand, we desire that our footsteps be made firm and that we be numbered among the just. We want our lives to count. We'd like history to esteem us as people who did more good than harm. Pilgrims that we are, we mean to trace the true pilgrimages.

As we dwell at length on the Bible, we notice certain trajectories. The prophet Micah echoes Isaiah's call to beat swords into plowshares even as Joel issues an invigorating call to beat them back into swords ("Let the weakling say, 'I am strong!'").[9] He draws on Isaiah's imagery, a vision of social justice. It's almost as if the prophets cut and paste, remixing the past to deliver a new song, a new word of the Lord. There is an interaction of imagination. It isn't as if Ezekiel, for instance, passes out with pen in hand and later awakens with a finished scroll and a sore arm. It isn't automatic writing.

There are praise songs extolling the goodness and the bountiful loving-kindness of the Lord, and then there's Jeremiah being told by the Lord that he will be transformed into a terror to himself and everyone he knows. Jeremiah insists—irreverently? blasphemously?—that God has done him wrong, has deceived him, and that it would have been better if he'd been miscarried in the womb (Jeremiah 20 and 15). We note that Jeremiah isn't praying a prayer of reverence to God. He's actually insisting that God has failed to revere human life enough. He's castigating God for what he takes to be God's Uncle Ben-like behavior, a series of crimes against humanity by a celestial tyrant. And while I'd sanction the employment of a stronger word in an honest attempt at exegesis—to get at the prayer that is essentially a curse recorded in our scripture—I will simply observe, with a hint of sanitation, that Jeremiah is telling God, "You really screwed up this time."[10] When I consider the place of such prayer-speech preserved in the psalms, the lamentations, and the cries of the prophets, I'm reminded that the biblical witness does not summon us to censor ourselves in prayer. It demands and even exemplifies the candor at work when Tori Amos observes that it's as obvious as rain that, sometimes, God just does not come through.[11] We're called to call it like we see it, just as the author of Ecclesiastes does. We aren't called to fake or pretend in any way. We're called to say what we see. God won't be sought or found by lying optimism.

Not everything in the Bible, I like to tell my students, is appropriate to inscribe on a poster picturing a basket full of puppies. Unearthing the context of particular phrases won't always make the words make more sense. Instead, it can challenge or defy what sense we thought we had of what's appropriate and godly. The Bible's witness has an annoying way of subverting one's theology and loosening one's doctrinal presumptuousness. Needless to say, there are prayers that might not seem appropriate to pray. Should we pretend such content isn't there? Should the Bible come with a parental advisory warning sticker? Should we leave Bible reading to the professionals? Is there even such a thing as professionals when it comes to the Bible—this assortment of people crying out to the Lord with joyful and not so joyful noises?

If we're going to read the Bible well, appropriate its language faithfully (*always* an open question, incidentally), and have a go at good interpretation, we will note these trajectories and tensions, not try to explain them away as if God might be embarrassed by the dissonance. Our presumed faithfulness, the rightness of our interpretation, will never be a given. To read the Bible well, we will need to be committed to the conversations and the sacred questioning the biblical text records.

"Do not answer fools according to their folly, or you yourself will be just like them," we read in Proverbs 26:4. Very well then. We'll try to take that in. Next proverb: "Answer fools according to their folly, or they will be wise in their own eyes" (26:5). What's up with that? Do or do not? We might be hesitant to say the word *contradiction* aloud, but given the way people talk about the Bible, its reliability, its inerrancy, and its plain meaning, this is enough to leave one feeling like a bit of a fool. Maybe there's a poetic subtlety at work. Maybe there's a time for both. Or to everything there is a season, or something like that. Maybe we need to keep returning to the questions.

Or consider the vision of Isaiah, in which the Lord says to the people of Judah,

> "The multitude of your sacrifices—
>> what are they to me? . . .
> I have no pleasure
>> in the blood of bulls and lambs and goats.
> When you come to appear before me,
>> who has asked this of you,
>> this trampling of my courts?
> Stop bringing meaningless offerings!
>> Your incense is detestable to me."

> ISAIAH 1:11–13

All right. No more incense. Got it. But who was it who asked for these blood sacrifices? The answer, according to one way of reading it, is straightforward. God did, as would seem to have been clearly recorded in the first chapter of Leviticus. What do we do with this? Is Isaiah saying something different? Notice that he doesn't deny the fact of animal sacrifices as a part of the Judaic tradition, but Isaiah does say (or says that the Lord is saying) that this practice isn't in keeping with what the Lord wants. Do Amos, Micah, Hosea, and Jesus flip the script further, picking up on Isaiah, when they bring in talk of mercy and not sacrifice, social justice over ceremony, as if "the knowledge of the Lord" has more to do with how we treat the poor than our solemn assemblies?[12] Jesus said, "You have heard that it was said. . . . But I tell you . . ."[13] Are we to sense a transition, a radicalizing of tradition, an earth-shattering instance of reading well? For the sake of your tradition, Jesus warned his resisting hearers, you're making void the word of God.[14]

How Do You Read It?

With eyes and ears for this sort of thing, we will have to resist the temptation to read the scriptures flatly, as if any verse can be extracted and deployed to say "what God says," as if there is no ethical progression or moral development or widening eschatology within the collection. If we do read it flatly, if we use accounts of slaying Canaanites to diminish the ethical demands of Jesus' Sermon on the Mount, we will be reading it wrongly. Ironically enough, we'll be using the scriptures to minimize what the word of God is saying. We might even be corralling particular verses (and ignoring others) to more effectively avoid the difficult questions put to us by the Jesus we otherwise call Lord. We might swear by it, quote it, read excerpts on a daily basis, and post particular verses on billboards, but we will have yet to appropriate the biblical witness well or interpret it faithfully. We will have yet to take it seriously.

"What is written in the Law?" Jesus asks an expert in the law who'd asked him how one might inherit and enter into the life that never ends. A question with a question followed by another one, the big one, the question of interpretation: "How do you read it?" (Luke 10:26).[15] This is always the question for those of us for whom the meaning of the written word is never entirely self-evident. What are we going to let it mean? Or to put it a little more provocatively, what are we going to try to make it mean? What will it mean now? Because it won't interpret itself. Interpretation has been done and will be done badly and unjustly. We're about to appropriate—will it be appropriate? How shall we go about going by the book(s)? Will the how of our reading and the practice it engenders be a just and faithful witness to God's way in the world? God help us and have mercy on us. This work of reading the words well—of trying to do them justice—is never done.

Interpretation is the possibility of the living word living within us—making a redeeming, transforming claim to all that lays unexamined and dead within our mental fiber. Will we let the double-edged indictments of the scriptures cut us to the quick, creating problems in the lives we are living? Or will we enlist the words to serve only in our projects of self-congratulation, skipping the bits that question our beliefs and practices? Will we read the Bible only to reaffirm our own take on the world? Tradition stops here, we sometimes seem to say. We have arrived. We're done.

How broad is the path of those who use the scriptures (religious professionals, politicians, Elmer Gantrys, hypnotists) and how narrow is the path of those who actually receive it, who refuse to reduce the redeeming revelation of God to pet projects and power plays. To interpret well requires a response to the ethical imperative that is interpretative uncertainty, a response that involves reading the Bible expectantly, attentive to all the myriad ways we have yet to hear what the Spirit of God is saying. Such uncertainty is probably the prerequisite for seeing and hearing anything, for knowing that you haven't gotten to the bottom of anyone or anything, for seeing eternity in a grain of sand. Uncertainty precedes discernment. In the sweet light of uncertainty, we renounce striving for possession by way of the biblical illiteracy[16] that only listens to its own voice; we reject the need to shrink-wrap revelation to fit a target market or a voting bloc; we repudiate the nonprofit that presumes to speak exclusively for the moral values of the Creator of the cosmos, as if one tradition or interest group could say and therefore police for all time what the Bible means.

Don't Answer

The good news of God's living word isn't the property of any one theology, ethnicity, nation-state, or even a particular generation's moment in time. As we develop a sense of self-consciousness concerning the inevitable limitations of our own interpretations, it is appropriate to note that the act of interpretation makes us nothing less than conduits of revelation. This should both invigorate and relativize our sense of ourselves as we're reminded of the blessedly finite earth-boundness ("on earth as it is in heaven") of all our talk of kingdoms and powers and glory. I think of Leonard Cohen's song "The Future," which includes a riff where he asserts that he's the little Jew who wrote the Bible. Consider this snippet of his conversation with Jewish *Book News*:

> The honey of poetry is all over the place. It is in the writing of the *National Geographic*, when an idea is absolutely clear and beautiful; it's in movies; it's all over because the taste of significance is that which we call poetry, when something resonates with a particular kind of significance. We may not call it poetry but we've experienced poetry. It's got something to do with truth and rhythm and authority and music.[17]

Cohen speaks like a man who's lived a life or three within the always ancient, ever-self-renovating tower of song. In a similar vein (and in words worth contemplating as we consider the possibility of religio-poetic continuity, of appropriating sacred traditions well and appropriately), I'm struck by this sensibility within James Joyce's *Ulysses*: "People do not know how dangerous love-songs can be.... The movements which work revolutions in the world are born out of the dreams and visions in a peasant's heart on the hillside. For them the earth is not an exploitable ground but the living mother."[18]

Might we occasionally be guilty of exploiting texts and traditions to score points, gain power, and top off angry emails? Are we hearers or users? Are we receiving the living and lyrical witness of scripture, or are we drawing on it as one more available resource in our daily ego trips? We bear false witness when we make an idol of our own grasp, our own historical moment, our own particular credo. If we're to believe that there are better interpretations yet to be done and answers we have yet to articulate, we will need the psychic wherewithal to let our provisional interpretations be slowly replaced by better—more faithful—ones and the psychic wherewithal to allow our minds to be changed by the love songs we have yet to really hear.[19]

Jesus often refused what was in his time the reigning interpretation of scripture. As is the case with the prophetic tradition he draws on, I believe his refusal was an act of faithfulness that transcended the insufficiently faithful readings of his contemporaries. He insisted that the words mean more than they had up to that point ("Today this scripture is fulfilled in your hearing").[20] He was in line with the way interpretation works. The meaning always lies before us. As it is reported in Nehemiah 8:8, the good teachers of oral and literary tradition give the sense of the scriptures and make the meaning clear. It is by way of good interpretation that words are made to give meaning—made to make sense—so that we can understand and change our way of thinking. It is by humility—and still more humility—that we can dwell within a living, sacred, redeeming culture that both precedes and exceeds little old us.

It seems that it was especially important in Jesus' mind that our words, our perceived holds on the holy, not form static concepts in such a way that we become settled in our understanding. Love and justice should not become givens, as if we've already arrived at a sufficient understanding of what's good. While he was willing to be called a teacher by his interlocutors, he evidently resisted the appellation of "good": "Why do you call me good? No one is good—except God alone" (Mark 10:18). This report might serve as a reminder that we'd do well to maintain a sense of ongoing deferral when it comes to decreeing our doctrines, our accomplishments, our histories, our traditions, and the interpretations through which we perceive them as good or awesome or somehow ethically sufficient.

Go easy on the presumption of the good, he seems to say, as if our haste toward fixed concepts might become an obstacle to actually trying to put into practice the things the "good teacher" says. Listen again. Interpret further. "Christ" isn't his last name. And skipping straight to "Christ" without thinking things through might all too conveniently gloss over the ways the teachings of Jesus of Nazareth slowly pull our common sense apart. Have we begun to consider what his announcement of a very different kingdom might mean for the way we order our world? Does our personal, privatized "Christ" leave us alone in our little ethically compromised kingdoms of shallow, unexamined interpretations? Our need to keep our speech tentative, never crowning our understanding as a mission accomplished, draws deeply from the Jewish concept of the messianic, the ought-to-be that's always still-to-come but also, in an unendingly revolutionary sense, already here. The kingdom is among you and within you and always just ahead, for God's sake.

In an anecdote that speaks to the open-endedness we do well to maintain in our talk of the Day of the Lord, a divine reckoning, or the Shape of Things to Come, Elie Wiesel once witnessed Martin Buber speak with great interpretive wit in a conversation with some Christian clergy who had dropped what was potentially a conversational bomb. Why don't Jews, they wanted to know, accept Jesus as Messiah? Buber offered an imaginative word:

> What is the difference between Jews and Christians? We all await the Messiah. You believe he has already come and gone, while we do not. I therefore propose that we await Him together. And when He appears, we can ask Him: "Were you here before?" ... And I hope that at that moment I will be

close enough to whisper in his ear, "For the love of heaven, don't answer."[21]

"For the love of heaven," he says. How devastatingly tactful. And what a clarion call by way of a joke, which, like all great jokes, is both more than a joke and, if we're to receive the sense given, no joke at all.

There are people out there (I'm one of them) who live in hope of everlasting redemption. And people who hold this strange notion by way of verses, suras, or sutras live with the constant risk, the occupational hazard, of believing that their tradition, their version of the news they call good, owns the copyright on the redemption of human history. Buber's wit calls on all such copyright claimers to take it easy. And for the love of whatever peaceable kingdom you proclaim, come out of your isolated subculture and learn. Watch. Wait. And at least every once in a while, practice your right to remain silent. Know when you don't know. Have the wit and the human kindness to say so. Practice tact.

What do I mean by tact? Julia Kristeva offers the best definition I know: "To hear true, along with forgiveness. *Forgiveness*: giving in addition, banking on what is there in order to revive, to give the depressed patient (that stranger withdrawn into his wound) a new start, and give him the possibility of a new encounter."[22]

Our experience of whatever religious tradition (call it an interpretive community) we most readily align ourselves with very likely ties into a sense of deep forgiveness (where we got and are getting forgiven) and a sense of new encounters, over and over again, in the texts that are infinitely provocative and newly enriching whenever we turn to them. Nearly every religious tradition is in some sense a summons to tactfulness because these traditions challenge us to "hear true." I sense this reviving challenge in Kristeva's equating of tact with forgiveness (banking on the *given* to revive *again*), Buber's characterization of a conspiracy of expectation and vigil Jews and Christians ideally have in common, and Jesus' admonition to avoid haste and presumption when we consider the good. There are so many ways of seeking the kingdom to come. So many ways to be hospitable. So many ways to be—and try to be—a good interpreter.

The Glad River

The new song, the image on the nightly news, the email that promises enlargement or enhancement, the army recruitment advertisement, the request that everyone stand for a pledge of allegiance, the face of the stranger on the street—all are invitations to ethical, poetic, and inevitably religious responses. All of these calls to worshipfulness are, to one degree or another, an invitation to join a story. And it isn't as if interpretation is something we begin to do once we decide to interpret. We're already engaged. We're at it long before it occurs to us to ask ourselves what we're doing. Our interpretations are like dreams that stay with us.

I recall eavesdropping on an excited conversation between a friend whom I suspect mulls over the Bible, predestination, and the doctrine of the Trinity even in his sleep—let's call him Travis—and a fellow we'll call Biff. Travis is very into his Presbyterianness, and Biff doesn't like it. Biff is all about being nondenominational and even wonders if Travis is more excited about Calvinism than he is about Jesus. So after a whole lot of back-and-forth, Biff thinks he has Travis cornered.

"So tell me, if you couldn't be a Presbyterian, what would you be?"

Travis only pauses for a moment before blurting out, "Ashamed!"

I absolutely love this response. Not because I'm especially

geeked over Presbyterian traditions but because Travis is insisting that his attachment to a particular interpretive community isn't something he could take or leave. As far as he can tell, this is the best way *he* knows of—the best framework—to be faithful to the coming kingdom of God. It's the way he feels called to work it out, and, for Travis, it is a matter of passion.

To Travis's credit, he loves working it out, rehearsing his understanding thus far again and again. He loves it when people disagree with him, because it appears to be the best avenue for a conversation to break out. And he loves conversations. His mind is, in many ways, redemptively unsettled. He believes his questions concerning meaning and salvation and the ways of God are generally worked out with fear and trembling and self-deprecating laughter.

I can't say for certain, but I suspect Travis's hold on Presbyterianism is such that he knows it might have gone differently. He doesn't think his alignment with this interpretive community is primarily a result of his own objective study—as if he's undertaken careful research on every other tradition before arriving at the one true faith—but he knows where he's landed, for whatever reason, and is determined, by the God whose graciousness surpasses our interpretations, to wear it well.

Wearing it well requires an awareness that is a sort of necessary agnosticism, the not knowing that leaves room for faith—faith that isn't knowledge but that is, nevertheless, enough. And lest faith become the stick with which we hit the less faithful, I'd like to unpack our talk of how much faith we have, speaking specifically of our beliefs. Do we have an objective grasp on our beliefs? Like interpretations and dreams, might beliefs be a little more elusive and dependent on our mood swings than we think? Does God's grace to us depend on keeping our beliefs in line? Did the imprisoned John the Baptist receive the word (and believe it) in time to believe enough of the right things about Jesus just before he lost his head? Will we?

"I do believe; help me overcome my unbelief!" cried the father of the boy with an evil spirit (Mark 9:24). This verse has remained adhered to the wall above our kitchen sink for many years, and as it meets my eyesight, I wonder if I've come to view it as a redeeming escape clause of some sort when I fall back into the debilitating feeling that God is angered by honest confusion. I can't imagine Uncle Ben responding very well to this prayer: "Whaddayamean? Do you believe or don't you?" But these days, I think of it as a paradigmatic prayer. I believe an awful lot a lot of the time, and I even believe that when I don't, God's grace is sufficient. Belief comes and goes, and God will lovingly sort it all out somehow. Even our darker moods, I believe, will be redeemed. All is grace.

I've even been adopted by more than one believing community, but I don't think that these adoptions or the beliefs that seem to come naturally to me from time to time could ever be a cause for boasting. I just hope and pray that anyone looking into my life, now or later, might generously conclude that I'm a faithful recipient and practitioner of the grace in which these communities strive to be in continuity. I think of Will Campbell, who I'm sometimes vain enough to consider a kind of mentor, and his characterization of community in the novel *The Glad River.* Community is "a bunch of folks getting along for some reason.... It just happens. We don't make community any more than we make souls. It's created."[23]

I Don't Think That's What It Means

I'm often loathe to employ the word *community* because I know it's sometimes harnessed to create false impressions, to get people behind a building fund, to make people feel like they're leading something. "Community" can become a self-deluding mantra made all the more maddening by the fact that, despite the advertising, it's often absent. It's as if the possibility of genuine community disappears the more someone starts saying it's happening. Like Christianity and poetry, we should probably let it be a verdict rather than a word of self-description.

Most of us are hell-bent on finding community anyway. The prospect that it might happen over drinks or in Sunday school or at a sporting event gets many of us out and about when the weekend comes because, on some level, we're eager to exchange interpretations. We tune in, turn on, and Google to glean from one another's progress via Facebook profiles. Most of us, most of the time, are searching for community.

I end with two stories that come to mind when I think of how conflicting interpretations can both call attention to the absence of community and plant the seeds of new life-giving communities. The first begins in the foyer of a church building.

My friend Alec knows the Bible very well, and it can get him into trouble. Not because he prattles on about it or steers conversations that way, but because he finds himself in circles that think of themselves as church communities and have the nonprofit status to prove it. Alec shows up and lingers with no small amount of hope, gets involved, and then gets disillusioned as he watches people who, in his opinion, make a general mockery of everything the biblical witness urges on us in terms of how we treat each other. Unless he's looking to become a hermit, I want to tell him, he had better get used to it.

One Sunday morning, the pastor stopped Alec in the foyer to ask him about one of Alec's friends he hadn't seen in months. What was up? Why hadn't he been around? Alec didn't want to get into it. The friend's life was in shambles, but, truth be told, it had been steadily falling apart even as he was a faithful and enthusiastic attendee. As it happened, this particular congregation wasn't adept at or dedicated to cultivating redeeming relationships among its members. As Alec saw it, the way a person could show up, put on a brave face, say a word or two about the Lord, and live a life of unexamined dysfunction was staggering. Alec suspected that the pastor wasn't asking about all of that, so he simply said his friend wasn't doing too well.

"Well, I wish he would start coming again," the pastor said.

Hoping for an opening and alive to the possibility of a breakthrough, Alec reluctantly went for it: "To tell the truth, he's been coming for decades, and it hasn't made much difference."

"Well, God's word will not return void," the pastor said, alluding to Isaiah 55:11.

Wincing a little and at a loss for words, Alec countered with, "I don't think that's what it means."

This wasn't the beginning of a conversation. It wasn't the moment when the pastor received a revelatory word about his own words. It was the end. And it brings to mind all the ways we who read the scriptures can quickly become people who give no ground to anyone. We can't. The metaphysical facts we think we stand on—our interpretations—have become essential to our fragile ego structures.

People like Alec pray for the occasion or the nerve to get into better conversations, something approaching the beloved community they read about and hope for. Like me, Alec is a sucker for almost anything that calls itself Bible study. It usually goes badly, because often the people in these circles have yet to know how to listen to each other. But occasionally it goes well, and when it does, it can be the best conversation in town. It keeps Alec going back for more because Alec really believes that the word of the Lord will not return void.

My second story pertains to something I saw on television. It was *The Daily Show* with Jon Stewart, featuring Jim Wallis as the guest. Wallis, as it turns out, also believes that the word of the Lord will not return void. Because he doesn't view the evangelical tradition to be well served when its self-professed adherents are indistinguishable from Republican Party activists, he is sometimes referred to as a "progressive evangelical" — but how, really, could there be any other kind of evangelical? Anyway, Jim Wallis appeared, and I knew they were going to talk Bible. Stewart began by making self-deprecating references concerning his Jewishness, and Wallis quickly observed that the humor and truth telling of the biblical prophets is a direct predecessor to the kind of thing Stewart is often up to. "So maybe you're one of the prophets, Jon."

Stewart responded, "If the Hebrew prophets were influenced by *Laugh-In*, I would say yes. If not, I don't think so."

Wallis laughed, then traced an evangelical trajectory that went from the Bible's three thousand verses on economic injustice to the abolitionist movement to Abraham Joshua Heschel to Martin Luther King Jr. In response to Stewart's prodding, Wallis said the Bible is "a super book for Jews."

Stewart responded with the observation that, according to rumor and what he takes to be popular evangelical opinion, that noteworthy detail still isn't enough to get them into heaven.

And with this, Wallis turns his attention to Matthew 25, starting with verse 31, a passage that has everything to do with the world to come and nothing to do with what anyone says they believe. There is no checking of belief in the story Jesus tells. How we treat the poor, the sick, and the stranger is, in Wallis's words, "our test of how much we love God." Our actions are our creeds. Whatever you've done for the least of these, Jesus says, "you did for me." You only love God as much as you love the poor among you. Or as my hero Steve Stockman, chaplain at Queen's University, Belfast, put it, "Look after the poor or go to hell."[24]

And in a move I hadn't even thought to hope for, Stewart senses something stirring in Wallis's words and gets in on the interpretive drift. "So you are saying, that's everybody. Faith without works is nothing."

"It is dead," asserts Wallis, referring to James 2:20.

"And works without faith" — Stewart finishes in a high voice — "is still pretty good."

And the interview ends amid uproarious laughter.[25]

Think about it. In a bit of exegesis that is both profoundly funny and completely true, Stewart offers an analysis that is deeply biblical. Faith without works, like it or not, isn't faith to begin with. And what we do, practically speaking, might be accompanied by occasional explanation when it's requested. But the work, if you like, is faith enough. Witness enough too. The only witness, actually. Witness isn't a personal profession of faith. Actions speak, and profession, at best, merely elaborates on actions, explaining the why and the how. We need not add how strongly we believe in God. We're doing what we believe, and we're not doing what we don't. The biblical witness is resoundingly with Stewart on this matter.

Another story about "who believes what" comes from a Jewish source in the eighteenth century, Moses Mendelssohn. It's an anecdote involving the saintly sage Hillel the Elder, whose superior generosity is being contrasted with his less magnanimous rival Shammai:

A heathen said: "Rabbi, teach me the entire law while I am standing on one foot!" Shammai, whom he had previously approached with the same unreasonable request, had dismissed him contemptuously; but Hillel, renowned for his imperturbable composure and gentleness, said: "Son, love thy neighbor as thyself. This is the text of the law; all the rest is commentary. Now go and study."[26]

Finally, seventeenth-century Portuguese Jewish philosopher Baruch Spinoza had the following advice involving the notion that love of neighbor is the fulfillment of the law: "Every man should embrace those [dogmas] that he, being the best judge of himself, feels will do most to strengthen him in love of justice. Acceptance of this principle would, I suggest, leave no occasion for controversy in the Church."[27]

I hope the understated seriousness and the sad hilariousness of this bit of sage advice is getting though. When we note that Spinoza was issued the writ of *cherem* (a kind of excommunication) by his Jewish community and considering the controversies that grip churches, mosques, and temples, we might give his wisdom a deeper look. However you need to interpret the scripture to do right by others and thereby love God, have at it. You aren't doing the one if you aren't doing the other.

What will help you to give your otherwise theoretical faith legs? Would reading the book of Job as if it were an allegory allow the Sermon on the Mount to change your buying habits? If so, by all means, read it as an allegory. Does the thought of Jonah residing in the belly of a large fish inspire you to share your resources with people deprived of access to food and medical attention? Does inerrancy of the Bible assist you in being good to homeless people? Does it prompt you to offer free tutoring to underprivileged children? If so, move deeper in your commitment to the doctrine of inerrancy. Read as you need to read to be invigorated and encouraged to do what you need to do. Then believe as if your life depends on it. Get worked up. Quickly. Move your interpretations in the direction of more righteous practice, and don't look back. Read as you need to read to be invigorated and encouraged to do justly. Do what you need to do. Love your neighbor. Think what it takes. This is the text. Let it mean love. The rest is commentary.

· · ● ● ● · ·

Questions for Further Conversation

1. How might the term *agnostic* be employed most redemptively? In the interest of honesty, when might it be necessary to describe ourselves as agnostics? Are there issues about which you yourself are agnostic?

2. Is "God, rid me of 'God'" a good and faithful prayer? What hesitations or hopes do we bring to the possibility of praying it?

3. What's the trouble with believing that we're saved by right belief? What does it say about the purposes of God and the scope of God's saving economy?

4. How does faith stop short of knowledge, and why does this often make us uncomfortable? How might our desire to think and speak beyond interpretation, beyond the fact of our humanness, do damage? Where does the con game fit in? Why are we tempted to lay it on thick with guarantees and oaths and promises?

5. How do the voices in the Bible employ the process of appropriation? What kinds of questions will accompany acts of faithful appropriation as we attempt to make good use of the Bible?

7. It has been said that the only right way to interpret the Bible is to do what it says. Do you agree or disagree? Why?

The Past Didn't Go Anywhere*

Questioning History

How far back can we trace? In African thought,
the consensus is that after the seventh generation we
can no longer distinguish between history and myth.

J. M. Coetzee, *Diary of a Bad Year*

All sorrows can be borne if you put them into a story
or tell a story about them.

**Isak Dinesen, *The New York Times Book Review*,
November 3, 1957**

Confession. I read books in public in the hope that someone will ask me what I'm reading and why. Sometimes I even enjoy talking about what I'm reading more than I enjoy reading. A good portion of the fourth chapter of this book was generated out of the time an especially kind Starbucks employee questioned me so relentlessly concerning the book I was reading that I found myself trying to explain commodity fetishism to him and to myself.

A day when someone asks me a good question is a good day.

I can't help but think I'm not alone in this. Why do people bring their "work" to coffee shops if they aren't secretly hoping

---

*I owe this title to the work of the great storyteller-historian, one-man-revolution Utah Phillips, whose recorded voice was put to inspiring effect by Ani Difranco in a recorded production of the same name.

that someone will ask them what they're up to? There's no shame in this game. Positive reinforcement, in some sense, makes the world go round. We want to be seen reading Naomi Klein and Cornel West and Howard Zinn. We want inquiring minds who want to know about us and how devastatingly intelligent and conscientious we are.

It was in this spirit that, as a younger man visiting some near and dear relations, I sat on a couch reading (note that I was *really* asking for it) Dee Brown's *Bury My Heart at Wounded Knee: An Indian History of the American West*. In time, the trap was sprung—someone walked up and asked, "What are you reading?"

I went for it with gusto. Irretrievably lost cultures. Genocide. Histories written by the winners. Conquest. American legacies built on the blood of the poor and disenfranchised even now. Crimes against humanity undertaken in the name of Christ and Manifest Destiny. The least we can do is learn their names for God's sake. "Know what I mean?" I paused to take a breath.

"How do you know it isn't biased?" my audience of one inquired.

That word again. *Bias*. "What if it isn't?" I managed to keep from saying in a defensive fashion.

I happen to love this particular woman, and I didn't know what to say. I understand, in my better moments, that she is pouring out her life as a sacrifice to God and other people. Truth be told, my anxious armchair activism pales in comparison to the way she goes about the difficult work of loving others without talking about it. She doesn't go in for theory. So I was at a loss as to how I might speak the truth in love in light of the rant I'd begun. Whether we speak the truth, Brian McLaren once said, is an ethical matter, but how much of the truth we tell is a matter of wisdom.

Comfortable Illusions

So I'll begin again with the question I was probably hoping for. Why do I read this kind of book? To better engage the principalities and powers of this present darkness? Yes. To avoid being an accidental fascist? Sure. To rage against the machinations of totalitarianism? Certainly. But let's go with being transformed by the renewing of my mind and not settling for the versions of history that serve only to justify domination. Reading with prayer and laughter and self-examination is often like fighting off demon-possession. Incidentally, saying no to the demonic is always a good thing.

Reading history yields the realization that deeply sincere people have gone to houses of worship, looked after their families, and prayed intensely while also participating in unthinkable atrocities. With this is mind, I read in the hope that I might participate in the redemptive movements of history, the kind that will look redemptive centuries from now. It's an attempt to rise above bias by refusing to view as "biased" everything that makes me feel funny about my background, my voting record, the actions I fund via my government taxes.

It's overwhelming—get ready for a mind twister—to try to want to know what I don't want to know, but I'm moved by what I take to be a healthy anxiety. There is a reigning historical deafness buzzing away in my own mind and in the way the world gets talked about, and I'd like to be part of the counteraction. Like many people born on this side of the economic divide, I have the luxury of philosophizing over how I might enter into some semblance of solidarity with two-thirds of the world, those people for whom history often feels like a nightmare. How do I avoid being yet another uncaring face in a long line of blissfully ignorant people whose action and inaction are harnessed to keep other people down? How do I become a part of the counteraction?

I find these questions deeply invigorating and inextricably connected to my desire to be one of those who mean to be faithful to Jesus' way of doing things. With this in mind, I joke with my students that most of us have some acquaintance with various official histories, *hist*ory proper. But it might be many years before we begin to cobble together a popular sense, for instance, of *her*story. I'll get a knowing nod from one or two, a puzzled look from a few, and anger with me from a good many for putting it that way. They have enough to worry about. It's too much. This knee-jerk defensiveness is that self-justifying impulse I hope to resist, and I hasten to add that the same impulse often seems to run through my veins as well. It's not simply the part of us that doesn't want to hear; it's the mind-set that kicks in to actively not hear. In an especially excellent phrase, sociologist Pierre Bourdieu calls it the "self-legitimating imagination of the 'happy few.' "[1] Like good interpretation, looking deeply into history probably won't be a self-legitimating activity. It will always involve dwelling at length on the difficult questions.

A favorite exchange that captures this sort of thing in literary form comes to us from William Gibson's novel *Spook Country*. Gibson is especially good at delivering dialogue that with humor and scintillating clarity illuminates the state we're in:

> "That's quite a plane," Milgrim had said.
> "That's what money will buy you, in America," Brown had said, firmly. "People say Americans are materialistic. But do you know why?"
> "Why?" asked Milgrim, more concerned with this uncharacteristically expansive mode of expression on Brown's part.

"Because they have better stuff," Brown had replied. "No other reason."[2]

I especially like this capturing of the awkward moment when what started off as small talk moves into an "uncharacteristically expansive mode of expression," when one talker suddenly moves toward a logic-defyingly awesome generalization. Milgrim is an extremely well-informed, incredibly well-read fellow who, for the moment, happens to be a drug addict. His dependence on Brown, who is more than willing to rough him up from time to time, preempts the possibility of Milgrim's ever talking back. But this only enhances the reader's amusement as the slapstick escalates. Milgrim can't risk provoking Brown's inner-Rush Limbaugh because he's afraid he'll get smacked for it. Milgrim's eyes widen as Brown glosses over the rest of the world, betraying his fervent religious commitment to America's ethical, technological, cultural, not-to-be-questioned superiority over other cultures. It's in the air these days. You're either with us or against us.

Bias, in this sense, is shorthand for insufficiently positive feedback and whatever history might make my head hurt. I'm perfectly capable of reducing the accumulated wisdom of centuries (be it Islamic, Buddhist, Native American, African, or Confucian) to bias. "Bias" is the history that challenges me to question my own sense of history, my flawed and finite sense of the meaning of my own story, my pronouncements as well as my pronunciations.

I research Native American culture in an attempt to avoid being conformed to the patterns of dominating, enslaving, genocidal powers, in an attempt to be transformed by the renewing of my mind. It's a spiritual act of worship, further dabbling in the possibility of emancipation conversations. It's tantamount to a spiritual conversion—repentance, turning my mind around. Familiarizing myself with history and herstory is one immediate and available way of being busy getting born instead of being busy dying. It's an introduction, new every morning, to various forms of cosmic plainspeak. May the beat go on and on.

This sense of a redeeming rhythm demanding renewal and vigilance brings to mind a favorite quote I'd like to see on plaques or cross-stitched for prominent display in any church, college, university, hospital, or media corporation that markets itself as having something to do with Jesus of Nazareth. It comes from David L. Edwards, whose breathtakingly broad and miraculously accessible take on Christian history has been enormously helpful in my attempts to think and imagine historically. It's called *Christianity: The First Two Thousand Years*—isn't that a nice subtitle? He hazards an amazing word on the meaning of Jesus' resurrection. I don't know if Edwards affirms a literal resurrection, but as I receive the punch of his words I also note that I kind of don't care. Edwards won't let literalists, nonliteralists, or illiteralists evade the question of the meaning of Jesus. The question before us is how the Son of Man will matter for us in our visions of success, progress, freedom, and justice. Check it out:

> Very strange events convinced these people that Jesus was truly and gloriously alive despite his terrible death. Many thought then, and have continued to think, that what the Christians believed was an illusion, but if that was the case it may still be reckoned the most influential of all the experiences which rightly or wrongly have persuaded people that human existence is after all not ultimately pointless or merely tragic. And if it was an illusion, it was not comfortable.[3]

Edwards understands that Jesus is a hard act to swallow. The existential reverberations of Jesus' career are with us still, growing in bandwidth every day. Given the new world order—the regime change—Jesus announces, even the rumors of his resurrection are enough to give honest people pause. Quite a story either way. Resurrection isn't a comforting illusion when we bring it to bear on our standard procedures. And even if we insist it's a metaphor, the metaphor takes on a life of its own as it generates a Jewish peasant movement that turns the world upside down. That movement has managed to give life to a robustly revolutionary and civilizing way of regarding human beings. There are so many ways of being a fan of this Jesus. So many ways of getting in line with what Jesus was talking about. So many ways of letting Jesus impact our estimation of the stranger, the slave, the enemy.

We have to distinguish this movement from so-called Western civilization and self-described Christian civilization, with its crusades and heresy trials and bowing down to the idols of nationalism. And at the same time, Jesus' different way of being a human being also won't be rightly distinguished from his vision of what it means to be faithfully Jewish.[4] Still, this Jesus movement persists as an enduring, world-conquering civilization that shares resources instead of squandering them, forgives wrongs instead of avenging them, and attempts solidarity and reconciliation with perceived enemies instead of dropping bombs on them.

I think of comedian Eddie Izzard's assertion that while he doesn't believe that Jesus was God's son, his life was nevertheless the most wonderfully earth-shattering and controversial story there is of "a bloke who tried to help."[5] While Izzard's affirmation might not pass creedal muster for many, it can signal the beginning rather than the end of the conversation concerning the redeeming significance of Jesus in history, a conversation that in a certain sense has hardly even gotten off the ground.

Edwards understands that Jesus' movement, which kicked into high gear with rumors of Jesus' resurrection, is no more comforting for the proud of heart now than it was then. Like W. H. Auden, Edwards might affirm that he feels strongly compelled to follow this Jesus, even given the fact that what he insists on as a lifestyle can feel so ridiculous and revolting. Do we want the economy Jesus announced to arrive? We might recall, too, that most of the earliest surviving manuscripts of Mark's gospel end on a similarly enigmatic note. The women who followed Jesus discover an empty tomb and their response is understandably emotional: "Trembling and bewildered, the women went out and fled from the tomb. They said nothing to anyone, because they were afraid" (Mark 16:8). The end.

These Jewish peasant women weren't afraid and bewildered because of the spiritual significance of what they'd stumbled on. They were shaken because what was known, what was familiar and verifiably normal, had been forever cast into doubt.

To be sure, they weren't fans of the status quo, of might making right, and of the execution of revolutionaries who dared to call the rightness of the Roman Empire into question. But now all bets are *really off*. What's dead doesn't necessarily stay that way. God might not be on the side of the people with "better stuff," and the whole story of masters and slaves might just be a powerful fiction, a story not so convincing anymore. Perhaps the arm of the Lord is long and perhaps it bends toward justice. The course of history has been powerfully called into question. And if we're paying attention, we'll discover strange tidings of comfort and joy branching out in unexpected directions. The tidings have a way of questioning, reevaluating, and (in time) rearranging any and every economy, every perceived have-to.

Centers of Gravity

The charge of "historical revisionism" is often used to avoid facts of history that make our own supposed successes—be they claims of ownership, the pillaging of natural resources, accumulated wealth, or military conquests—feel a little less morally corrupt.

As someone who has graded a number of high school students' rough drafts over the years and who tries to earn a living by writing well, I think revision is a fine thing. It's right up there with redemption in my book. In fact, I'm counting on it. And when it comes to history, doing it redemptively, especially in light of how Jesus throws everything off balance, may be our only hope, an ethical imperative. How is justice possible if we aren't committed to rethinking the past over and over again? Are we open to the prophetic work of deconstruction? Are we open to removing the effects of brainwashing?

If we're dead set against rethinking official histories, I suspect we have yet to look deeply at the revisioning that went on within Israel's prophetic imagination as it developed in the Bible and the decentering of political power that happened when the Jesus movement got hold of people. Revolution depends on revision. I'd say we pray for it whenever we pray for a certain kingdom to come here on earth. Isn't the act of prayer itself an act of revisioning? Does revision strike us as a little too closely aligned with redistribution? Do we actually want the kingdom to come soon and very soon?

The kingdom that is coming, to which I aspire to bear faithful witness in the meantime, demands the revision of history. If I refuse to revise or to allow my sense of history to undergo the transformation that only comes from reading repentantly—with a determined interest in cultures whose voices have been lost or silenced—I have yet to grasp the significance of the Lord's Prayer. It might be worth asking if I've undergone a conversion at all. I might believe I've appended Jesus into my life as a kind of spiritual accoutrement, but if I give one nation, culture, political party, or news network the right to decide my history for me—to decide, for instance, who my enemy is—I have yet to respond deeply to the call away from my tribal allegiances and the worship of false gods.

We need to cast aside for a moment the misrepresentation of the word *evangelical* and restore to it a flavor of good news, as John Howard Yoder does when he speaks of the necessity of evangelical revisionism, the reappraisal of history in light of our growing understanding of the meaning of Jesus' good news.

> The reason history needs to be reread is not merely that every generation must claim the right to begin writing world history from scratch ... but that at certain points there is specifiable good news about the human condition, the goodness or the newness of which those who hitherto have been controlling the storytelling had not yet appropriated.[6]

With a prophetic eye on the schemes of disinformation propagated by those who go about "controlling the storytelling," be they rulers who order hits on truth tellers, priests who slay prophets, or PR teams who work reality control amid news cycles, Yoder understands that there is always good historical work to be done. There are acts of remembrance and feats of attentiveness that are seamlessly connected to good news proclamation and practice. So much has been lost, but all manner of forgotten voices can be found again. History is a salvage operation that challenges and redeems our imaginations. We are called on to exercise our historical memories redemptively.

Novelist William James advised aspiring writers to try to be the kind of person "on whom nothing is lost."[7] I believe something similar is at work in the questioning of history. Yoder claims that the good news of Jesus frees us to bring a liberating voice to the past and the present and enables us "to enter any world in which people eat bread and pursue debtors, hope for power and execute subversives."[8] We get to be on the lookout for what might have been and imagine visions of what might yet be. The "silenced" of history might not be forever silenced. They might return with a lyrical word or two, with a newly authoritative "Once upon a time ..."

The history of redemption will not merely be the memory of states and other wielders of the sword. In God's economy, there are no closed books. And the work of remembering well, interrogating the past, having a go at retrieving and redeeming what was lost in the clash of power-mad uncivilizations, might be the vocation of a politics of resurrection. Contrary to popular talk of personal, private salvation, I believe the blessedness of this good work is in large part what getting saved is for.

Or as the Peruvian theologian Gustavo Gutiérrez put it, "To be converted is to know and experience the fact that, contrary to the laws of physics, we can stand straight, according to the gospel, only when our center of gravity is outside ourselves."[9] This is the opposite posture of what we've referred to as the self-legitimating imagination. Against the tendency to seek out histories, genealogies, and news reports that seem to buttress our fragile ego structures, Gutierrez advises us to derive our sense of blessedness from the Beatitudes. Strictly speaking, they aren't about the innate goodness of the poor and disenfranchised; they're about the goodness of God, who sides with them. The God made known in Jesus. The God who doesn't do history like we do. The God whose affectionate attentiveness extends to the minute particulars—to sparrows, lilies, and the hair on people's heads. This God doesn't believe in the term *collateral damage*. This God does body counts. Do we?

The not-so-redemptive dreams of righteous conquest and the myths of redeeming violence often stay with us in our big countries. We inherit them, and if we fail to test them, we become custodians of death-dealing actions. We defend them as if they were what had to be done, as if no true patriot would doubt or question what had to be done. But as Gutiérrez and the biblical witness urge, we have to seek our centering elsewhere. We have to get unbrainwashed. We have to relativize our attachments to the kingdoms of this world if we're to be conscious of and awake to the world to come. We have to lose our history to find it.

You Are Not Your History

Reality, Philip K. Dick reminds us, "is that which, when you stop believing in it, doesn't go away."[10] It is the work of the prophet—the poet, the songwriter, the teacher, the preacher—to seek out reality and to never stop questioning it. The Bible isn't a collection of voices that learned, over thousands of years, to stop questioning, to silence protests and lamentations. It is a relentless kicking against the status quo, even and especially when the prophets fear that it's their one true God who's somehow endorsing it. The biblical tradition keeps kicking back, crying out loud, and asking, How long until righteousness reigns? How long will we have to sing these songs?

Will Campbell, in his chronicling of race relations in the American South and as a white Baptist minister who worked with Martin Luther King Jr. and James Lawson in the civil rights era, observed that when you believe in tragedy, as opposed to an economy of just deserts where people get what's coming to them, you can't take sides.[11] You can't demonize the opposition as if yours is the only morally sound voice in the room. The angry white Southerner has to be enlisted in the dismantling of racist mechanisms. The redeeming story requires a redemptive posture even toward the enemy.

For those who mean to follow Jesus, this isn't the adoption

of quiescence. In fact, it's the opposite. It's the empathy without which there can be no moral action. Developing a sense of the tragic, a sense of the undeserved and needless suffering of people in our world, is the only way one can be a good rememberer, a redeeming agent within the history that's even now speeding past us, developing a judgment on our getting, our spending, and our inaction.

As we try to remember, we might have peculiar interests — be they separatist or Sufi mystic or samurai — but an exclusive focus on the "big names" will mean that we lack the evangelical tact Yoder and Gutiérrez urge on us. The good news of history biblically speaking is that the winners don't win. Read how Yoder put it:

> When Paul wrote that the word of the cross is weak to those who look for signs, but God's saving power to those who believe, he was promoting not otherworldly mysticism but the kind of political reality which brought down Bull Connor in 1963, Ferdinand Marcos in 1986, and Erich Honecker in 1989. I don't know what particular regime Arthur Cleveland Coxe was thinking about when in a hymn he penned the question, 'Oh, where are kings and empires now of old that went and came?' ... The rest of the hymn was less fitting, as Coxe went on to describe the church as unshaken and immovable. The point is rather that the church's being shaken and moved, being vulnerable, defines or constitutes its participation in the travail of the Lamb who was slain and is therefore worthy to receive power and wealth and wisdom and might and honor and glory and blessing. That suffering is powerful, and that weakness wins, is true not only in heaven but on earth. That is a statement about the destiny not only of the faith community but also of all creation.[12]

The redeeming rememberer, recorder, chronicler, or lyricist of our time will have to live in determined expectation of all manner of things being redeemed—or, as Julian of Norwich put it, "All shall be well, and all shall be well, and all manner of things shall be well."[13] The good rememberer won't discriminate between the mundane and what "matters" because, in view of the age to come, she senses that she doesn't have to. The German literary critic Walter Benjamin captured this historical sensibility well:

> A chronicler who recites events without distinguishing between major and minor ones acts in accordance with the following truth: nothing that has ever happened should be regarded as lost for history. To be sure only a redeemed mankind receives the fullness of its past—which is to say, only for a redeemed mankind has its past become citable in all its moments.[14]

Only in redemption is the past fully citable. It is only by feats of sympathetic and imaginative attentiveness that we begin to retrieve and redeem the past. I believe Yoder and Benjamin are largely on the same page in their understanding of history. Both pitch their tents within the sense of vocation—lyrical and historical—attested to in the words of the Beat writer Jack Kerouac: "And so I struggle in the dark with the enormity of my soul, trying desperately to be a great rememberer redeeming life from darkness."[15]

The good remembering, the histories that RE-member in a world that seems committed primarily to DIS-membering, is the work forever before us. It is the work that redeems life from darkness. Along these lines I recall an exchange between Flannery O'Connor and her friend Betty Hester. A prolific and profound author, though she was never published, Hester characterized her own troubled history as "a history of horror." In the letters the two women exchanged, Hester eventually shared some especially disturbing details. O'Connor rushed her response: "I can't write you fast enough and tell you that it doesn't make the slightest bit of difference in my opinion of you, which is the same as it was, and that is a solid and complete respect." O'Connor continued:

> If in any sense my knowing your burden can make your burden lighter, then I am doubly glad I know it. You were right to tell me, but I'm glad you didn't tell me until I knew you well. Where you are wrong is in saying that you are the history of horror. The meaning of the redemption is precisely that we do not have to be our history, and nothing is plainer to me than that you are not your history.[16]

Among the tragedies Hester had chosen to share was the fact that, as a child of thirteen, she had tried to persuade her neighbors to contact the police in an attempt to prevent her mother's suicide. The neighbors refused, assuming it was another of her mother's spells of delusion. Hester's mother committed suicide, with her daughter being the lone witness.

This kind of memory challenges my understanding of how redemption retrieves what was damaged and lost and dims the hope of all manner of things being made well. Such histories of horror stagger my powers of hope and belief. But I believe in, hope in, and try to affirm what O'Connor terms "the meaning of redemption" and what Yoder, Benjamin, and Kerouac envision as the cosmic recovery in which nothing will be lost and nothing will go unredeemed. Our commitment to remembering well, to the details of what really happened in tragic personal histories, war zones, and under the watch of negligent governments, is, it seems to me, inescapably tied to the struggle to think, speak, and listen redemptively. To these histories of horror we are called to bring our questions, our powers of witness, and our hopes that life will yet be redeemed from darkness. Only good remembering can re-deem. Will even this be somehow redeemed? Will what has been DIS-membered be RE-membered? How long, O Lord? Help our unbelief. Let the whole of the kingdom come.

"Have more talk of these sad things," asserts the last man standing to the audience at the conclusion of *The Most Excellent and Lamentable Tragedy of Romeo and Juliet*. What befell the two star-crossed lovers in their last attempt to be true to one another and to be together was so irretrievably ill-timed and so unspeak-ably sad that a well-executed performance won't leave a dry eye in the house. It can hardly be talked about. It's just too much. Nevertheless, "Have more talk" is the Shakespearean imperative. Crushing truths are lightened by their acknowledgment. Remem-ber again. Remember rightly. Re-vision. "Once upon a time" one more time.

Among the founders of Charter 77, the Czech thinker-activist Jan Patočka, once observed that history is life that no longer takes itself for granted.[17] Like Shakespeare's words, I take this to be a call to ethical remembrance, to bring the difficult past into the space of the talkaboutable, and at the same time a summons to remember that today's reigning dysfunction is not inevitable. In Patočka's case, he would not live to see the culmination of his activist work in the Velvet Revolution of 1989, but his definition of history, as I understand it, is based in a determined liveliness that insists, again and again, that the way things are is not the way things have to be. Redemption draws nigh.

Questions for Further Conversation

1. What constitutes appropriate use of the word *bias*? How might we become more alive to the way our own biases and prejudices stand in the way of perceiving reality? Are there ways of confessing and overcoming bias?

2. How has news of the risen Jesus impacted the world's understanding of human existence? What revolution did Jesus radically further concerning the net value of the peasant, the slave, and the enemy? Where does the revolution stand today?

3. Oscar Wilde once observed that the best thing one can do for history is to revise it. Is he right? Why or why not?

4. What does it mean to not take sides when it comes to remembering history rightly? What do we gain when we choose empathy over judgment?

5. How is it that Jesus' gospel involves the hope that "the winners" won't take all and won't ultimately write history? How does this impact your understanding of Jesus' good news?

6. Can you think of instances in which good remembering has contributed to the redeeming of life from darkness? How do you differentiate between good remembering and bad remembering?

9

We Do What We're Told

Questioning Governments

If the law is of such a nature that it requires you to be
an agent of injustice to another, then I say, break the law.
Henry David Thoreau, "Civil Disobedience"

The church has an obligation not to join in the incantation
of political slogans and in the concoction of pseudo-events
but to cut clear through the deviousness and ambiguity
of both slogans and events by her simplicity and her love.
Thomas Merton, *Faith and Violence*

In the weeks following September 11, 2001, the United States government referred to its military campaign in Afghanistan as "Operation Infinite Justice." The enlistment of such language on the part of any nation-state, especially one that, in its advertising, locates itself as being *under* God, struck me as deeply problematic. The name was soon changed to "Operation Enduring Freedom," allegedly in response to concerns from clerics within the Islamic tradition regarding the words *infinite justice*. The secretary of defense at the time, Donald Rumsfeld, noted that "in the Islamic faith, such finality is considered something provided only by God."[1]

Wait a minute. Does such blasphemous language only step on Muslim toes? Anybody else concerned about a governing body's delusions of grandeur? Why didn't anybody else cry foul? Are Americans in danger of developing Stockholm syndrome in our relationship with the government, leaving "infinite justice" and other matters of "such finality" to mere mortals, whose governing is ostensibly dependent on our consent? Why no corrective word?

Loyalty to the country always, loyalty to the government when it deserves it. So said Mark Twain, and it is a reminder to me of the bad habits by which we let those we employ to run the government do our thinking for us. We have to resist the power plays of our government. We have to resist in the name of real patriotism. Otherwise we're letting the law, as it stands, prevent the possibility of real order. And real law and order, real justice, is something to which no nationality owns the copyright. It is the prerogative of the coming righteous reign of God.

I'm of the opinion that Martin Luther King Jr. will probably be remembered as the greatest American who ever lived, the one whose prophetic posture toward the land of his sojourn helped usher in an America worthy of celebration. He loved the hope of America enough to refuse to worship it. He was determined to mine the open-ended language of the Constitution for all it might be worth. King embodies an evangelical tension, a tension that gets glossed over when people get worked up over American flag lapel pins. In the rush to claim affiliation with King's brand, it is often overlooked that the same King whose gravesite is featured in presidential photo ops passed his final moments in a Memphis hotel room working on a sermon titled "Why America May Go to Hell."[2]

When governments brand themselves the ultimate arbiters of "infinite justice," deprive terrorist suspects of due process, overthrow democratically elected governments via covert operations, and dedicate resources to high-tech mechanisms of self-justification, they sabotage the democratic society they were supposed to facilitate. When people forgo the right to question the governing bodies of the country within which they were born, they become cogs in the dysfunctional exercise of political power. The dysfunction runs on fear, and as Bertolt Brecht observed, the rule of fear isn't just a matter of the masses being ruled by fear; fear rules the rulers too. There is no meaningful political deliberation—no dialogue, no conversation.

History demonstrates that governing bodies respond most swiftly to questions and demands voiced by direct action, especially action to which the government feels forced to respond. These actions often fall under the heading of "nonviolence," but this mustn't be confused with passivity or an unwillingness to risk bodily harm. In fact, a willingness to make oneself vulnerable to some degree of harm is at work in all of these actions. Personal harm can be the price one has to pay for the right to question the government. The power of governments is dependent on the obedience of the people, and we have both the ability and the obligation to reconfigure and redeem that power. The works of the government are our works. Our government budgets—local, state, and national—are our mission statements. As Jim Wallis insistently reminds us, budgets are moral documents, our acts of worship[3]—where our treasures are and where our hearts are, as Jesus so provocatively put it. What we do is never *not* worship.

Say It!

The commitment to questioning everything is a sacred obligation. The ramifications of believing this sort of thing can get personal. I wouldn't characterize the following story as an instance of direct action on my part, but it is a tiny example of the mind-set I believe I have to maintain if I'm to remain capable of questioning certain authorities.

I was teaching in high school in those anxious days of the government-sanctioned spirit of "infinite justice" when word went out among students and parents that I was refusing to participate in the Pledge of Allegiance. But this wasn't true. I hadn't refused, because no one, then or now, had asked me, with the threat of firing or even a severe look of disapproval, to say the pledge. As it happened, the tradition of reciting the pledge at our school had lain dormant for years, but the reappraisal of any number of social mores in light of the September 11 attacks now included at the request of at least two students a reinstitution of the pledge recital to accompany other forms of daily worship. And as far as I can tell, the question of whether Mr. Dark would participate essentially arose out of a lesson plan I'd developed and taught that—the Lord be praised—had somehow remained branded in the minds of certain young.

Among the surviving elegies of the Anglo-Saxon oral tradition that come to us via *The Exeter Book* is a piece called "The Wanderer." (Tolkien draws from it in one of Aragorn's songs in *The Lord of the Rings*, and U2 gives us a fantastic postmodern version channeled by Johnny Cash at the end of what I take to be an underrated masterpiece album of 1993, *Zooropa*.) The speaker is a warrior rendered homeless by a tragic turn of events whereby his hearth lord has died. With his lord dead, all possibility of coherence is gone. His sustenance, his shelter, and the ethical framework that forms his understanding of who or what he should live for, die for, and kill for have been obliterated. And now he wanders, fantasizing bitterly over that remembered moment of maximum moral clarity, arguably the greatest moment of his life, when he was awarded for his proven worthiness by being allowed to kneel, grasp his lord's knee, and, as the poem went, pledge his liege unto him.

When we got to this part in the poem, I observed as a point

of possible interest that in some cultures little children are made
to speak similar oaths to certain authorities without even knowing the meaning of the words. They're bred to pledge their liege
away without question. So sad really—can you believe it? This
was usually enough to win an approving smile from one or two
students who were on the hunt to find something to complain
about, as well as from those who wanted to challenge the comparison. Either way, it yielded a great discussion and generated
lots of questions that I stubbornly refused to answer. Should they
have been made to say the pledge as children? I said I didn't want
to step on anybody's religious upbringing.

This particular lesson plan returned to haunt me. People talked
("Are you going to quit?), and my principal, to his credit, stayed
true to the school's policy of living out what is sometimes called
the Matthew 18 principle: If you have a problem with someone,
talk to that person, not to others. The result was conversations via
telephone and in hallways on the evangelically directed civil disobedience of Dietrich Bonhoeffer and Martin Luther King Jr. that
continue to this day. During the Pledge of Allegiance, I stood up
and placed my hand over my heart and prayed the Lord's Prayer
in my head as other people pledged other words. Sometimes I'll
quietly say some words and change others (as I often do with
hymns I can't conscientiously say aloud) and generally try hard to
avoid giving offense that comes when people sense you might be
questioning their unacknowledged religion.

The idea that anyone would conclude that I'm not patriotic
because I refuse to pledge my loyalty so casually is troubling, especially when a more thoroughgoing patriotism involves seeking
the welfare and peace of the land—and the people—of one's sojourn. But when people are willing to keep talking and questioning, such conflicts can occasion a bit of good news. In my case, I
hope I facilitated a conversation about the possibility of Christian

witness within a high school that aspires to be recognized by the watching world as Christian. During the dialogue, I remained free to worship in spirit and in truth.

Sacred Phone Books

My resistance to offer my allegiance to flags isn't primarily a matter of what I take to be the idolatry involved so much as the pledging part—an oath. And this returns us to the question of what we do—our liturgy, our worship, our ways of being in the world. The difficulties of trying to be a just, attentive witness are ever before us. And the question of what such witness might entail amid the well-funded liturgies of nation-states and corporations that have already enlisted us is a question many of us have hardly begun to ask.

Liturgy is a religious-sounding word for what is simply *the work of the people*. And bad government, which does the work of the people, is bad liturgy. Both good liturgy and bad liturgy depend on our action and cooperation. Our personal liturgy affects—either constructively or destructively—larger liturgies of groups, movements, governments, and civilian populations. The bad ordering of an unjust government is only overturned, only redeemed, only reworked, into better and more redemptive ways when we stop cooperating with its bad orders.

Cooperating with a government because it is the government is like pledging allegiance to a phone book. It is giving a government a religious allegiance of which it can't possibly be worthy. A phone book orders people's names and contact information, but it doesn't bear witness to their infinite value any more than passports or deportation documents do. What do we do with the governing bodies under our jurisdiction when their allegiance to the general welfare of humans is deficient or destructive? What are the governments we fund undertaking in our names? What is being done in my name? How can we bend our international lawmaking powers in the direction of justice?

We bear witness. Or, more soberingly, we attempt to assume responsibility for the witness we already bear by way of our governments. We listen closely for the witness of others, thinking hard about the reality of other people, perhaps especially the nameless ones often on the receiving end of the raw, unchecked power exercised on them and funded by people like us. We mustn't allow governments to decide who our enemies are or to dictate policies whereby some lives are more sacred, more worthy of our attentiveness, than others. Governments respond to our dictates, and our consent (or what often appears to be a kind of manufactured consent) directs their doings. We're responsible for what's being done in our name. How shall we conduct our witness?

Practice Resurrection

There are so many kinds of witnesses — poets, prophets, priests, activists, and other agents of awareness. Those who dare to imagine a different world. Those whose hopes for a better world to come energize and invigorate different ways of thinking and doing things now. Artisans of the possible, I call them.[4] People like Peter Chelèický, a fourteenth-century Bohemian farmer, who wrote that the person who obeys God has no need to heed the godlike pretensions of earthly authorities (church or state) that in their powerfully deluded ways often rip at the fabric of true religious practice. Seek first God's kingdom, that regime that most radically values all human beings. Be willing to be held in contempt by the powers that be — even lethal contempt. Question the order of things. Bring cosmic plainspeak to the ears of those in power. Choose this day whom you will serve. Or, as Wendell Berry puts it in "Manifesto: The Mad Farmer Liberation Front," take a moment out of every day to do one thing that won't compute on anybody's marketing scheme. Prophesy a profit in planting for harvests that won't come in your lifetime. Love people who, to your mind, don't deserve it. In Berry's invigorating phrase, "Practice resurrection."[5]

Consider the Vietnamese witness Thich Nhat Hanh and his organizing of relief efforts and nonviolent action during the Vietnam War. In the foreword to Hanh's 1967 book *Vietnam: Lotus in a Sea of Fire*, Thomas Merton described Hanh as "a contemplative monk who has felt himself obliged to take an active part in his country's effort to escape destruction in a vicious power struggle between capitalism and communism," and a man who "speaks for his people and for a renewed and 'engaged' Buddhism that has taken up the challenge of modern and Western civilization in its often disastrous impact upon the East."[6]

Reprinted in the book is a letter Hanh wrote to Martin Luther King Jr., a letter locating South Vietnam's Buddhist community's struggle for equality alongside America's civil rights movement and explaining the traditional context of acts of self-immolation on the part of Buddhist monks.[7] While I believe we rightly hesitate in championing these acts, I also believe we suffer from tragically misplaced religious allegiances if we're unmoved by their attempt at witness, their power to call certain death-dealing liturgies (the carpet bombing of rural villages, for instance) into question. We might do well to expand the sphere of what offends us and broaden our definition of obscenity.

Hanh explains that these acts of self-immolation weren't to be understood as instances of suicide (as the Western press had reported) but attempts "to perform an act of construction, i.e., to suffer and die for the sake of one's people." For all their scandal, Hanh insists they were assertions of goodwill:

What the monks said in the letters they left before burning themselves aimed only at alarming, at moving the hearts of the oppressors and at calling the attention of the world to the suffering endured then by the Vietnamese.... To express will by burning oneself, therefore, is not to commit an act of destruction but to perform an act of construction, i.e., to suffer and to die for the sake of one's people.... I believe with all my heart that the monks who burned themselves did not aim at the death of the oppressors but only at a change in their policy. Their enemies are not man. They are intolerance, fanaticism, dictatorship, cupidity, hatred and discrimination which lie within the heart of man.... These are real enemies of man — not man himself.[8]

Out of this profound sense of the anger, violence, and tragedy that arises from our ignorance concerning the interconnectedness of all life, Hanh asserts, "Nobody here wants the war. What is the war for, then? And whose is the war?"[9]

Against the complacency of those who see the escalation of violent conflicts as inevitable and necessary, Hanh turns the tables by illustrating how the bloodshed is born of a kind of militant ignorance, of nobody assuming responsibility for themselves, of a majority not even wanting the war they're perpetuating and staying the course by default. By Hanh's account, the monks who burned themselves were refusing the despair of the status quo by giving their lives as a public service announcement, an experiment in making people aware — and thereby were mobilized toward compassion. They acted with a depth of understanding and a profound ethical commitment to life and freedom that scandalizes the cynicism of the aggressors who claim to make war to protect life and freedom.

Hanh isn't apologizing for the monks or romanticizing death. He seeks instead to articulate the meaning of their actions. Their acts are a summons to a more robust realism, a more profound awareness of the consequences of our decisions, of what's being done beyond our perceived borders in the name of security. To make too sharp a distinction between other lives and our own is a false witness. To label entire populations — or even sections of the globe — as "enemy" is bad theology, and no government that does so can claim to be operating in any mindful way "under" God. To allow an all-too-human governing body to describe the world for us is to hand over our God-given duty to the likes of a phone book or a demonic stronghold. We have to take our thinking back.

The same summons is communicated by Iraqi Christians who publicly pray that American Christians might consider more deeply their understanding of the body of Christ. Does our understanding of this communion move beyond national boundaries when it really counts? Do our imaginations, the way we think about other people, acquiesce to the idolatrous and destructive divisions of nation-states? The defensive distance we maintain between ourselves and the people we see in images of war and deprivation is a deadly construct. The social incompetence of our governments is our incompetence, our work, and our responsibility.

The question of our governing is the question of our liturgy, worship, and witness — the question of what we deem sacred. Does our sense of the sacred include the average Palestinian, the Chinese peasant who builds structures for the Beijing Olympics for slave wages, the Ugandan child soldier? Are some people less sacred than others? Will we stand beside them, look them in the eye, and help them? Are people mere numbers, or are they valuable bearers of the image of God? What are we willing to sign off on? What do we underwrite? A determined dwelling on these questions is the way redeeming and revolutionary history is written — this is our liturgy.

Body Politics: Artisans of the Possible

Much can change in a short time. Women in America were denied the right to vote less than a century ago. What led to the change? Prayer, speeches, hunger strikes, marches, daily picketing, and arrests. And the leaders, women who forced the topic into public view—Elizabeth Cady Stanton and Susan B. Anthony. The final push came from Alice Paul (1885–1977), who formed the National Woman's Party and refused, as a Quaker and a woman with a PhD in economics, to allow her government's policies to continue to keep women out of the voting booth. As an artisan of the possible, she is an exemplary figure within what the poet Philip Metres refers to as "a poetics of nonviolent community."[10]

Political scientist Gene Sharp characterizes nonviolent action as "a generic term" that can prove deceptively definitive if we let it be anything less than a way of somehow conducting conflict "by doing—or refusing to do—certain things without using physical violence."[11] The National Woman's Party grounded ethical innovation in communal resistance. While Alice Paul's final prison hunger strike and the bureaucratic response of force-feeding her might afford the most cinematic moments of her struggle, it's important to keep it all in the context of the long, deliberate strategizing of the National Woman's Party. They had learned that letting themselves relax in their work would consistently lead to the relaxation of the wider culture (and the relaxed posture of President Woodrow Wilson) on the issue of suffrage. As Inez Hayes Irwin describes "their system" whereby they pushed for a constitutional amendment, the movement "worked on Congress by a series of electric shocks delivered to it downwards from the President, and by a constant succession of waves delivered upwards through the people." The fasts undertaken by the activists became the necessary means to maintaining momentum. "The pressure never ceased for a moment. It accumulated in power as ... this work went on."[12]

One way of characterizing this growing pressure (and it seems to be a common aspect of all nonviolent confrontations, from Moses to Jesus to Gandhi to King) is the dramatizing of the tension between an established power—with its self-proclaimed status as the maintainer of the common good—and another power that calls this status into question, making moves that might sober, demystify, or disenchant a public still in the other power's thrall. By dramatizing this tension as it grows, it becomes possible for more people to see that the reigning power's claims of justice, progress, good order, and consensus are not what they seem.

Abstract nouns such as *freedom* and *security* are defined—and undermined—by actions taken in their name. To take one recent example, the "State Peace and Development Council," the military regime that rules Myanmar (formerly Burma) can and does bring lethal force to its own citizens in the name of "peace and development." But the council began to be deprived of its advertising power when Buddhist monks excommunicated the council's leadership in the name of another, higher public order. Who owns the copyrights on public order and peace and development? Who represents civilization? Whose power is primarily defined by their willingness to use violence and lethal force against their own people?

The tension between people and governments is eventually played out on the field of rhetoric. The National Woman's Party could have quit their protests once President Wilson committed the country to a declaration of war that plunged the United States into World War I. The tension for the country, one could have easily argued, would become too much. What chance would a social revolution of women have against the cries of "Support the Troops!" and "My Country Right or Wrong!" But somehow, via commitment and conviction, the National Woman's Party continued its push for woman's suffrage and continued to outnarrate the White House publicity machine. In front of the White House, they ritually burned papers containing the president's lofty words in open demonstration of his devastatingly empty rhetoric concerning democracy for all.

When the government resorted to unlawful imprisonment of the women—viewed as legitimate by many wartime "patriots" —the movement showed the public what was being done under Wilson's supposed moral leadership. When Paul herself was arrested, she carried a banner inscribed with Wilson's own words that promised democracy, ostensibly for the whole of humankind, which she employed toward her vision for democracy at home: "THE TIME HAS COME TO CONQUER OR SUBMIT. FOR US THERE CAN BE BUT ONE CHOICE. WE HAVE MADE IT." She had this to say as she was carted off to prison: "I am being imprisoned not because I obstructed traffic but because I pointed out to President Wilson the fact that he is obstructing the progress of justice and democracy at home while Americans fight for it abroad."[13]

Deprived of certain inalienable rights within Occoquan Workhouse (including the right to *not* be segregated according to race), the women (a young Dorothy Day among them) escalated their resistance through hunger strikes and in some cases by refusing to be released. Their willingness to suffer drew public attention. They refused to let themselves be defined as criminals and maintained to the end their identity as prisoners of freedom. The violence enacted on them, which they were determined to endure, focused public anger on the country's justice system and its use of violence to prevent individuals from existing democratically in a democratic society. Such a fascist public image, especially in wartime, was a public relations disaster for the Wilson administration.

The specific abuse used on Alice Paul as the ringleader seems to have been pivotal in unsettling the nation's complacency. Force-fed during her hunger strike, confined to the psychopathic ward, and subjected to sleeplessness by shrieking mental patients and a nurse instructed to shine a light on her face once every hour, Paul was determined to be obedient to her vision of a better world even unto death. Her witness—little known in popular accounts of American history—is a powerful reminder of how one light can illuminate the dark discourse of a governing body and can force change.

Governments can and must be questioned. This is how democratic revival happens. President Wilson was forced to recommend that women be accorded the right to vote, although he pitched it as a necessary war measure that he supported. The work of questioning the words and imagery of the powerful goes on. Language is never owned. Such words as *freedom*, *evil*, *truth*, and *terror* often have to be wrestled back to recover more redemptive meanings.

There's a lesson here. Artisans of the possible have the means to unmask the unjust business of the power wielders. Leaders are making it up as they go along, manufacturing new realities to justify the death-dealing policies they've already put in place. As the Dalai Lama recently put it in response to a violent crackdown by the Chinese government, "Ultimately, the Chinese government is clinging to policy, not looking at the reality. They simply feel they have gun—so they can control. Obviously they can control. But they cannot control human mind."[14]

Artisans of the possible engage and rearrange, sometimes almost spoofing the reigning rhetoric of control. These artisans are guided by a wider sense of human history than governments seem capable of. They respond to the mechanisms of unredemption, which, in Jesus' words, literally know not what they do.[15] The person in the United States I often view as the patron saint of such artistry is Dorothy Day, a founder (with Peter Maurin) of the Catholic Worker Movement. Catholic priest and peace activist Daniel Berrigan recently described her witness this way:

> Dorothy Day taught me more than all the theologians. She awakened me to connections I had not thought of or been instructed in, the equation of human misery and poverty and warmaking. She had a basic hope that God created the world with enough for everyone, but there was not enough for everyone and warmaking.[16]

Like Dorothy Day's work, Berrigan's work as an activist and a poet is criticized for its ineffectiveness on the structural level. Homeless people get fed, draft files get burned, weapons of mass destruction get destroyed, and people get arrested, but what really changes? This is where the longer, more biblical view of history comes in. And Berrigan seems to be its most eloquent spokesperson:

> The good is to be done because it is good, not because it goes somewhere. I believe if it is done in that spirit it will go somewhere, but I don't know where. I don't think the Bible grants us to know where goodness goes, what direction, what force. I have never been seriously interested in the outcome. I was interested in trying to do it humanly and carefully and nonviolently and let it go.[17]

Do we have an ear to hear this evangelical word? Or are we so wedded to the cult of effectiveness and relevance that we think of Day and Berrigan only as "radicals"?

Creative Maladjustment

Such determined and radical mindfulness — robust, improvisational, and marked by an ever-renewed commitment to the well-being of others (even the aggressor)—is what I've come to associate with the vision of the "beloved community" most frequently identified with the civil rights movement. It is an alternative form of governance that calls into question the less worthy forms. It exposes the bad politics and bad religion involved in the habitual devaluing of human life that pervades our societal status quo. It challenges us to keep our God talk inescapably social. This is a version of people power, a body politics worth examining, practicing, and celebrating in all of its poetic and prophetic potential.

Even if we claim to be ready to follow the path of Jesus and we affirm that redeeming love is the only real means to revolution, I suspect it isn't appropriate to describe ourselves as nonviolent in advance of practice, as if a professed commitment to nonviolence guarantees that it will be so. It might be more appropriate to describe the hope in terms of a struggle—the struggle to respond redemptively to aggression and repentantly when we're made to see the ways that violence stems from ourselves. Like claims to Christianity, a commitment to nonviolence, when spoken of too presumptuously, can become largely theoretical and even self-defeating. One thinks of self-described pacifists who prove to be remarkably contemptuous, hateful even, of anyone who questions or disagrees with them. Might nonviolence, like Christianity, be more helpfully considered as a verdict instead of a tightly held, self-proclaimed boast?

Martin Luther King Jr. issued a call to creative and constructive maladjustment that might be helpful as a statement of intention and invitation: "I never intend to adjust myself to the tragic effects of the methods of physical violence and to tragic militarism. I call on you to be maladjusted to such things."[18] There will always be new, death-dealing norms at work in the global market and in "foreign affairs" concerning which we will do well to feel maladjusted, just as there will be new and unforeseen ways of performing and acting directly out of our evangelical refusal to be "well-adjusted" to them.

I'm also moved by the call to live in truth, to refuse cooperation with falsehoods (the anticreativity of violence), and the political possibilities of determined affirmation and imaginative magnanimity. In his characterization of his own democratic movement's nonviolent struggle with Slobodan Miloševiæ's regime, Srdja Popoviæ is especially apt: "Their language smelled like death. And we won because we loved life more."[19] By esteeming life, even the lives of those who wish us harm, with an unconventional intensity of affection, we resist evil without being overcome by evil methods. Or as the apostle Paul puts it, we "overcome evil with good."[20]

This love of life will have to exist seamlessly with an intense and determined awareness of present goings-on, and such awareness doesn't come naturally to me. It's a difficult and paradoxical task to try to seek out, for instance, the inconvenient truths of who bears the price of inexpensive food and my personal contributions to landfills. But when I exist in a state of historical deafness (deaf to what came before and deaf to the history happening all around me), it's as if I was literally born yesterday, and I find myself believing anything the powerful sellers and spinners of news need me to believe to sustain their interests. Against this possibility, I want to practice and contribute to the sustaining of a counterculture of lively awareness — counter to any ideology that would reduce human beings to "illegals," "enemy combatants," or mere "resources."

The work of education toward and within this awareness is never done. It's as if I require a fresh exorcism every day if I'm to consistently snap out of the unreal, almost surreal, aloofness that reigns over my culture, the very aloofness that legitimates the status quo by paying it no mind. I'm reminded of Howard Zinn's observation (made in his recollection of the Freedom Schools of 1964) that "education can, and should, be dangerous to the existing social structure."[21] Zinn, who was an adviser to the Student Nonviolent Coordinating Committee at the time, believes that Freedom Schools throughout Mississippi, often established by students, called into question the meaning of public education—its goals, its ends, and its understanding of a job well-done. Zinn believes the memory of that time still raises the questions. What forms of soul-numbing adjustment are we inculcating, through a variety of media, even now? What sorts of evil are we getting used to?

Socially Disruptive Newness

I've been haunted by this question of evil—and a collector of stories of resistance—ever since I went to a movie theater to watch *The Mission* by myself as a teenager. A Jesuit is strapped to a cross and sent over a waterfall in South America, and Jeremy Irons' Father Gabriel climbs back up, extending and embodying good news to the Guarini tribe that would eventually seek conversion to the way of life they'd so violently refused. Within this cultural interface, I was pummeled by one scene after another of Christlike witness. As I tried to recover from the devastating final images of the film, I was struck by the fact of a historical movement of radical patience. It was a discernible continuum, and I wanted to be a part of it. I wanted to try to be a practitioner of God's mercy as well as a recipient.

I'd read the Bible. I'd always been a churchgoer. I'd been baptized. But I don't think I'd ever been made so powerfully aware of the possibility that Christianity in some sense is a countercultural movement of nonviolence. If this was true, it was clearly objectionable subject matter. The Jesuits portrayed in the film weren't just loving their enemies theoretically or, in a depoliticized sense, spiritually; they were loving their enemies even as these enemies acted as enemies. In keeping with their conversion and against all practical sense, the Guarini embraced and received the murderer of their kin. This was something entirely new. "God is love," the Jesuit affirmed with a tremble in his voice, knowing that it put him on the wrong side of the firepower of The Powers That Be. This wasn't just a matter of holding some interesting private, personal religious opinions about what happens to people when they die; this was life *before* death. A different culture, a different politics altogether. An undermining of the status quo. I wanted to tell people about it, and I found I couldn't share my enthusiasm for the film without getting allied or associated with the path of nonviolent resistance ("Are you a *pacifist* or something?"). This could get messy.

In considering people like Martin Luther King Jr., Will Campbell, James Lawson, and the Jesuits of *The Mission*, I was confronted by individuals whose bottom-line reality differed radically from what had been presented to me as obvious, sensible, and logical in everyday discourse, including among Christians. I was being confronted by a different kind of conversation in which love alone is credible. I had to make room in my head and heart for what they were up to. I had to make room in my perception of myself, others, and the news of the day. This Christianity was revolutionary, and it functioned by its own logic, irrespective of what was routinely determined to be appropriate, seemly, or realistic. It didn't need my affirmation or anyone else's, but it was there in stories demanding it and awaiting my response each day.

This Christianity is alive to me whenever I walk around downtown Nashville and note that I'm frequently standing on the very spot where the lunch-counter sit-ins of 1960 occurred.

The events were popularly rendered in David Halberstam's *The Children*, and his account masterfully conveys the sense that the movement was birthed in a process of conversational discernment among like-minded African American students concerning which aspect of Nashville's segregated culture might be best suited for an orchestrated appeal to the city's conscience. There was constant discussion and an ongoing hashing-out of ideas about how to respond to new developments, how to preserve the momentum. Around that time, when King was asked if a mere boycott might better serve the public image of the movement, he insisted, as the Nashville contingent of the civil rights movement had long maintained, that it is sometimes appropriate to dramatize an injustice to deprive it publicly of its credibility, confronting it and thereby delegitimizing an otherwise all-too-accepted evil.

Dramatization is the way of nonviolent confrontation. It makes people see their evasions of conscience. King's colleague and leading strategist of the sit-ins, James Lawson, would later describe how the sit-ins eventually led a wide variety of Nashvillians to boycott downtown businesses still refusing service to blacks. When such operations are carried out well, Lawson observed, everyone and anyone can get involved.

This brings new meaning to Jesus' observation concerning the movement that is God's coming kingdom, namely, that whoever is not against it is somehow for it.[22] Those who witness such dramatizations locally, even if they hadn't given much thought to everyday injustices, will either be scandalized by it or moved, in however small a fashion, to align themselves with it. The pull of the event appears to become nonoptional, and the movement, like the biblical tradition it draws on, is somehow made available to all. It generates an invigorating, innovative hospitality toward anyone who is paying attention and a kind of democratic dignity to anyone with ears to hear and eyes to see.

When "the spiritual forces of wickedness," to employ Lawson's phrase,[23] are largely invisible to certain groups, it never occurs to them to disavow these forces. Even when an awareness does creep in, it seems to some that there's nowhere to go and no way out. In a locale where there once appeared to be no possibility of break-through, the sit-ins revealed a redeeming possibility. Suddenly, as word of what was happening began to spread, the masses found themselves invited and enlisted to begin to dislodge from their midst—and their hearts—one concrete manifestation of evil. And the culture that had funded this particular evil was reduced in power, paralyzed long enough to examine itself. Civil rights activist Bernard LaFayette Jr. said in the documentary *A Force More Power-ful*, "We had a philosophy, which was the power of nonviolence. . . . Our willingness to suffer outweighed anything they had."[24]

A society can be awakened by the power of nonviolence. Henry David Thoreau wrote, "If the injustice is part of the necessary friction of the machine of government, let it go, let it go: perchance it will wear smooth—certainly the machine will wear out. . . . Let your life be a counter-friction to stop the machine."[25]

I find it helpful and necessary to add that this counter-friction, if it's to be faithful to a Christian nonviolence, must make constant appeal to and acknowledgement of the opposition's worth. The one whose lifestyle serves as a counter-friction will sympathetically hold up a mirror to the wounded conscience of the violent culture. And as was the case in the Nashville sit-ins, the culture will be made to see that it is in danger of losing its soul. As Thoreau put it, "Is there not a sort of blood shed when the conscience is wounded? Through this wound a man's real manhood and immortality flow out, and he bleeds to an everlasting death. I see this blood flowing now."[26]

A deep-seated sympathy with and good-humored affection for the aggressor must have been present in one famous exchange between James Lawson and an angry young man as the two stood outside a Nashville restaurant as students were being arrested. When the young man spit in Lawson's face, Lawson regarded him calmly and asked for a handkerchief. The young man was so surprised, he handed the handkerchief to Lawson before he realized what he was doing. Lawson thanked him and wiped his face, then asked if he owned the nearby motorcycle. In no time, they were discussing horsepower.

The Nashville sit-ins rendered the status quo untenable and violence ineffectual. And in countless similar exchanges that came to be associated around the globe with the name of Martin Luther King Jr., activists would often manage to regard their violent opposition with a degree of mirth and affection. The aggressors, acting out of fear and anger, were shown love and respect in return. In the New Testament sense, an earthbound evangelism that showed love for the enemy was taking place. Scenes of enlivening justice were staged in cities like Nashville, Montgomery, Selma, and Little Rock. And justice, as Cornel West reminds us, is simply and deeply "what love looks like in public."[27]

Imagery of Infinite Possibility

In Richard Attenborough's film *Gandhi*, there's a scene drawn from an early encounter in Gandhi's career that gives a sense of how an openness to unforeseen possibilities is crucial in nonviolent protest. Gandhi is leading a procession of Indian mine workers in South Africa who are striking on behalf of their jailed comrades. It appears he is armed only with the principle of nonresistance his group has agreed on and whatever powers of improvisation might come to him when trouble starts. The man who presumably owns the mines approaches and tells them they've been warned and better move along, and Gandhi responds, "We have warned each other."

Gandhi had no plan of response—none save a willing determination to suffer violence without responding violently. When policemen mounted on horses appear with their batons in the air, Gandhi appears as frightened as the miners. Then from the back an unnamed miner shouts, "Lie down!" Gandhi adds his voice to the shouting, and the men get down on the ground. The horses, trained to do no harm, resist their riders' intentions. One horse even throws off a sergeant as he shouts, "For-*ward*!"

In the face of conflict, Gandhi maintained his principles of creative nonviolence and was always open to the unexpected. How does one live life perpetually open to unforeseen alternatives? How does one develop a knack for the unexpected response that defuses a situation? How does one get to the point where such responses come naturally? How do you become a person who will ask the man who spit in your face for a handkerchief?

James Lawson—who had the wits to ask for a handkerchief—has observed that we have to collect within our lives an imagery of infinite possibilities.[28] Governments and other forms of culture are redeemed through the work of those who can see infinite possibilities. Lawson insists that everything we have that is worthy of the name of civilization—all societal progress, all signs of redemption—are the fruit not of governments and their militaries but of the long, hard, and more enduring work of women and men throughout history who have refused to respond violently to violence. Artisans of the possible won't let those who hold power define for them the available means of response. Artisans of the possible conjure new means. Artisans of the possible sense that the means to redemption are, like the reign of God, without end.

What lies before us? Our options aren't limited to quiescence or aggression. Violence begets violence. As Gene Sharp put it, "Violence against violence is reinforcing."[29] But there remains the possibility of "political jiu-jitsu"[30] in which opposing forces can be made to partake in their own undoing—or better still, their own rehabilitation.

Bad governments await the tactical responses of the people. The ship of state can be turned around. Power is never monolithic or absolute. Power structures, like nation-states, lose power when we withdraw our consent and act on our alternative visions. We can defuse power with power. Gene Sharp again: "Political power can be viewed as fragile, always dependent for its strength and existence on a replenishment of its sources by the cooperation of a multitude of institutions and people—cooperation that may or may not continue."[31] As Leonard Cohen put it, democracy might even come to the USA.[32]

Literacy of Hopefulness

When I bring these observations to bear on the phenomenon of "public opinion"—opinion that is carefully engineered and entirely manufactured—I'm moved toward a sense of renewed vigilance and hopefulness. Each time our consent is marshaled toward state-sponsored atrocities, we must turn our attention to the testimony of activists, soldiers, displaced nationals and other refugees, and humanitarian organizations. We must listen to the artisans of the possible and allow ourselves to hear and to be called out. To action.

What do you do when you're living in and helping to sustain a nation-state that ignores the ethical imperatives of human rights? What do you do when you disagree with your own government? Are you forced to accept its legitimacy as absolute? Or do you withdraw your consent? What do these things entail?

These questions come to me self-administered. They are religious questions, and it might be a good idea to write them on a piece of paper to post on your refrigerator. Japanese culture scholar William R. LaFleur calls us to the work of prophetic and questioning discernment: "Our task should be that of exposing the specific metaphor, representation, or religious idea that causes or sanctions cruelty.... Wittgenstein showed that we cannot live without pictures. We can and must, however, constantly monitor our pictures to see what they are doing and neglecting to do."[33]

To undertake this task of sacred questioning is to live out a determined commitment to see clearly the systems of our age or, to put it in biblical terms, to struggle against the powers of this dark world.[34] It's a commitment to become aware of what's going on, consciously and unconsciously, and to deconstruct the unredeeming accounts and analogies that otherwise would leave us assuming that the impossible living conditions of the poor and the war-ravished are beyond the scope of our reasonable concern. The work of prophesying against these collective illusions is the liturgical duty of rearranging these power equations in such a way that justice and mercy might enter people's lives.

The artisans of the possible, the artisans of hope, ground their questions in a hopefulness they inherited from forebears who transcend the divisions of ethnicity, national borders, and religious traditions. Gandhi read Jesus through the eyes of Tolstoy. King and Lawson read Jesus through Gandhi and Howard Thurman's *Jesus and the Disinherited*. For many Americans of my generation and background, news of King and his Jesus came our way initially via the music of U2.

Such artisans understand that no government, sect, or network owns the copyright on freedom, dignity, or, that most questionable phrase, economic development. Such copyright claimers are the criminal element that refuses to view global resources as a public commons under God. They would prefer to privatize and personalize any higher divine law that might call their kleptocracies into question. Their language game has long required that we keep religion out if it. But this only serves to give politicians and financial moguls a pass when it comes to their own eminently faith-based decision making in waging war and arranging tax-funded bailouts for gambler-speculators on Wall Street. No one is held accountable when the unacknowledged religion of "free market" idolatry proves to have been an ill-informed guesswork. (Did the con men con themselves?) It is precisely the prophetic tradition (call it religious if you must) that unmasks the con, speaking truth to the breathtakingly corrupt with an eye on the deeper economy of a kingdom to come, that sense of economy that is with us even now, enlivening our social transactions, if we have the wit to discern it.

Our call is to be people whose pro-human actions break the silence and break through barriers. We learn to ask good questions as we mimic the redeeming questions of those who have come before us. We learn to cultivate better hopes, better imaginings, a larger sense of general welfare. We join a literacy of hopeful resistance that refuses to be co-opted by any nationalistic ideology, marketing scheme, or outmoded economic policy that gets carried out—lest we forget—in our name, with our funding, through our negligence.

We are called to align ourselves with the creative force of the redeeming God who is on the side of what Ziggy Marley calls the one-word prayer, "justice."[35] This is the prayer for a way out when there seems to be no way. Martin Luther King Jr. issued this very summons:

> When our days become dreary with low-hovering clouds of despair, and when our nights become darker than a thousand midnights, let us remember that there is a creative force in this universe, working to pull down the gigantic mountains of evil, a power that is able to make a way out of no way and transform

dark yesterdays into bright tomorrows. Let us realize the arc of
the moral universe is long but it bends toward justice.[36]

This arc that King discerns within the cosmos is at the core of
what it might mean to be evangelical — an announcer in word
and deed of good news for all of creation and verified in the
resurrection.

Lest resurrection be misunderstood as primarily involving a
disembodied other-world bliss that leaves this-world dysfunction
behind, unaddressed and unredeemed, like a crumpled plastic
water bottle to be inherited and worried over by future generations, Rowan Williams offers this more robust evangelical account of resurrection practice: "The resurrection is a moment in
which human beings are reintroduced to each other across the
gulf of mutual resentment and blame; a new human community
becomes possible."[37]

This vision of human community won't be contained by the
borders of ethnicity, citizenship, or economic class that governments reinforce under our direction. Artisans of hopefulness,
mostly anonymous and unremembered, have long lived and loved
and extended hospitality beyond the legal fictions of so-called
sovereigns and nation-states. Prophets and poets have announced
a wider economy of human meaning than power mongers can
afford by questioning the dark yesterdays of official histories in
the name of brighter tomorrows. Jesus insisted that this wider
economy is coming and is already among us, ever ancient, ever
new. When we sense its movement, we allow ourselves to be
moved by it. The question of caretaking begins to inform our
doing and speaking and spending. We take care differently and
gird ourselves with a mindfulness and begin to outnarrate the
murderous and plundering powers that know not what they do.
Such determined mindfulness has a way of changing everything.
Resurrection happens.

· · ● ● ● · ·

Questions for Further Conversation

1. What's the problem with employing a phrase like "infinite justice" to sell a war? Is it idolatry? Why or why not?

2. How is the work of government liturgical? What conflicts come to mind when you consider the practice of worship as a nonoptional, 24/7 activity?

3. In what way was the career of Alice Paul a resurrection practice? What examples come to mind when you think of today's scene? Who would you deem an artisan of the possible?

4. What does Daniel Berrigan mean when he notes that doing good, biblically speaking, won't yield an easily discerned forecast? Who are some examples of people who did the good they discerned as faithful without knowing what good would come of it?

5. Some feel compelled to be creatively maladjusted to certain policies and standard operating procedures perpetuated by governments and economic systems. Do you include yourself in that group, and how might you make your maladjustment known?

6. When you consider the phrase "socially disruptive newness," what examples come to mind, past or present? How does this connect with keeping in mind an imagery of infinite possibilities? What could you change in your daily routine to access this imagery more frequently?

10

Sincerity as Far as the Eye Can See

Questioning the Future

There are known knowns. There are things we know
that we know. There are known unknowns. That is to say,
there are things that we now know we don't know.
But there are also unknown unknowns.
There are things we don't know we don't know.
Donald Rumsfeld, press conference at NATO headquarters,
Brussels, Belgium, June 6, 2002

We witness the advent of the number. It comes along
with democracy, the large city, administrations, cybernetics.
It is a flexible and continuous mass, woven tight like a fabric
with neither rips nor darned patches, a multitude of quantified
heroes who lose names and faces as they become
the ciphered river of the streets, a mobile language
of computations and rationalities that belong to no one.
Michel de Certeau, *The Practice of Everyday Life*

I probably spend too much time thinking about Cormac McCarthy.
As I see it, the man gives the alarm. He's one of my artisans. His is
the cosmic plainspeak. McCarthy is doing the business.

Consider *No Country for Old Men*. Here is Uncle Ellis, the wise

Yoda figure, and Sheriff Ed Tom Bell stops by for a visit. Sheriff Bell is at a crossroads on his pilgrimage (I'd say there are no nonpilgrimages in McCarthy's worlds), and he's trying to weigh some things out. Obligation. God. Duty. Early retirement. Grace. Justice. Warring on terror.

The memory of Sheriff Bell's father and his own crime-fighting career is in the air. Was fire ever successfully fought with fire? Will the sheriff be true to his father's memory if he decides not to live or die by the sword any longer, to retire from trying to war on terror? What does wisdom require?

The two men speak occasionally out of the silence of what they know the other is thinking. Uncle Ellis suspects that we speak vaingloriously whenever we open our mouths, that false witness is inevitable so it is probably wiser not to speak at all. But Uncle Ellis decides to venture a word: "You can be patriotic and still believe that some things cost more than what they're worth. Ask them Gold Star mothers what they paid and what they got for it. You always pay too much. Particularly for promises. There ain't no such thing as a bargain promise."[1]

Bargain promises. "There ain't no such thing." McCarthy's characters live in the realm of ancient lore, Greek tragedy, and existential quandary, a realm the reader comes to understand we've been in all along. There are costs, covenants, testaments, and keepsakes, as there have always been. Our world of "great bargains," "low prices," "satisfaction guaranteed" was always a false world, as deluded and fantastic as a national security strategy that solemnly decrees that it is the responsibility of the United States to undertake to "rid the world of evil."[2] In the Bible, in Shakespeare, in board meetings and press conferences, our vows and vouchers outrun our powers of avowal, our ability to control events.

Even if we mean to somehow disavow the hope that the world can be redeemed through violence, as Sheriff Ed Tom Bell does, we're still left with our religiosity and what we feel compelled to do in the hope of living meaningfully, and our religiosity has nowhere to happen but here. Our pilgrimages, journeys, and jihads are under way. They are what we're doing even when we don't think we're doing it.

The fact of human interface that exceeds our ability to compartmentalize our appearances to one another with words such as *class*, *religion*, *economics*, and *ethnicity* is especially evident in the Paul Haggis film of explosive intimacy, *Crash*. The questions of who we are and how we might redemptively orient ourselves haunt every moment of the film. One scene features an Arab American store owner who, with his daughter's reluctant help as a translator, is trying to purchase a firearm for the purpose of fending off armed robbers. The two argue back and forth in Arabic over his decision while they're supposed to be deciding which free box of bullets to accept. The store owner, a veteran of the Vietnam war, unable to follow the exchange, becomes increasingly perturbed over all they might be saying. Finally he says, "Yo, Osama! Plan a jihad on your own time. What do you want?"

But even a casual examination of the word reminds us that jihad doesn't work that way. Never has and never will. Like any struggle to live a life after God, jihad is alive and signaling in all we say and do. In a certain sense, we're never not doing jihad. Like any religious practice, it is inescapably social. It knows no neat separations. It won't ever be private because it can only be played out in the public square that is our sweet, old, messed-up, God-loved world.

No Country for Old Men, like all of McCarthy's novels, generates recognition of such scenes. It's nothing personal. It's just religion. It's what's going on. It might be redeemed, reformed, or reevaluated, but there's no getting around it.

God Speaks

As fine as *No Country* is, *The Road* stands as McCarthy's finest novel. It's the story of a man and his son pushing and sometimes carrying an old grocery cart toward the ocean across a devastated countryside bereft of vegetation and peopled, we begin to understand, by humans exactly like us, but who have resorted to eating each other. It is not easy reading, but it is profoundly good.

As we consider *The Road* I'd like to view it in light of a passage from Charles Marsh, whose work on the connection between religious faith and social justice in the civil rights era and in the present day is remarkably incisive:

> If only holiness were measured by the volume of our incessant chatter, we would be universally praised as the most holy nation on earth. But in our fretful, theatrical piety, we have come to mistake noisiness for holiness, and we have presumed to know, with a clarity and certitude that not even the angels dared claim, the divine will for the world. We have organized our needs with the confidence that God is on our side, now and always, whether we feed the poor or corral them into ghettos.
>
> To a nation filled with intense religious fervor, the Hebrew prophet Amos said: You are not the holy people you imagine yourselves to be. Though the land is filled with festivals and assemblies, with songs and melodies, and with so much pious talk, these are not sounds and sights that are pleasing to the Lord. "Take away from me the noise of your congregations," Amos says, "you who have turned justice into poison."[3]

In McCarthy's *The Road*, an unnamed father and his son travel in a world largely destroyed by activities that once passed, we assume, as "economic development" and by the horrors unleashed under the brand of homeland security. The father and son seek out sustenance and study what little they can see in the ashen daylight congealing over the landscape. Of the father, McCarthy writes, "He knew only that the child was his warrant. He said: If he is not the word of God God never spoke."[4]

There was a time when I would have regarded this line as horribly sacrilegious. Now I treasure it as profoundly biblical. God speech divorced from love for human life is the speech of Nobodaddy, the false god who authorizes and underwrites environmental devastation, antipersonnel weapons, and cutthroat economies. The word of the living God is never less than an ethical summons, a call to *take care*, to gather up and strengthen the life that remains, to reorder, redeem, and remember.

William Blake calls on us to discern the human body, any human body, as "the human form divine."[5] The worth of every human life is beyond our powers of measurement. The boy in *The Road*, simply because he is a boy, constitutes hope for the world, a hope *for* a world, a sustainable legacy of moral coherence, and in this sense a bearer of divine value. As the father strokes his blonde, tangled hair, he thinks to himself, "Golden chalice, good to house a god."[6] The treasuring of the child and the elevation of his fragile form escalate as the story progresses, particularly when the father and son encounter an elderly man, an accidental soothsayer, who has somehow survived even though he appears too weak to conquer and devour anyone. The old man tells the father, "There is no God and we are his prophets."[7] As if in response to this enigmatic statement, the father later regards his son and asks the man, "What if I said that he's a god?"[8]

With this question, the possibility of bearing life by being true to life remains alive and signaling, a religiosity of care, of lived reverence, that is our only home and our only hope. The father had drawn from this thread previously when he observed, "On this road there are no godspoke men. They are gone and I am left and they have taken with them the world."[9]

I hope to God that the term "godspoke men" enters our popular discourse. I believe the father's words have a double meaning. In a fashion that resonates with Charles Marsh's vision, it was the godspoke men whose gut feelings amounted to a "God speaks to me" and who forfeited goodwill and stewardship and destroyed the world. Did we expect such bad faith from some other quarter? Who is quicker toward anger and violence than the proudly religious? It is the unacknowledged covetousness and power-mad presumption of the all-too-religious that has "made of the world a lie every word."[10]

But in another sense entirely, there were other people, differently religious, those who carried the possibility of poetry in their hearts and minds. These "godspoke men" who bear redeeming human witness in an ancient "You are your brother's keeper" sense of the divine appear, in the world of *The Road*, to be gone. And they took the world of hope, the possibility of coherence, with them. The culture that deeply valued human life has gone. And yet, there's the child, his warrant. God's word if God still has one.

Consider the scene in which the father has built a fire and, despite the cold, bathed his son in the open air in an attempt to cleanse him of the physical evidence of a gross and violent scene:

> The boy sat tottering. The man watched him that he not topple into the flames. He kicked holes in the sand for the boy's hips and shoulders where he would sleep and he sat holding him while he tousled his hair before the fire to dry it. All of this is like some ancient anointing. So be it. Evoke the forms. Where you've nothing else construct ceremonies out of the air and breathe upon them.[11]

Evoke the forms. Order life. Breathe upon the hieroglyphs that they might glow again and bear witness. "You have to carry the fire.... It's inside you," he tells his son. "It was always there. I can see it.... You have my whole heart.... You have to practice.... Goodness will find the little boy. It always has. It will again."[12]

The Road is grim and shocking in the sobriety of its earthbound hopefulness. If religion is that fiery delusion that neglects the responsibility to see things as they are, the novel is antireligious. But if religion is justice—justice that begins with responsibility—the book may be the most deeply religious novel of our time. Are we looking for bargains or promises? Do we want our satisfaction guaranteed? Did we think redemption would be easy?

Jacques Derrida asserted that "religion is responsibility or it is nothing at all."[13] This challenges me. Like *The Road*, this sentiment invites me to place my center of gravity somewhere other than in a hope for my private salvation. It begins to liberate my imagination from the egotistical and draws me toward the fragile and precious world we're in—the world I believe God so loves.

All Things Go

The Road is often characterized as an apocalyptic novel, a novel of destruction and hopelessness. But I employ the word *apocalyptic* differently. I understand *apocalypse* to refer to revelation—to an unmasking and unveiling. The apocalyptic genre challenges the way things are, the regimes we're wrongly settling for, and the death-dealing and reductionistic economies of meaning. John's Apocalypse in the book of Revelation subverts and interrogates the imposed disorder of Rome's imperial pretensions—and all such power-mad pretensions in the name of a new world on the way. In this sense, apocalyptic expression issues a challenge to the all-too-overwhelming present in the name of a more hopeful, though perhaps dimly perceived, life-giving future. It kicks us alive. With this meaning in mind, I affirm *The Road* and so much else as apocalyptic. That includes whatever manages to dislocate my imagination in a more redemptive direction. It's the stuff of country songs, cartoons, paintings, plays, and folk expression. This world, the way it's being run right now, can't stand for long. A change is going to come. It has to come. We need apocalypse now.

With the coming apocalypse in mind, let's move on to the word *eschatology*. To put it simply, eschatology is whatever we have in mind when we think of The End. The eschaton is the end of everything. Eschatology names not only our vision of the future, our worldview concerning what's ultimately important, but also the ends that justify our means in the meantime. It's where all of our hopes and fears are invested. One's eschatology is whatever one thinks is coming. It's what is at work in our acts of jihad. The term *eschatology* names the notions that make our worlds go round. Every advertisement that seeks to lay hold of our minds, be it for car insurance, a political campaign, hummus, or a hybrid, is appealing to our eschatological sense, our feeling of what's coming. Competing eschatologies vie for our votes, our investments, and our consumer confidence. Our economic policies are our eschatologies.

Our eschatologies comprise our accounts of the ultimate end, of where history is headed, of what will become of us as individuals. They reveal what we suppose or insist to be the shape of things to come, be it survival of the fittest, the meek inheriting the earth, winners taking all, God's kingdom come, united we stand, the healing of nations, or every man for himself.

Everybody has an eschatological sense. Your eschatology is what you're waiting for and where you're headed or think you're headed. It cuts to the heart of your politics, your religion, your sense of what matters.

One eschatology at work is the nihilistic assertion that the judgments of history and future generations need not give us pause because we won't be around to see them. When the journalist Bob Woodward asked President George W. Bush the question, "How is history likely to judge your Iraq war?" his response was telling: "History, we won't know. We'll all be dead."[14] In P. T. Anderson's *There Will Be Blood*, Daniel Plainview, played by Daniel Day-Lewis in the film, serves as a powerful caricature of this eschatology. Winning is his only verifiable value. "I have a competition in me," he observes. Pitched on the terrain of our international discourse, the film's witness is horrifically relevant. Plainview is a man of wealth and, in the most limited sense, taste, but he will lay his soul and everything that dares touch it to waste. In time, he heeds only his own sense of unbridled competition, reducing the whole of creation, including the life of his adopted son, to the raw material for more competition. He can't speak of his workers or his customers as "people" without noting the strange sound of the word on his lips and laughing. "I want to earn enough money [so] I can get away from everyone," he confides to an associate. By the film's conclusion, the shell of the human he has become has made a lie of every relationship he ever had. He has perverted his own memory and won't abide the presence of anyone who questions it.

The vision of a beloved community articulated by James Lawson and Martin Luther King Jr., the assertion that humanity is made for something more than unbridled competition, brings word of a different eschatology. While the brutality of a mercantile world is with us always, there's also the counterrevolution of God's kingdom that insists that redemption is under way, that the renewal we pray for will be visible and made known in the land of the living.[15] This striving toward community, civil rights leader

John Lewis asserts, "is as inexorable, as irresistible, as the flow of a river toward the sea."[16]

Our eschatologies drive what we do. They underwrite our practices. If we hold certain ideas as fundamental, nonnegotiable, ultimate, and never to be denied or questioned, then we're fundamentalists, and our eschatology reveals the content of our fundamentalism. Are we up for rethinking our sense of the ultimate? Could we do with some revision?

To Be Evangelical

Eschatology is the big ideas we don't like anyone to question. It is the space where meaningful witness transpires. In this sense, eschatology is also the site of conversion. If a belief has long had a strong hold on our hearts and minds and we find ourselves imagining the future differently, our hold on that belief is beginning to loosen. Our eschatology is changing.

I mean to assert, in word and deed, an eschatology born of faith in the perpetually redemptive posture — a posture that is never not redeeming — of the God of Abraham, Isaac, Jacob, and Jesus. It is an eschatology of earthbound hospitality and hope grounded in a determined and practiced faithfulness to a God whose affection for all of life is without limit, a God whose own faithfulness is primarily discerned in the lived witness of people having a go at living lovingly and justly.

This vision of the future, this eschatology, differs radically from the Uncle Ben God who intends to destroy the world and put most people in hell forever, an eschatology that I pray will become increasingly less convincing in the world of my children and my children's children, an eschatology most reprehensible in its neglect of creation, complexity, and the beautiful human beings who, in Larry Norman's phrase, "have been left behind."[17]

"Like all other knowledge, eschatology is always determined by its concerns, while at the same time it also determines those concerns."[18] So says Jürgen Moltmann, reminding us that eschatology will often be the why of what we do, even as our doing will inform our eschatology. For instance, if we believe ourselves to be a remnant whose confessed doctrine separates and distinguishes us from unbelievers whose lack of such doctrine will consign them to eternal torment, our Christian practice will be tightly wrapped within this eschatology.

A church marquee states, "Son-block Prevents Burning!" According to this eschatology, Jesus functions simply as a get-out-of-hell-free card, as the one who performed his function by coming and dying so that we won't have hell to pay. Such devastatingly low regard for the meaning of Jesus can play into our understanding of The End. This eschatology is what largely passes for Christianity in much of popular discourse, with a God ready to destroy creation and consign most of humanity to endless torture.

Believers in this version of coming events await this nightmarish scenario they're, perhaps reluctantly, sure must be stated in the Bible somewhere. They think they'll have to learn to like it if they're going to have a shot at being saved. Even if they don't want it all to end this way, God's will isn't to be questioned.

What can we do? How do we counteract witness to the nonredeeming Uncle Ben God who holds all human life in contempt and is determined to destroy it with everlasting fire? How do we retain and perform a witness that holds all creation as sacred and human life as incalculably valuable? Where might we locate a good news eschatology, an evangelical eschatology?

I mean to reposition that hot-button term *evangelical* as the "good news" that questions all versions of the future, with an insistence on prioritizing conditions that sustain human life. All those ways of ordering the world that crumble under such interrogation, whether they brand themselves conservative, democratic, religious, or civilized, aren't teaching the "good news." They aren't in any discernible way "evangelical."

To give further sense to this repositioning, I now turn to the strange, inspiring, paradoxically popular, intentionally evangelical work of U2, that band of lively troubadours who reside among the artisans of the possible.

We Are the World

Like many of my friends, I find it hard not to turn on the television when I hear that U2 is scheduled to make an appearance. We go way back—all the way back to my days as a fifteen-year-old Tennessean, when they got me thinking hard about Martin Luther King Jr., compelled me to look up *apartheid* in the dictionary, and drove me to wonder over the weirdness of Elvis of Tupelo; and they were probably the first band I found myself getting defensive about. For better or worse, I can't account for my understanding of the world or my reading of the Bible without acknowledging the impressions U2 made on me over the years. They're an -ism over which I remain (forgive me) uncynical. A few years ago, the latest U2 epiphany felt just about guaranteed when I heard Bono would appear on Fox's *The O'Reilly Factor*.[19] How on earth was this going to play out?

I worried a little for my hero. Would Bono's testimony hold up for the cameras? So much of what I hold dear was at stake because Bono is having a go at the gospel. He appears to believe that Jesus' good news proclamation—ever ancient, ever new, and ever cosmic—is actually about a better way of treating people, all kinds of people. He doesn't see it sequestered away from whatever we call politics, religion, or economics because Jesus' good news proclamation changes everything, disrupting the seemingly settled and overturning the sense we call common. Will the content of Bono's news translate into Fox's best-selling news product? How does one keep the good word alive amid the flood of words and images in the marketplace? Is an evangelical eschatology transmittable? How will Bono fare with O'Reilly?

As it happens, not bad. "I'm a non-partisan guy," Bono begins. "I've stopped rooting. I'm rooting for people that don't have a vote and for people whose faces we don't see." And when O'Reilly observes that Bruce Springsteen, a close friend of Bono's, is campaigning for John Kerry, Bono holds fast: "I'm not going to do that. I love Bruce Springsteen, but I'm not going to do that. I put all that behind me when I went to work for the world's poorest and most vulnerable."

Bono won't allow himself to be positioned or the word of his testimony to be characterized as yet another instance of liberal spin. His good news word, his *euangelion*, is too big to be cut down to any manageable size. In the meantime, O'Reilly is the service provider for what inquiring minds think they want to know. His job description is to unmask partisan passions and unearth the angle of his guests. And so O'Reilly brings up the oft-repeated mantra that insists Europeans hate America and asks if Bono, who is from Ireland, really believes America is a great country. Bono replies, "I'm like an annoying fan. I'm like the one that reads the liner notes on the CD. I'm the one that—I read the Declaration of Independence before a speaking tour we did on AIDS in the Midwest. I've read the Constitution. I've read these poetic tracts.... The United States that I love is like the Statue of Liberty with its arms open, give me your tired, your poor and huddled masses. It's not the continent behaving like an island."

Unbelievably good television. Bono draws on America's past to question its sense of the future. He won't even let his concerns on Africa be reduced to what O'Reilly calls "a cause." "It's an emergency," Bono says. "How can three of these a week, three Madison Square Gardens [the setting for the interview with O'Reilly] a week, how can—you know, a giant stadium every two weeks disappearing, you know, a preventable, treatable disease like AIDS, how can that not be an emergency?... It's not on the news. It's not on the agenda here. It's the greatest health crisis in 600 years, but it's not on the news."

Bono was offering a very different version of what's newsworthy. He was offering a broader sense of homeland that includes the rest of the non-American world seated in the hot spot of highest viewer ratings. The man was bearing witness to the sacred integrity of every human life. Bono flipped the script by suggesting that the real story might not be evil versus good, but death versus resurrection.

Bono speaks as someone who is trying—and by his own account mostly failing—to take the Jesus business seriously. He speaks as an evangelist. He's haunted by the crisis of grace that leaves no room for pride or self-satisfied talk in the face of other people's trials and tribulations. Bono invites everyone to think hard about the tragic state of affairs whereby wealthy nations maintain a stranglehold on the livelihoods of generations of Africans. He says their resources are locked into the payment of interest on Cold War debts while their companies are locked out of access to global markets. If we aren't moved toward a big rethink, Bono leads us to wonder what we mean when we describe ourselves as God-fearing. Who or what are we praying to when our concept of God is divorced from these matters? What do we have in mind when we speak of a strong economy, success, victory, hope? Do we assume that the graciousness of God means we can benefit from the oppression of other people without being responsible for it?

Bono is very good on the "we" as he invites us and himself to live a life of worshipful acknowledgment of a God who desires mercy and not sacrifice. We get to carry each other. We get to discover all the ways in which what we thought was freedom and liberation was mostly just greed. If we aren't interested in such discoveries and asking the hard questions that precede them, we aren't fixing our eyes on the hope set before us in the life of Jesus, and we aren't really, in any way, evangelical.

Bono calls our practices and his own into question in the name of God's promised future. While our economies often presume that life is a zero sum game in which history's winners control resources and decide the future, Bono proclaims that the Lord will not honor the boundaries of our economic models. He calls on anyone who will listen to renounce the artificial equilibriums of unjust orderings and to be guided by the spirit of this Lord who loves and cherishes the poor and vulnerable in all the ways the world doesn't, the spirit of the Lord who anoints people like Isaiah and Jesus and anyone properly described as evangelical to bring good news to the poor. God is with us, Bono asserts, if we are with them. How long, the evangelist always asks, until the brokenhearted are mended, captives are released, the blind receive sight, and the oppressed go free?[20]

Is my enthusiasm for Bono's activism out of control? Probably. But for all the unseemliness of a wealthy pop star presuming to preach on economic policy, I'd like to assert that our divisions, once again, won't hold water. The folk tradition knows no boundaries. Redemption songs (all we've ever had) are personal, political, and poetic. They're offered in the hope of extending the possibility of authenticity or, as Linus once said of a pumpkin patch, sincerity as far as the eye can see. Bono even stands firmly in the punk tradition. I have in mind the words of Joe Strummer of the Clash: "Punk rock means exemplary manners to your fellow human beings."[21] Could one be more verifiably evangelical than that?

Peer Pressure Is Forever

To my mind, Bono's plainspeak (in word and song) reminds us that God's economy differs radically from ours. The gospel punctures our presumption that our economies are successful and winning insofar as they increase financial profits, if only for a moment. Whenever such puncturings occur—via cartoons, music, film, or literature—it's always good news, because it drives us to ask if anyone anywhere really profits from this piratelike seizure of the world, not only in the future, but even now. Instead, we are called to cultivate a culture that sustains life rather than plundering it.

Those who aspire to be artisans of the possible, genuine evangelicals, will concern themselves with funding and sustaining human projects. But as we saw in the previous chapter, these redeeming subcultures have nowhere else to happen but within a commodifying and largely commodified world that perverts the human form in every imaginable way. This is the world we're in—a culture of militant self-interest devoted to the unexamined, unending acquisition of material wealth.

Beyond whatever laws our elected officials cobble together to legitimate this ethically problematic eschatology, even a casual consideration of the biblical witness serves to remind us that, from the evangelical perspective of God's economy, which presides above and in spite of the pretensions of nations, such unchecked aggression against creation and the human life it sustains is best characterized as the work of organized crime, even when wrapped in flags and ceremony. What does the Lord require of our doing and buying and trading? Do justice, love mercy, walk humbly, the prophet Micah insists.[22] But this evangelical witness will face constant challenges when the laws of our land are primarily committed to what the Slovenian philosopher Slavoj Zizek calls state-sponsored "unabashed economic egotism."[23] This phrase names widespread policies generated out of the escalating, damaging narcissism of a small percentage of the global population. Our mythologies of economic "progress" are often composed of statistics and equations ostensibly "reality based" but tragically divorced from the common good, from the health and livelihood of most human beings. Are we willing to have our concept of the good questioned by those who dwell outside of our economic models? Would we be willing to adjust our standards of living to better accommodate the raising of theirs? What do we mean by globalism?

These questions bring to mind the one-dimensional eschatology of fake redemption, which Canadian journalist Naomi Klein refers to as "disaster capitalism," a fundamentalist form of capitalism that commits to "the elimination of the public sphere, total liberation for corporations, and skeletal social spending" and creates a system that is ultimately "not liberal, conservative, or capitalist, but corporatist."[24] To the extent that we leave this system unengaged and uninterrogated, it sets up global green zones (think gated communities) and vandalizes our physical and psychic landscapes in the name of economic "development." With a perverted vision of success and profit, this ideology of cutthroat marketeering condemns much of the world to the status of red zone, that realm consigned to what Bono refers to as "stupid poverty,"[25] often barricaded away from sight, still awaiting the promised benefits of globalization, the free trade that has yet to yield trade justice.

When we broaden this eschatology to include the less edifying aspects of American foreign policies, we begin to see the picture anthropologist Talal Asad sketches when he refers to "a project of universal redemption" that informs the mostly unstated conviction "that some humans have to be treated violently [and millions left behind] in order that humanity can be redeemed." Having articulated this principle, Asad traces how it breeds the very violence it proposes to protect "freedom-loving" people against. Suicide bombings and other forms of terrorism often mirror Western violence. In this sense, they are inextricably connected to "a modern Western tradition of armed conflict for the defense of a free political community: To save the nation (or to found a state) in confronting a dangerous enemy, it may be necessary to act without being bound by ordinary moral constraints."[26]

Might we do well to bring our sacred questions to the unavowed world religion at work in what passes for global capitalism with all its calls to worship and all the human sacrifices it deems somehow necessary? In the daily high-powered news blitz, functionaries declare missions accomplished in press conferences *now*, only to write books *later* about how strange it felt to not tell the truth *then*. Where is the hungering and thirsting after righteousness, justice, and what's true? What would it mean for the news to be faithful to the bright light of the good news—the *euangelion*—of the biblical witness now and then? What are we waiting for?

Against the eschatology that seeks to gain security for the homeland even if it means the forfeiting of all redeeming soul, I believe there's an emerging eschatology, ever ancient, ever new, and evangelical in the right sense of the word. This eschatology is more concerned with sharing the resources that are God's than squandering them. Viewing the earth as a public commons isn't a novel idea; it's more like a restoration of sanity. It isn't a question of charity but rather of ordering our bad economies in the direction of justice, of a sustainable future. John Howard Yoder spells it out:

We are not called to make the bread of the world available to the hungry; we are called to restore the true awareness that it always was theirs. We are not called to topple the tyrants, so that it might become true that the proud fall and the haughty are destroyed. It already is true; we are called only to let that truth govern our own choice of whether to be, in our turn, tyrants claiming to be benefactors.[27]

Those who deny this truth, even as they hold sway in our own heads, are ever with us. But we can press back. We can let a different world break through in the way we talk and act and conduct ourselves. If the kingdom of God is that space where none of us are protected from the joys and demands of sociality, maybe it's also the place where none of us feel like we have to. Perhaps in an eschatological sense, it's the only space there is. The geography (or cosmography) of the future.

Sight of My Own Blood

Ursula K. Le Guin, in a strange and very short story called "The Ones Who Walk Away from Omelas," speaks to our eschatologies. Omelas, or place of happiness, we come to understand, is a sovereign state where everybody knows your name, every citizen is well fed and satisfied, and a profound care and artistry inform all architecture, all work, and all leisure. Well-being, depth of feeling, and even hilarity are in every corner of this global green zone in which people know what life's about and a sense of dignity infuses every moment of existence from the womb to the tomb. No secret police, no guilt, no advertisements, no weapons. Just cultivation, development, and beautifully well-balanced abundance.

There's always a "but." And this "but" involves a sight every citizen of Omelas is made to see when he or she comes of age.

It's an initiation rite reserved for that stage of development when people are ready to be realistic, capable of understanding certain necessities and ready to receive an explanation concerning the cost of their freedom.

Somewhere underneath the grandeur of Omelas, a child is kept in a dark, windowless room with a locked door and almost no light. People come to see the child, but no one is allowed to communicate or interrupt the child's fear and suffering, born of neglect and malnutrition. Each day the child is allowed a half bowl of cornmeal and a replenished water jug, placed within reach as the door closes. The child's resigned silence is sometimes broken with promises of good behavior upon release—a release the people of Omelas grimly understand must never be allowed to occur.

> Some of them understand why, and some do not, but they all understand that their happiness, the beauty of their city, the tenderness of their friendships, the health of their children, the wisdom of their scholars, the skill of their makers, even the abundance of their harvest and the kindly weather of the skies, depend wholly on this child's abominable misery.... There is nothing they can do.... These are the terms ... this [is the] terrible paradox.[28]

In her narration, Le Guin makes clear that the people of Omelas understand how terribly unjust and bitter this is, but they understand too that freedom is messy. They would have to accept the loss of their lifestyle to allow the child full access to health and nurture. But the child, they reason, is too far gone, too accustomed to its suffering squalor, to ever be fully blessed and incorporated into the public benefits of Omelas. Decorum requires that this fact be faced but only stated among those brave few with the stomach to handle the truth. In the scales of history, the price of one never-to-be-redeemed soul for the needs of the many is worth it.

But there's always another "but." It is said that there are those who refuse the equation placed before them by the elders of Omelas. Some adolescents reach the initiatory rite of seeing the child—facing the facts—only to disavow this state of affairs and walk away from all they've ever known. Others, after years of consenting to it, experience a moment of clarity and make the same exit.

> They keep walking, and walk straight out of the city of Om-
> elas, through the beautiful gates. They keep walking across
> the farmlands of Omelas. Each one goes alone ... out into the
> darkness of the fields ... ahead into the darkness, and they do
> not come back. The place they go toward is a place even less
> imaginable to most of us than the city of happiness. I cannot
> describe it at all. It is possible that it does not exist. But they
> seem to know where they are going, the ones who walk away
> from Omelas.[29]

Le Guin's story enriches the notion of a called-out people, whether we recall the Abrahamic call out of the land of Ur, Siddhartha Gautama's exodus from the pleasure palaces, Muhammad's retreat from Mecca to Medina, or the Greek term *ekklēsia*, "the called out," which the English New Testament translates as "church." I hope to be affiliated with those who walk away or disengage from death-dealing economies. But I don't want to claim affiliation in a manner that would blind me to my own complicity in that which destroys life. Even as we walk away from our Omelas, we wear the city's fine clothes and comfortable shoes.

Le Guin reminds me that the regime change I pray for when I pray the Lord's Prayer is an economy, a kingdom, that could never be private. It never excludes and never stops redeeming. Or as the ancients put it, the kingdom is the creative work of a God whose center is everywhere and whose circumference is nowhere. The boundaries we erect and the prison walls we defensively construct won't hold.

Against the Omelasian economies of our own day—in which we refuse to recognize the sight of our own blood in the lives of those we call "collateral damage," the masses on the strangled end of "global trade," and the people who die because they were born in the wrong place—the Lord's Prayer posits an evangelical economics that is good news, first of all, for the least of these. This prayer Jesus teaches us to pray and the kingdom it extols have conjured—and continue to conjure—heretofore unimagined civilizing possibilities among people and the ways they order themselves, expanding the sphere of peace in the direction of justice, of a hospitality without frontiers.

We might note that Salem, the backward variation of Omelas, is a name the prophets have for Jerusalem, and that Salem itself is derived from shalom, the real peace that troubles our imaginations, especially when the peace we talk about is a sham. While I don't believe in compulsory prayer, I confess I'd like to make Le Guin's tale compulsory reading for people in high school classrooms, people overseeing international monetary funds, and people who shape governmental policies. Actually, I want everyone to read it.

John Berger, the British literary expatriate turned French farmer, offers an excellent word on the generative power of stories, which, like prayers, call us out of the consensual fictions that constitute our unjust economies: "A story refers life to an alternative and more final judge who is far away. Maybe the judge is located in the future, or in the past that is still attentive, or maybe somewhere over the hill, where the day's luck has changed ... so that the last have become first."[30]

Here Comes Everybody

The sacred questioning I've championed in this book always returns us to what we might call the human interest story, the story that, from the media's marketing viewpoint, draws everyone in with its sense of common humanity. I'd like to use the term to question how it is we can so easily deny the interests of real humans when we think they might somehow challenge or call into question the way we conduct our lives.

What status will we accord all human beings? What are our controlling interests? Do we still find other humans interesting, or do we regard them with a cold eye for "use value"? Do we genuinely believe they're all endowed by God with certain inalienable rights? Does what William Blake called "the human form divine" still appear within our stretched attention spans?

The call to be humanly interested in one another continues. Regarding the saying "I'll do anything humanly possible," poet Adrienne Rich suggests that it might imply a summons to ethical vigilance: "What's 'humanly possible' might be what we bring to the refusal to let our humanity be stolen from us."[31]

I associate ethical vigilance with the Hebrew word *halakha*, which refers to *the way* of life to which Jewish traditions bear witness. It's *halakha* that forms and sustains a set of beliefs or a creed. It is the way that is faithful, and the just shall live by it. Paradoxically, the way that is founded on faith is also the way that constitutes faith itself. It makes a way, as Martin Luther King Jr. might put it, when there is no way. Like love, it always redeems and reconstitutes by remembering and RE-membering human life.

In view of the demands of *halakha*, the remembering way, and the hope of human interest, we don't have to wait for what passes for economics (The Economy, they call it) to mature before we look to deepen our awareness (what Bill McKibben calls the Deep

Economy) by asking if what we call "growth" takes into adequate account the human misery index of the rest of the world and future generations left to survive amid the devastation wrought by our so-called economic success. No profit (religious or economic) will be gained in the long term by impoverishing the world in which we reside, the world that sustains us despite whatever language we use to boundary it all up, commodifying our otherwise common wealth, the world entrusted to us to be received and cultivated lovingly.

In the interest of engaging the neuroses and the bad religion that keep us resentful and resistant to the suggestion that the only thing to do with a common wealth is to share it, I have what I take to be an evangelically winning anecdote. My story occurred at a family reunion.

I once had an aged relative who wouldn't suffer anyone he took to be a fool, and his least favorite ship of fools was crewed by his family. With persuasion, he managed to appear at the gathering. But as soon as he could, he made his way into a spare room and took a very long nap. He came. He saw. He slept. And got away with it. At least no one could say he hadn't shown up.

After his nap, his sister spotted him and said, "Where have you been?"

"I was asleep," he replied with the ease of a wit who knew he need fear no attempt at reprimand. But he wasn't done with her. "And you know what?"

"What?"

"One of these days I'm just gonna keep on sleeping."

The macabre note of this remark might require some explanation. This relative was extremely well versed in the biblical witness and all manner of religious controversy. Both were intertwined within this family's culture in such a way that conversation in this direction was highly unpleasant (hence the bad energy of reunions). "*I* won't have to deal with *you*, and *you* won't have to deal with *me*," he seemed to say in a Daniel Plainview way. "Anyone care to dispute it?" He'd thrown down the gauntlet, and, as his sister excused herself, I decided to pick it up.

"And you know what you're gonna find when you wake up?"

"What?"

"More people."

And he laughed until he coughed. He knew I was taking a shot at his meanness by way of an appeal to a coming redemption, a more long-term reunion than this business with families, we might say. And it won't play to our tastes. It's a larger hospitality than most of us feel we can afford most of the time. It's the common decency that is the only eternal life worth talking about. If hell is other people, as Jean-Paul Sartre observed, it is probably also the case, as C. S. Lewis's *The Great Divorce* proposed, that heaven is too.[32] We'd better get used to it. There's no getting away from each other, God help us. And if we aren't up for finding one another interesting and valuable now (relatives, coworkers, enemies, immigrants), why do we suppose we'll want the human community then? Relationships are what we've got, the currency, we might say, of the kingdom that is here and coming. Were we hoping to get away from everyone?

I suspect there's something a little demonic in finding others boring or unworthy of our interest. Something profoundly antithetical to the life to come that Jesus describes, something resistant to the hospitality to come, the good graces on which we've all along depended. Contrary to many Bible-wielding motivational speakers and popular end-times novels, we do not know the details of how the eschaton will sort out. But the messy fact of other people, near and far, reminds us that all grace is social. Bringing it back down to people (not disembodied souls, after all) will keep the good news seriously imaginable, seriously having to do with what we do with people — how we do by them — now. The good news of God's economy is inescapably social. Ready or not.

In a strange book called *Finnegan's Wake*, James Joyce gives us a male protagonist, an Everyman, whose flawed but often magnanimous soul is his only hope. He is called HCE, which stands for many things: his proper name, Humphrey Chimpden Earwicker; Howth Castle and Environs; and Haveth Childers Everywhere. But the one I like the most is a phrase sometimes referred to as James Joyce's definition of a genuinely catholic church, one that serves as a sign of all manner of things being made well and all manner of souls being hospitably received. Joyce explains it as a nickname afforded by the people who knew HCE well:

> It was equally certainly a pleasant turn of the populace which gave him a sense of those normative letters the nickname *Here Comes Everybody*. An imposing everybody he always indeed looked, constantly the same as and equal to himself and magnificently well worthy of any and all such universalisation ... from good start to happy finish the truly catholic assemblage gathered together.[33]

Here comes everybody. What do we have in mind when we pray for a kingdom coming? A melting pot or a global green zone or a gated community or a refugee camp? Do we want our wills and our economies to be transformed by the God who will redeem the entire cosmos? Have we drawn certain lines in the sand that won't survive this regime change? Do we think we know who's in and who's out? Who is with us and who is against us? Do we imagine that the infinite hospitality of God will be contained in what Samir Selmanovic calls "God-management systems"?[34] And how will grace and mercy operate?

The visions we live by, whether asserted in song, made plain in poetry, or longed for in prayer, often conjure up more questions than answers. On good days, the questions are an occasion for joy and mirth, not fear or dread, and we ask them of each other the way our children ask, with the avid look of someone getting ready for a good story. We ask the questions with a sense of renewed attentiveness and a hope for renewed invigoration in trying to be agents of redemption, good rememberers, and witnesses to the promise that all that is and was—and is even now damaged by our perversity—will be healed and made whole.

Like the recitation to one another of lyrics and scriptures and special phrases, the questions we put to ourselves and to each other are a means to trusting yet again in what we believe we've experienced and discerned of the steadfast love of God. We rehearse these matters in the hope that we might dwell, as the psalmist put it, in the house of God forever.[35] The space of God's dwelling isn't primarily a matter of what happens when we die but a way of naming the space we're in—a space where goodness, mercy, and hope spring eternal even now, a space that has to be believed to be seen. We discern ourselves and others within this space by way of consciousness raising, a cultivation of joy and wonder that often bursts forth only when we're alive enough to one another to ask questions within that sacred space of paying attention.

The questions make new worlds possible. Like well-told jokes, they let the air in. We get to put questions to each other and to the world we too often settle for. Questions make a way where we often fear there is no way in our families, our neighborhoods, and in our complicated relationships with people around the world affected by our consumption, our selling, and our voting. There are better ways of being in the world that await us by way of the questions we have yet to ask. It is by questions that we are born again and again.

· · ● ● ● · ·

Questions for Further Conversation

1. What difficulties face us when we attempt to perform pilgrimages, jihads, or acts of "spiritual development" on our own time or apart from other people? Why doesn't it work?

2. In a consideration of Amos's language, how might "the noise of congregations" be related to practices that "turn justice into poison"? How do certain forms of religion threaten living conditions? What do we make of "godspoke men"?

3. Do you believe religion, rightly understood, is a responsibility? Why or why not?

4. Describe your own eschatology. How does it differ from what you take to be the eschatology of other people you know?

5. What are Bono's evangelical commitments? Do they differ from yours? If so, how?

6. What tensions would you identify between the prerogatives of God's economy and the establishment of global green zones? How might they be maintained more evangelically?

7. What issues arise when you consider "The Ones Who Walk Away from Omelas"? Do you find the story helpful?

8. What quandaries (amusing or not so amusing) come to mind when you eschatologically consider the phrase "Here comes everybody"?

9. In your experience, has a question ever signaled a new world or a new way of thinking about the world? Tell the story.

End Note
That Means to Signal
a World without End

A friend passed away recently, a friend whose way of being in the world presented a challenge to everyone who knew him. His name was Harmon Wray. As a friend of prisoners, an advocate for prison reform, and an activist against the death penalty, his vision of cosmic redemption moved beyond the boundaries of many a comfort zone. He understood as much, and there was no note of piety or smug self-righteousness when he would remark, as if he was pulling over to help someone change a tire, "I don't believe God gives up on anyone, and neither should we."

At his memorial service, in story after story, Harmon's determined friendship and hospitality to those often considered beyond the pale were recounted. Richard Goode, a mutual friend, spoke of Harmon's commitment to the possibilities of restorative justice and his work at the Riverbend Maximum Security Prison in Tennessee. Since 2003, Harmon led a project whereby faculty from various Nashville schools conducted classes comprised of both local students and inmates. As Richard described it, Harmon's career was a commitment to "the socially exiled and disinherited." And as he shared what Harmon's friends from Riverbend had to say about him, the shape of his life began to fit almost seamlessly within a vision of God's promised future, what Miroslav Volf has called "the final social reconciliation."[1] Because Harmon viewed the coming kingdom as something of an already/not-yet-done deal, he often remarked to the inmates that they were his church.

The week before Harmon's death, Dean Shoemaker, a Riverbend inmate, told Richard that after he arrived there, he was told by his cellmate that he would do well to become acquainted with Harmon at the first available opportunity. While Shoemaker hadn't been especially interested in furthering his education, he attended Harmon's class anyway and ended up engaging him in a one-on-one conversation. As Harmon asked him questions, Shoemaker made mention of the fact that both of his parents had died and casually noted that from here on out there was no one left who loved him.

Without hesitation, Harmon said, "Well, I love you."

And for the first time since he'd been incarcerated, Dean Shoemaker broke down in tears.

Exchanges like these not only characterize Harmon's life but also, as it was recalled during the service, serve as a call to the practice of witnessing. We are to enact and facilitate such redeeming occasions, to remain alive to them. An opening occurs, and within it, the faithful will locate themselves. The love of God is made manifest in these moments or, we might say, not at all. The call awaits our response.

In some sense, the service questioned, as Harmon often did, the audience's sense of decorum. Harmon held everything up to a kind of redemptive and redeeming skepticism. But his seeming irreverence had everything to do with his determination to value people, all people, the way he believed God valued them. When it came to *due* reverence, Jesus was his model. He was even skeptical of his own sense of reverence, lest it mistake itself for practice. He wouldn't credit much. It all remained tentative. To Harmon, whatever endeavors he was up to would remain open to question, even when they seemed to be successful. Because the good, in order to remain good, would always involve more questions.

The Rev. Ken Carder spoke in a bemused fashion about the tension involved in taking seriously, as a witness, a person like Harmon. He spoke of the present world and the coming world and the fact that the world to come is forever impinging on this one. Carder noted that we've all made compromises with this present world. He said that, when it comes to the compromises he's made with this world, nobody reminded him of them more than Harmon did.

He noted the difficulties Harmon had in finding funding for his work in restorative justice and how his lack of certain credentials added to the difficulties. He emphasized that these issues were not Harmon's fault but were merely further instances of the resistance Harmon met when he tried, as a faithful witness, to bring God's world into this one. When Carder said that the world Harmon sought to represent will prevail, the applause was deafening.

I dedicate this book to Harmon's memory in the hope that this work will somehow be in continuity with Harmon's practice. Harmon was compelled by the notion of living life on earth as it is in heaven—a good news revolution that informed Harmon's speech, his thinking, his visions, and his love for others.

Notes

Chapter 1: Never What You Have in Mind

[1] Blaise Pascal (1623–1662) famously weighed out the pros and cons of believing in a God who may or may not exist. Given the consequences of *not* believing in a God who *does* exist (perhaps with an Uncle Ben-ordained future in mind), Pascal observed that we might be best off believing in God even if we are proved to be wrong. I mean to challenge the idea that God is upset, one way or another, over not being believed in (as if giving intellectual assent to God is somehow worthy of divine commendation). Ultimately, I believe Pascal issues the same challenge.

[2] Gerard Hughes speaks of "an identikit picture of God," which formed in his mind during his conversations with university students in his years as a chaplain. It became the story of "good old Uncle George." I don't know why I came to remember it as Uncle Ben, but I insist that I intend no disrespect to Peter Parker's Uncle Ben, who remains so worthy of imitation and so sound in his advice concerning the great responsibility that comes with having great power. "Good old Uncle George" can be found in the first chapter of Hughes's book *Oh God, Why? A Spiritual Journey towards Meaning, Wisdom, and Strength* (Abingdon, Oxfordshire, UK: Bible Reading Fellowship, 2000), *www.gerard whughes.com/oh_god_why_chapter1.htm*. (Accessed August 21, 2008.)

[3] Proverbs 6:16–17.

[4] 1 Corinthians 13:12 KJV.

[5] William Blake put the matter even more provocatively by asserting that Jesus died an unbeliever. I feel a rather strong sense of love for William Blake.

[6] 1 John 4:20.

Chapter 2: The Unbearable Lightness of Being Brainwashed

[1] Matthew 9:17; 16:24–25.

[2] Romans 6:6–7; 7:6; Galatians 2:20.

[3] Romans 12:2.

[4] Flannery O'Connor, *The Habit of Being* (New York: Farrar, Straus, and Giroux, 1979), 478.

[5] Bob Dylan, *Chronicles: Volume I* (New York: Simon & Schuster, 2004), 217.

[6] You will see this genre-transcending term of affirmation again. After trying to convince myself for a few weeks that I made it up, I Googled my way toward the humbling awareness that it first entered my mind via a description of (you guessed it) Dylan's flowing conversational prose. Thank you, Jon Dolan (see his "New Scorsese Documentary Only a Pawn in Dylan's Game," *Village Voice*, September 27, 2005, *www.villagevoice.com/screens/0539,dvd1,68557,28.html*). (Accessed August 21, 2008.)

[7] Matthew 7:20.

[8] A close examination of what we're doing is the only way any of us can know what our religion (think about it) is.

[9] Salman Rushdie, *The Satanic Verses* (New York: Picador, 1988), 100.

[10] C. S. Lewis, *An Experiment in Criticism* (Cambridge: Cambridge Univ. Press, 1961), 19.

Chapter 3: Everybody to the Limit

[1] It's all "speculative presentism" (Gibson's tongue-in-cheek phrase) now.

[2] William Gibson, *Spook Country* (New York: G. P. Putnam's Sons, 2007), 237.

[3] McLuhan (1911–1980) was the Roman Catholic media critic who dropped the famous assertion that the medium *is* the message. As I return to his work again and again, I find it difficult to overestimate his powers of observation.

[4] Gibson, *Spook Country*, 237.

[5] Have a look at ReligionFacts.com, *www.religionfacts.com/jesus/image_gallery/200_alexamanos_graffito.htm*. (Accessed August 21, 2008.)

[6] The phrase emerges from the head of homicide detective Meyer Landsman in an extremely funny and altogether moving tale of Jews, Tlingit, and political conspiracies in the Alaskan Panhandle. Landsman "feels weary of ganefs and prophets, guns and sacrifices, and the infinite gangster weight of God. He's tired of hearing about the promised land, and the inevitable bloodshed required for its redemption" (Michael Chabon, *The Yiddish Policemen's Union* [New York: HarperCollins, 2007], 368).

[7] Merold Westphal, *God, Guilt, and Death* (Bloomington: Indiana Univ. Press, 1987), 12.

[8] Thomas Merton, in a letter to James Forest (William H. Shannon, ed., *The Hidden Ground of Love: The Letters of Thomas Merton on Religious Experience and Social Concerns* [San Diego: Harcourt Brace Jovanovich, 1993], 294).

[9] Shannon Hale, *The Goose Girl* (New York: Bloomsbury, 2003), 165.

[10] Jim Ridley, "The Terrible Infant Speaks: Harmony Korine Talks about His New Movie *Mister Lonely* and Growing Up in Nashville, Then and Now," *Nashville Scene,* May 8, 2008, *www.nashvillescene.com/2008-05-08/news/the-terrible-infant-speaks/.* (Accessed August 21, 2008.)

[11] W. H. Auden, "Purely Subjective," in *The Complete Works of W. H. Auden: Prose: Volume 2,* ed. Edward Mendelson (Princeton, N.J.: Princeton Univ. Press, 2002), 184–97.

[12] W. H. Auden, "Address on Henry James," in *Complete Works of W. H. Auden,* 302.

Chapter 4: Spot the Pervert

[1] Leonard Cohen, in his song titled "Democracy" (1992).

[2] James Joyce, *Finnegan's Wake* (New York: Viking, 1958), 273.

[3] Philip Rieff, *Charisma: The Gift of Grace and How It Has Been Taken Away from Us* (New York: Pantheon, 2007), 38.

[4] Placed alongside Shakespeare's investigative visions, the products of formalized "Arts and Sciences" often appear to be nothing more than footnotes. T. S. Eliot once observed that all each generation of readers and theatergoers can hope for is to be a little less wrong than the last generation concerning the deep wisdom Shakespeare is showing us.

[5] Or if you aren't up to the memorization, try the same activity with the Lord's Prayer.

[6] *Star Trek,* "Amok Time," airdate September 15, 1967; stardate 3372.7.

[7] Matthew 10:39.

[8] Romans 7:19.

[9] I added this wonderful word, *transmogrification,* to my word bank thanks to a *Calvin and Hobbes* cartoon strip. God bless Bill Watterson.

[10] U2, "Fast Cars," lyrics by Bono and the Edge (2005).

[11] Elias Canetti, *The Human Province* (London: Picador, 1986), 115–16. Canetti also said that one becomes a better person by reading Kafka but *minus* a sense of pride over the fact. If one reads the good stuff *really* well, one can hardly become a snob about it. Snobbery and deep wisdom don't generally coexist.

[12] Hugh Kenner, *The Pound Era* (Berkeley: Univ. of California Press, 1971), 53.

[13] I recently cajoled an otherwise keen student who dared to speak dismissively of libraries in my presence. It occurred to me to suggest that stepping inside

a library is like receiving a magical walkaround tour of an especially well-furnished iPod. She saw my point and conceded.

[14] Jon Pareles, "A Head for Figures," *The Scotsman*, December 22, 2007, *news .scotsman.com/features/A-head-for-figures.3615062.jp.* (Accessed August 21, 2008.)

[15] I'm never sure what people mean by "popular culture," but if it's *people's* culture, I'll happily apply it to my own concerns and enthusiasms. It's what *people* are *cult*ivating. What else is there?

[16] Josh Modell, "Interviews: Win Butler," March 14, 2007, *www.avclub.com/ content/interview/win_butler_of_arcade_fire.* (Accessed August 21, 2008.)

[17] Ibid.

[18] Daniel Berrigan, *Night Flight: War Diary with 11 Poems* (New York: Macmillan, 1968), 136.

[19] Win Butler has expressed an admiration for John Kennedy Toole's *A Confederacy of Dunces* and its predecessor, *Neon Bible*, but his appropriation of the title, he noted, is not a reference to anything within the novel.

[20] William Blake, "The Everlasting Gospel," in *William Blake: Selected Poetry*, ed. Michael Mason (New York: Oxford Univ. Press, 1996), 263.

[21] Greg Kot, "Band of the Year: An Interview with Arcade Fire," *www.popmatters .com/pm/features/article/31307/band-of-the-year-an-interview-with-the-arcade-fire/.* (Accessed August 21, 2008.)

[22] Rowan Williams, *Christ on Trial: How the Gospel Unsettles Our Judgment* (Grand Rapids: Eerdmans, 2003), 29.

[23] Ursula K. Le Guin, *Four Ways to Forgiveness* (New York: HarperPrism, 1995), 1.

Chapter 5: The Power of the Put-On

[1] Ron Suskind, "Without a Doubt," *The New York Times*, October 17, 2004, *www.ronsuskind.com/articles/000106.html.* (Accessed August 21, 2008.)

[2] William Blake, "Songs of Experience: London," in *William Blake: Selected Poetry*, ed. Michael Mason (New York: Oxford Univ. Press, 1996), 124.

[3] Paul Simon and Art Garfunkel, "The Boxer" (1969).

[4] Bill Moyers, "Bill Moyers Interviews Jon Stewart," July 11, 2003, *www.pbs .org/now/transcript/transcript_stewart.html.* (Accessed August 21, 2008.)

[5] Charlie Rose, "An Interview with David Letterman," February 16, 1996, *www.charlierose.com/shows/1996/02/16/1/an-interview-with-david-letterman*; *www.geocities.com/davidletterman82/CharlieRose1996Interview.html.* (Accessed August 21, 2008.)

[6] Edward R. Murrow, *In Search of Light: The Broadcasts of Edward R. Murrow 1938–1961*, ed. Edward Bliss Jr. (New York: Knopf, 1967), 354.

[7] Ibid., 363.

[8] Ibid., 364.

[9] Bob Dylan, *Chronicles: Volume One* (New York: Simon & Schuster, 2004), 95.

[10] Ezra Pound, *ABC of Reading* (New York: New Directions, 1960), 29.

[11] Lawrence Ferlinghetti, *Poetry as Insurgent Art* (New York: New Directions, 2007), 4.

[12] Cid Corman, "Poetry Is," *Lilliput Review*, no. 103 (April 1999).

[13] Herman Melville, *The Confidence-Man* (New York: Penguin, 1990), 14.

[14] G. K. Chesterton, *Orthodoxy* (Vancouver, B.C.: Regent College Publishing, 2004), 56.

[15] Paul Klee, *The Inward Vision* (New York: Abrams, 1959).

[16] I would add that the community that formed around the life and teachings of Jesus believed themselves to be in continuity (as Jesus did) with Moses and the prophets.

[17] Flannery O'Connor, "A Good Man Is Hard to Find," in *Flannery O'Connor: The Complete Stories* (New York: Farrar, Straus, and Giroux, 1971), 132.

[18] Ibid.

[19] Denise Levertov, "Some Affinities of Content," in *New and Selected Essays* (New York: New Directions, 1992), 4.

[20] Pete Seeger, in his description of how he got his version of "The Water Is Wide," *www.livingmusic.com/catalogue/albums/pete/tracks/waterwide.html*. (Accessed August 21, 2008).

[21] Johnny Cash, *Cash: The Autobiography* (New York: HarperCollins, 1997), 263.

Chapter 6: The Word, the Line, the Way

[1] It can also be done with numbers.

[2] Northrop Frye, *Words with Power: Being a Second Study of "The Bible and Literature"* (San Diego: Harvest, 1990), 285.

[3] Allen Ginsberg, *Spontaneous Mind: Selected Interviews, 1958–1996* (New York: HarperCollins, 2001), 92.

[4] Numbers 11:24–30.

[5] *Malcolm X*, DVD. Directed by Spike Lee, Warner Home Video, 1992.

[6] According to the Russian thinker Mikhail Bakhtin, it's Dostoevsky who perhaps captured this madness especially well (years ahead of Freud, I might

add) via *Notes from Underground* and all that followed. Certain smart-sounding people call the flow of self-conscious and unself-conscious meaning making *discourse*. Bakhtin puts it nicely: "One's own discourse is gradually and slowly wrought out of others' words that have been acknowledged and assimilated, and the boundaries between the two are at first scarcely perceptible" (*The Dialogic Imagination: Four Essays*, ed. Michael Holquist [Austin: Univ. of Texas Press, 1981], 345 n. 31). Watching your language is the strange and difficult work of keeping an eye on your own discourse, a work that is never done.

[7] I confess I gave up on the series when it became all too clear that there would be no cameo appearance by a dark-haired, troubled teenager from Gotham City named Bruce.

[8] Jacques Derrida, *Writing and Difference* (Chicago: Univ. of Chicago Press, 1978), 74.

[9] W. H. Auden, "In Memory of W. B. Yeats," in *Another Time* (New York: Random House, 1940).

[10] Amanda Petrusich, "Interview: Tom Waits," November 27, 2006, *www.pitchforkmedia.com/article/feature/39683-interview-tom-waits*. (Accessed August 21, 2008.)

[11] Ibid.

[12] 1 Corinthians 13:12 KJV.

[13] Matthew 5:37.

[14] Walter Brueggemann, *Theology of the Old Testament* (Minneapolis: Fortress, 2005), 206.

[15] Eugene Peterson, *The Jesus Way: A Conversation on the Ways That Jesus Is the Way* (Grand Rapids: Eerdmans, 2007), 25.

[16] Ibid.

[17] Ibid.

[18] Thomas Pynchon, *Mason & Dixon* (New York: Holt, 1997), 350.

[19] Czeslaw Milosz, *The Captive Mind* (New York: Vintage, 1990), 250.

[20] John Caputo, *The Weakness of God: A Theology of the Event* (Bloomington: Indiana Univ. Press, 2006), 31.

[21] Milosz, *Captive Mind*, 237.

[22] N. T. Wright, *Jesus and the Victory of God* (Minneapolis: Fortress, 1996), 176.

[23] Laura Miller, "Far from Narnia: Philip Pullman's Secular Fantasy for Children," *New Yorker*, December 26, 2005, *www.newyorker.com/archive/2005/12/26/051226fa_fact*. (Accessed August 21, 2008.)

Chapter 7: Survival of the Freshest

[1] "Let us pray to God that we may be free of 'God' " (*Meister Eckhart: The Essential Sermons, Commentaries, Treatises and Defense*, ed. Edmund Colledge and Bernard McGinn [New York: Paulist, 1981], 2000).

[2] Philippians 1:6.

[3] I suspect this is what Jacques Derrida has in mind when he makes the provocative and paradoxical observation that, in a certain sense, *only an atheist can have faith* in God. "When I pray," Derrida once noted, "I am thinking about negative theology, about the unnamable, the possibility that I might be totally deceived by my belief and so on" (*Derrida and Religion: Other Testaments*, ed. Yvonne Sherwood and Kevin Hart [New York: Routledge, 2005], 30). I have William Franke to thank for this word and for his rich and redemptively subtle reading of Derrida. A close reading of Franke's two-volume *On What Cannot Be Said: Apophatic Discourses in Religion, Literature and the Arts* (Notre Dame, Ind.: Univ. of Notre Dame Press, 2007) will profoundly benefit all parties in this immense conversation.

[4] Friedrich Nietzsche, *Beyond Good and Evil: Prelude to a Philosophy of the Future* (New York: Oxford Univ. Press, 1998), 22–23. As an avid student of the Bible, Nietzsche was particularly sensitive to the ways bad interpretation can be mistaken for or mindlessly championed as the word of God.

[5] I've read a decent amount of Nietzsche, but I owe my own awareness of this little dictum to the frequency with which it is referenced by the Italian philosopher Gianni Vattimo. I owe my introduction to Vattimo to the amazing cultural critic, musician, and blogger extraordinaire Barry Taylor.

[6] Ernst Becker, *The Denial of Death* (New York: Free Press, 1973), 23.

[7] *The Gospel According to America: A Meditation on a God-blessed, Christ-haunted Idea* (Louisville: Westminster John Knox, 2005).

[8] I draw or appropriate or thieve the phrase from Northrop Frye. It's a recurring theme in his work, but one especially accessible address is "All Things Made Anew," in *Reading the World: Selected Writings, 1935–1976*, ed. Robert D. Denham (New York: Peter Lang, 1991), 254–56.

[9] Micah 4:3; Isaiah 2:4; Joel 3:10.

[10] I invite the reader to compare these passages to Jesus' complaint of forsakenness in the course of his execution (Matthew 27:46) and the paradox Blake and Chesterton name as central to the popular symbol of Christian tradition, the cross. The literary critic Terry Eagleton has observed that the meaning of human history, in the Christian sense, is to be widely broadcast in the image of a wrongly executed political criminal. Do we have eyes to see?

[11] Tori Amos, "God" (1994).

[12] See Amos 5:21–24; Micah 6:6–8; Hosea 6:6; Matthew 9:13.

[13] Matthew 5:21–22, 27–28, 31–32, 33–34, 38–39, 43–44.

[14] Matthew 15:6–7.

[15] I was made to pay heed to this question and to talk about it the way I do by way of a favorite song-and-dance man, harmonica virtuoso, and very good friend, Buddy Greene.

[16] I owe this winning phrase to Fred Clark, the slacktivist (*slacktivist.typepad .com*). His thoroughgoing, critically engaging, weekly response to the biblical exegetical and literary malpractice of the *Left Behind* series is a tour de force that makes the blogosphere feel like a sign of the coming kingdom. One midrash leads to another in his ever-redeeming tangents. Salute.

[17] Arthur Kurzweil and Pamela Roth, "Leonard Cohen: Stranger Music: Selected Poems and Songs," *The Jewish Book News Interview*, October 31, 1994, *www.webheights.net/speakingcohen/jewish.htm*. (Accessed August 21, 2008.)

[18] James Joyce, *Ulysses* (New York: Vintage, 1961), 186–87.

[19] Repentance is the older way of putting it. A willingness to change our minds or to hold to our interpretations lightly is, as I understand Jewish and Christian traditions, a likely prerequisite to being saved.

[20] Luke 4:21.

[21] Quoted in Walter Brueggemann, *Theology of the Old Testament* (Minneapolis: Fortress, 2005), 403 n. 6.

[22] Julia Kristeva, *Black Sun: Depression and Melancholia* (New York: Columbia Univ. Press, 1989), 189.

[23] Will Campbell, *The Glad River* (Macon, Ga.: Smyth & Helwys, 2005), 76–77.

[24] Steve Stockman, "Bono's Faith: Challenged or Challenging," *Rhythms of Redemption*, *www.stocki.ni.org/u2/faith.phtml*. (Accessed August 21, 2008.)

[25] Jon Stewart, "Interview with Jim Wallis," *The Daily Show*, January 18, 2005, *home.san.rr.com/schroederfamily/JonStewartJimWallisInterview.html*; *www.thedaily show.com/video/index.jhtml?videoId=117748&title=jim-wallis*. (Accessed August 21, 2008.)

[26] Moses Mendelssohn, *Jerusalem: Or On Religious Power and Judaism* (Waltham, Mass.: Brandeis Univ. Press, 1983), 102.

[27] Baruch Spinoza, *Theological-Political Treatise*, 2d ed. (Indianapolis: Hackett, 2001), 161.

Chapter 8: The Past Didn't Go Anywhere

[1] Pierre Bourdieu, *Distinction: A Social Critique of the Judgment of Taste* (Cambridge, Mass.: Harvard Univ. Press, 1984), 31.

[2] William Gibson, *Spook Country* (New York: G. P. Putnam's Sons, 2007), 254.

[3] David L. Edwards, *Christianity: The First Two Thousand Years* (London: Cassell, 1997), 2.

[4] It might also be worth asking if it isn't often the case that many Jews, Buddhists, Muslims, and atheists take Jesus' way of being human more seriously than self-professed Christians who pride themselves on having received Jesus into their hearts as, as the saying goes, their "personal savior." I believe this saying has long been a false witness to the cosmic scope of Jesus' good news.

[5] Quoted in his performance at the Ryman Auditorium in Nashville on June 20, 2008.

[6] John Howard Yoder, "The Burden and the Discipline of Evangelical Revisionism," in *Nonviolent America: History through the Eyes of Peace*, eds. Louise Hawkley and James C. Juhnke (Newton, Kans.: Mennonite Press, 1993), 22.

[7] William James, "The Art of Fiction," *Longman's Magazine*, September 1884.

[8] John Howard Yoder, *The Priestly Kingdom: Social Ethics as Gospel* (Notre Dame, Ind.: Notre Dame Press, 1984), 62.

[9] Gustavo Gutierrez, *A Theology of Liberation* (Maryknoll, N.Y.: Orbis, 1973), 205.

[10] Philip K. Dick, "How to Build a Universe That Doesn't Fall Apart Two Days Later," in *I Hope I Shall Arrive Soon*, eds. Mark Hurst and Paul Williams (Garden City, N.J.: Doubleday, 1985), 4; *deoxy.org/pkd_how2build.htm*.

[11] Will Campbell, *Brother to a Dragonfly* (New York: Seabury, 1977), 225–26.

[12] John Howard Yoder, "The Paradigmatic Role of God's People," in *For the Nations: Essays Public and Evangelical* (Grand Rapids: Eerdmans, 1997), 35.

[13] Julian of Norwich, *Revelations of Divine Love* (New York: Penguin, 1999), the thirteenth revelation, chapter 27.

[14] Walter Benjamin, "Theses on the Philosophy of History," *Selected Writings, Volume 1: 1913–1926*, eds. Marcus Bullock and Michael W. Jennings (Cambridge, Mass.: Belknap Press, 1996), 256.

[15] Jack Kerouac, *Visions of Cody* (New York: McGraw Hill, 1972), 103.

[16] Steve Enniss and Jacki Lyden, "Flannery O'Connor's Private Life Revealed in Letters," NPR's *All Things Considered*, May 12, 2007, *www.npr.org/templates/story/story.php?storyId=10154699.* (Accessed August 21, 2008.)

[17] Erazim Kohak, *Jan Patočka: Philosophy and Selected Writings* (Chicago: Univ. of Chicago Press, 1989), 5.

Chapter 9: We Do What We're Told

[1] "Infinite Justice, Out—Enduring Freedom, In," BBC News, September 25, 2001, *news.bbc.co.uk/2/hi/americas/1563722.stm.* (Accessed August 21, 2008.)

[2] Townsend Davis, *Weary Feet, Rested Souls: A Guided History of the Civil Rights Movement* (New York: Norton, 1998), 152.

[3] Jim Wallis, *God's Politics: Why the Right Gets It Wrong and the Left Doesn't Get It* (San Francisco: HarperSanFrancisco, 2005), 241.

[4] I draw the phrase from Adrienne Rich's *Arts of the Possible: Essays and Conversations* (New York: Norton, 2001).

[5] Wendell Berry, "Manifesto: The Mad Farmer Liberation Front," in *The Country of Marriage* (New York: Harcourt, Brace, Jovanovich, 1973), 17.

[6] Thomas Merton, foreword to Thich Nhat Hanh, *Vietnam: Lotus in a Sea of Fire* (New York: Hill and Wang, 1967), vii.

[7] Martin Luther King Jr. nominated Hanh for the Nobel Peace Prize in 1967.

[8] Hanh, *Vietnam*, 106–7.

[9] Ibid., 107.

[10] Philip Metres, "William Stafford's *Down in My Heart*: The Poetics of Pacifism and the Limitations of Lyric," *Peace & Change* 29 (2004): 2.

[11] Gene Sharp, *The Politics of Nonviolent Action: Power and Struggle* (Boston: Extending Horizons, 1973), 64.

[12] Inez Hayes Irwin, *The Story of Alice Paul and the National Woman's Party* (Fairfax, Va.: Denlinger's, 1964), 32.

[13] Ibid., 292.

[14] "'Eighty Killed' in Tibetan Unrest," BBC News, March 16, 2008, *news.bbc.co.uk/2/hi/asia-pacific/7299212.stm.* (Accessed August 21, 2008.)

[15] Luke 23:34.

[16] Quoted in Chris Hedges, "Daniel Berrigan: Forty Years After Catonsville," *The Nation*, May 20, 2008, *www.thenation.com/doc/20080602/hedges.* (Accessed August 21, 2008.)

[17] Ibid.

[18] Martin Luther King Jr., "The Power of Nonviolence," in *I Have A Dream: Writings and Speeches that Changed the World*, ed. James M. Washington (San Francisco: HarperSanFrancisco, 1992), 33.

[19] Quoted in Peter Ackerman and Jack Duval, *A Force More Powerful* (New York: Palgrave, 2000), 489.

[20] Romans 12:21.

[21] Howard Zinn, *A Power Governments Cannot Suppress* (San Francisco: City Lights, 2007), 230.

[22] Mark 9:40.

[23] James Lawson, "Justice and Non-violence in Global Community," *Catholic New Times*, April 11, 2004, *findarticles.com/p/articles/mi_m0MKY/is_6_28/ai_n6244677*. (Accessed August 21, 2008.)

[24] Quoted in Michaela McCaughey, "MCC Presents Nonviolence Documentary," January 27, 2004, *media.www.ramcigar.com/media/storage/paper366/news/2004/01/27/News/Mcc-Presents.Nonviolence.Documentary-588692.shtml*. (Accessed August 21, 2008.)

[25] Henry David Thoreau, "On the Duty of Civil Disobedience," *www.literatureproject.com/civil-disobedience/civil-disobedience.htm*. (Accessed August 21, 2008.)

[26] Ibid.

[27] Cornel West, in an interview in *Call + Response*, a documentary film about global slavery, releasing in theatres October 10, 2008 (Fair Trade Pictures, produced and directed by Justin Dillon).

[28] I heard Lawson make this comment in a lecture in Nashville.

[29] Gene Sharp, *The Politics of Nonviolent Action: The Methods of Nonviolent Action* (Boston: Extending Horizons, 1973), 112.

[30] Ibid., 104.

[31] Ibid., 8.

[32] Leonard Cohen, "Democracy," from the album *The Future* (Sony, 1992).

[33] William R. LaFleur, "Body," in *Critical Terms for Religious Studies*, ed. Mark C. Taylor (Chicago: Univ. of Chicago Press, 1998), 51.

[34] Ephesians 6:12.

[35] Ziggy Marley, "Justice," from the album *One Bright Day* (Virgin Records, 1989).

[36] Martin Luther King Jr., "Where Do We Go from Here," Southern Christian Leadership Conference, August 16, 1967, *www.stanford.edu/group/King/publications/speeches/Where_do_we_go_from_here.html*. (Accessed August 21, 2008.)

[37] Rowan Williams, *The Dwelling of the Light: Praying with Icons of Christ* (Grand Rapids: Eerdmans, 2003), 31–32.

Chapter 10: Sincerity as Far as the Eye Can See

[1] Cormac McCarthy, *No Country for Old Men* (New York: Vintage, 2005), 267.

[2] President George W. Bush, speaking at the National Cathedral, Washington, D.C., September 14, 2001, *www.whitehouse.gov/nsc/nss3.html.* (Accessed August 21, 2008.)

[3] Charles Marsh, "God and Country: What It Means to Be a Christian after George W. Bush," *The Boston Globe,* July 8, 2007, *www.boston.com/news/globe/ideas/articles/2007/07/08/god_and_country/?page=full.* (Accessed August 21, 2008.)

[4] Cormac McCarthy, *The Road* (New York: Knopf, 2006), 4.

[5] William Blake, "The Divine Image," in *Songs of Innocence* (Mineola, N.Y.: Dover, 1971), 44.

[6] McCarthy, *The Road*, 64.

[7] Ibid., 143.

[8] Ibid., 145.

[9] Ibid., 27.

[10] Ibid., 64.

[11] Ibid., 63.

[12] Ibid., 234–36.

[13] Jacques Derrida, *The Gift of Death* (Chicago: Univ. of Chicago Press, 1995), 2.

[14] "Woodward Shares War Secrets, *CBS News: 60 Minutes,* April 18, 2004, *www.cbsnews.com/stories/2004/04/15/60minutes/main612067.shtml.* (Accessed August 21, 2008.) In speaking of nihilism in regard to these words spoken to one of America's most famous journalists, I don't mean to slander the word choice of an unpopular president or raise questions concerning his views on a literal resurrection or a kingdom coming. I only wish to contrast this sensibility and its impact on the environment, detainees, returning soldiers, and civilian populations with a more lively, verifiably conservative, and earthbound evangelical one, what environmentalist Bill McKibben calls a more durable and deep economy, a more intensely mindful sense of the world we're in and the future we're cultivating.

[15] Psalm 116:9.

[16] John Lewis, *Walking with the Wind* (New York: Simon & Schuster, 1998), 467.

[17] Larry Norman, "I Wish We'd All Been Ready," from the album *Upon This Rock* (Capitol Records, 1969).

[18] Jürgen Moltmann, *The Coming of God: Christian Eschatology* (Minneapolis: Fortress, 1996), 135.

[19] Bill O'Reilly, "Interview with Bono: Not Facing AIDS Crisis 'Foolhardy,'" *The O'Reilly Factor*, September 2, 2004, *www.foxnews.com/story/0,2933,131198,00.html.* (Accessed August 21, 2008.)

[20] See Isaiah 61:1; Luke 4:18–19.

[21] Quoted in Antonino D'Ambrosio, *Let Fury Have the Hour: The Punk Rock Politics of Joe Strummer* (New York: Nation Books, 2004), 176.

[22] Micah 6:8.

[23] Slavoj Zizek, "What Does Europe Want?" *In These Times,* May 1, 2004, *www.inthesetimes.com/comments.php?id=716_0_4_0_C.* (Accessed August 21, 2008.)

[24] Naomi Klein, *The Shock Doctrine: The Rise of Disaster Capitalism* (New York: Henry Holt, 2007), 15.

[25] Bono, "Because We Can, We Must," commencement address, University of Pennsylvania, May 19, 2004, *www.upenn.edu/almanac/between/2004/commence-b.html.* (Accessed August 21, 2008.)

[26] Talal Asad, *On Suicide Bombing* (New York: Columbia Univ. Press, 2007), 62–63.

[27] John Howard Yoder, *For the Nations: Essays Public and Evangelical* (Grand Rapids: Eerdmans, 1997), 211.

[28] Ursula K. Le Guin, "The Ones Who Walk Away from Omelas," in *The Wind's Twelve Quarters* (New York: Harper & Row, 1975), 282.

[29] Ibid, 284. Le Guin cites William James as an inspirer of the story, but when readers noted a resonance with a story told by Ivan Karamazov to his brother Alyosha in *The Brothers Karamazov*, she recalled reading Dostoevsky but found it difficult to return to (and therefore perhaps repressed it). Omelas appears to have been derived from the sight of Salem, Oregon in a rearview mirror. Where do ideas for stories come from? In Le Guin's words, "From forgetting Dostoevsky and reading road signs backwards, naturally. Where else?" (p. 276).

[30] John Berger, *Hold Everything Dear: Dispatches on Survival and Resistance* (New York: Pantheon, 2007), 101–2.

[31] Adrienne Rich, *Arts of the Possible*: *Essays and Conversations* (New York: Norton, 2001), 145.

[32] "Hell is other people" is from Sartre's 1944 play *No Exit*; C. S. Lewis, *The Great Divorce* (New York: Macmillan, 1946).

[33] James Joyce, *Finnegan's Wake* (New York: Viking, 1939), 32.

[34] Samir Selmanovic, "Commission or Invitation," *Signs of the Times* (August 2008), *www.signsofthetimes.org.au/archives/2008/august/religionmatters.shtm.* (Accessed August 21, 2008.)

[35] Psalm 23:6.

End Note That Means to Signal a World without End

[1] Miroslav Volf, "Enter into Joy! Sin, Death, and the Life of the World to Come," in *The End of the World and the Ends of God: Science and Theology on Eschatology*, eds. John Polkinghorne and Michael Welker (Harrisburg, Pa.: Trinity Press International, 2000), 264.

Acknowledgments

In a typically illuminating phrase, James Joyce observed that we never know whose thoughts we're chewing. Like the delusion of absolute authorial authority, a sense of unassailable originality is no small fiction. When it comes to the words in our heads, it's all appropriation all the time. And I hope these words of acknowledgment will render my borrowings a little less shameless. Among the myriad mortals not mentioned in the text but who would be right to note that their exchanges with me have contributed to the content contained therein are the following: Todd Greene, David Bazan, Trevor Henderson, Elizabeth and Brett Wiley, Mark McCleary, Gareth Higgins, Geoff Little, Joel Dark, Jon Foreman, Tom Willett, Richard King, Ken Locke, Jude Adam, Molly Jones, Ann Coble, Doug Meeks, Martina Urban, Brook Downs, Dave Bunker, Elizabeth Kaine, Chris Palladino, James Stewart, Hortense Spillers, Mark Masen, John Wilson, Jay Geller, Gabriel Ferrer, and Mark Woods, curator of "wood s lot" (*www.web.ncf.ca/ek867/wood_s_lot*), which I take to be the most inspiring website available to speakers of English. Words kindly employed and, in some cases, eyebrows raised in amusement over something I'd said (inspiring me to commit particular words to paper) have come at crucial points via Doris Dark, Steve Stockman, Lee Smithey, Warren Pettit, Mark Nicholas, Benjamin Sohr, Micah Weedman, Michael Lovett, Steve Mason, Rodney Clapp, David Masen, Gar Saeger, David Dobson, Jeff Rioux, Jana Riess, Richard Goode, David Harkness, John Lamb, Ken Heffner, Chris

Kelly, and the people of Timebeing. Sarah Masen, my partner in crime and matrimony, once inscribed in the margins of the galleys of an earlier text "Love thy reader" as an affectionate rebuke of the ways excess verbiage can get the best of me. And for the work of somehow redeeming and believing in me beyond my dysfunctional relationship with needless convolution, I here deliver a shout-out of thanks to Greg Daniel, literary agent extraordinaire, who vouchsafed the title unto me; Angela Scheff, whose powers of editing have saved me from repeat embarrassments; and Dirk Buursma, who straightened it all out. The present work owes its existence to their critical encouragement.

Share Your Thoughts

With the Author: Your comments will be forwarded to
the author when you send them to *zauthor@zondervan.com*.

With Zondervan: Submit your review of this book
by writing to *zreview@zondervan.com*.

Free Online Resources at
www.zondervan.com/hello

 Zondervan AuthorTracker: Be notified whenever your
favorite authors publish new books, go on tour, or post
an update about what's happening in their lives.

 Daily Bible Verses and Devotions: Enrich your life
with daily Bible verses or devotions that help you start
every morning focused on God.

 Free Email Publications: Sign up for newsletters on
fiction, Christian living, church ministry, parenting, and
more.

 Zondervan Bible Search: Find and compare
Bible passages in a variety of translations at
www.zondervanbiblesearch.com.

 Other Benefits: Register yourself to receive online
benefits like coupons and special offers, or to participate
in research.